An Eye
for
An Eye

The Place of Old Testament Ethics Today

Christopher J. H. Wright

InterVarsity Press
Downers Grove
Illinois 60515

*InterVarsity Press is the book-publishing division of Inter-Varsity Christian Fellowship,
a student movement active on campus at hundreds of universities, colleges
and schools of nursing. For information about local and regional activities, write
IVCF, 233 Langdon St., Madison, WI 53703.*

*Distributed in Canada through InterVarsity Press, 860 Denison St., Unit 3, Markham,
Ontario L3R 4H1, Canada.*

*Quotations from the Bible are from the Holy Bible: New International Version.
Copyright © 1978 by the New York International Bible Society.
Used by permission of Zondervan Bible Publishers.*

Cover illustration: Roberta Polfus

ISBN 0-87784-821-1

Printed in the United States of America

Library of Congress Cataloging in Publication Data

Wright, Christopher J. H., 1947-
      An eye for an eye.

      Bibliography: p.
      Includes index.
      1. Ethics in the Bible.   2. Bible.   O.T.–Criticism,
interpretation, etc.   I. Title.
BS1199.E8W74   1983   241.5   83-18651
ISBN 0-87784-821-1

18	17	16	15	14	13	12	11	10	9	8	7	6	5	4	3	2	1
97	96	95	94	93	92	91	90	89	88	87	86	85	84	83			

To
Elizabeth
(in the spirit of Proverbs 31:10–11, 28–29)
Catharine, Timothy, Jonathan
and
Suzannah
who shares her beginnings
with this book

Contents

Preface   9
Prologue   12

PART ONE:
THE FRAMEWORK OF OLD TESTAMENT ETHICS

Introduction: The ethical triangle   19

1. The theological angle   21
   God-centred origin   21
   God-centred history   24
   God-centred content   26
   God-centred motivation   29

2. The social angle   33
   The pattern of redemption   33
   The distinctiveness of Israel   35
   Israel as God's paradigm   40

3. The economic angle   46
   The land in Israel's story   46
   The land as divine gift   51
   The land under divine ownership   57
   The land as 'spiritual thermometer'   59

Conclusion: Covenantal, canonical, comprehensive   63

PART TWO:
THEMES IN OLD TESTAMENT ETHICS

4. Economics and the land   67
   Perspectives from creation   67
   Perspectives from redemption   74
   The land in Christian ethics   88

5. Politics and the world of nations   103
   'Every nation of men'   103
   The redeemed nation   108
   Israel and the nations   122

6. Righteousness and justice   133
   The vocabulary of justice   133
   The theological context   136
   The social context   141

7. Law and the legal system   148
   The main legal blocks   148
   The different kinds of law   151
   Reflections on Old Testament law   159

8. Society and culture   174
   Rejection and prohibition   175
   Toleration with control   175
   Acceptance and affirmation   183
   Christians and culture   187

9. The way of the individual   197
   The individual in community   197
   Personal responsibility   199
   Models of morals   201
   Failure and forgiveness   208

Bibliography   213
Index of biblical references   221
Subject index   223

Preface

Some authors preface their works with an apology or justification for adding another volume to the literature on their subject. At least I feel I am spared that duty since the subject of Old Testament ethics has scarcely any literature to add to. There are many academic articles and special studies, of course, that bear on the ethical significance of the Old Testament, as the biblio graphies show. But I am not aware of any recent attempt to present an overview of the subject as a whole. So, without pretending to have exhausted the subject in depth or detail, I have attempted to provide a comprehensive framework within which Old Testament ethics can be organized and understood. The student should find in the bibliographies sufficient resources to take his study to deeper and wider dimensions.

In the interests of the general reader I have avoided as far as possible the use of technical vocabulary and dense footnotes. The only technical term I have consciously allowed myself is 'paradigm' and its derivative, 'paradigmatic'. I can find no simpler word to express the points I wish to make concerning a method of understanding and applying the Old Testament. The term is fully defined and explained as soon as it rears its head in chapter 2 (see pp. 40 and 43). Likewise, one or two other more familiar items of theological vocabulary are explained as they arise.

Two other points need to be made. First, a glance at the table of contents will show that most of the material is concerned with social aspects of the ethics of the Old Testament. Only in the last chapter do we look at personal or individual ethics. This may be somewhat unbalanced, since undoubtedly a lot more could be said on the personal ethical demands to be found in the Old Testament. The emphasis is, nevertheless, quite deliberate, and based on the conviction that the *primary* ethical thrust of the Old Testament is in fact social. The Old Testament is the story of a people – God's people; and all the morally memorable tales of individuals are part of that wider story. God called a whole society to be 'a people for his own possession', to live before him in the midst of the nations of the earth. So, as our title indicates, the Old Testament is absorbed with what it means to be the living people of the living God.

The second point relates to the subtitle and the chapters in Part Two. I am convinced that the Old Testament, when properly understood and applied as part of the whole canon of Scripture, has a vital relevance for the whole range of our ethical concerns. My aim in this book is to point out ways in which it can be validly applied, to suggest directions for such applications, rather than to follow those directions through to detailed conclusions in each sphere. I am not an economist, nor a politician, lawyer, or sociologist, and claim no special expertise in these areas. But my hope is that Christians who do work in these and other fields will be stimulated by what is offered here to a more coherent and effective application of biblical theology and ethics to the particulars of their own environment.

Many of the ideas of this book were first aired and shared in the congenially critical context of various study groups of the Shaftesbury Project. I am most grateful to the members of those groups for their stimulus over the past years, and also to the Shaftesbury Project itself for permission to modify and revise material which they originally published as working papers.

I also wish to record my gratitude to the kind ladies of Tonbridge who typed the manuscript: Sheila Armstrong, Sue Bladon, Kathie Portlock and Frances Weller. My thanks also go to Brian and Megan Adams, Kenneth and Margaret Gubbins, Lawrence and Margaret Pope and David and Clare Wenham, who provided hospitality of various kinds for me during the writing of the book. I greatly appreciated the careful scrutiny of the Revd David Field and Dr Gordon Wenham who read the original typescript and made a large number of very helpful comments. Their suggestions helped me to clarify or improve what I wanted to say at a number of points. The book owes its indexes to the labours of some of my students at All Nations.

Only an author's family shares the full burden of the writing of a book, but my own family has gone beyond such patient forbearance and has turned some of the warmer principles of Old Testament ethics into a living experience of great joy. So with gratitude and affection this book is dedicated to them all.

CHRISTOPHER J. H. WRIGHT

Prologue

Put a group of Christians together, set them to talk about any of the great moral questions that are woven into the fabric of human life, and sooner or later someone will bring the Bible into the discussion. That will be true whether it is a small circle of friends meeting in a chatty home group, or an ardent knot of academic students, or a heavyweight ecclesiastical commission. It is also likely to be true whether the group takes a high view of the Bible, believing it to be the Word of God and full of authority and relevance, or, at the other extreme, regards the Bible as just one among many possible and equally valid sources for working out Christian ethical positions. Even those who dismiss the Bible as largely irrelevant to the problems we face today usually feel obliged to give lengthy explanations as to why they do so, thus confirming, even if negatively, the importance of the Bible in the Christian ethical tradition.

The trouble with the Bible, however, is that so much of it is Old Testament. And the trouble with the *Old* Testament is just that. It is *old*. Now, of course, for some things, oldness speaks of permanence and lasting, even increasing, value. For other things, oldness spells outmoded, obsolete and irrelevant. Which category does the Old Testament belong to?

At first sight, even the New Testament is unhelpfully ambiguous on this question. At times the Old Testament is affirmed to have permanent validity; at others it seems to be regarded as obsolete and ready to pass away. So then, if we feel obliged to take the Bible into account in some way and to some degree in our ethical arguments, what are we to make of the Old Testament?

Let's listen in on our imaginary group of Christians as they wrestle with an ethical issue. It is a somewhat mixed group, containing, in our imagination, representatives from each of the groups mentioned above. They are discussing one of the burning issues of our day – social justice for the world's poor and the matter of aid and development in the Third World. Someone feels it is time the Bible was brought to bear, thinking that an apt text or two should settle the argument:

'But the *Bible* says somewhere in Proverbs, I think, that "He who is kind to the poor lends to the Lord." And there are laws like, "Be generous to the poor and needy in your land." '

'Precisely,' comes a reply. 'It was for the poor and needy *in your land* – not everybody else all over the world. Charity begins at home. And even if that isn't in the Bible, you'll find the Jews kept their generosity to themselves and there are some pretty nasty texts about foreigners.'

They will probably go on swapping text and counter-text for a while, with little likelihood of convincing themselves or anyone else. Already the group has come up against the first blind alley in using the Old Testament (or any of the Bible) – that of simply quoting random texts that seem to be relevant. Not only is there the danger of everybody making the Bible say what they want it to, thus bringing its use into disrepute; there is also the danger of lifting texts right out of their context and applying them directly to very different situations and issues. This kind of short-cut use of the Bible often ends up as a short-circuit. Invalid or irrelevant quotations actually prevent the real word of God on a specific issue being heard.

At this point someone, perhaps a student, tries to raise the level of discussion to more substantial matters of biblical principle.

'Surely, since this is a subject which involves mankind as a whole and the resources of the earth, we have to go back to the stories of creation. They show us that man is accountable to God for each other and for the earth. So, simply because we are fellow men, created by God, and sharing the same earth, we have a duty to help the poorer nations to develop.'

'I agree,' adds another participant, 'and the good thing about taking a principle like that from the creation narratives is that they apply to all men – not just to Israel or the Christian church.'

'But that sounds like you're saying that the "Israelite" bits of the Old Testament are irrelevant to the issue, if all we need are the creation principles,' complains another. 'If that were the case, why have we got the rest of the Old Testament at all?'

'No, it's not a question of making a sharp division between creation and the rest,' returns the first, 'because even the creation stories and principles were given to Israel who already knew God as their Redeemer. We need both the creation principles and also the laws and institutions given to Israel to help them to live in a world that had fallen far short of the creation standards.'

Mention of the laws of the Old Testament rapidly brings another member of the group into action:

'But I understood that all the law of the Old Testament was fulfilled in Christ and no longer applicable to Christians at all. So how can you bring that into the argument?'

'*Some* of it was fulfilled by Christ,' corrects his neighbour. 'That was all the ceremonial laws about sacrifice and so on. Then there was the civil law, which was only meant to apply to Israel in any case. But there is still the moral law, which is unchanging, like God, and applies to all men.'

'I've heard that distinction before,' interrupts another voice, 'but I don't find it very helpful any more. When you actually read the laws in the early books of the Bible, they don't fall neatly into those categories. What would you actually classify as "the moral law", for example?'

'The Ten Commandments, I suppose.'

'But there is nothing explicitly in the Ten Commandments about giving help to the poor, is there? Yet a moment ago you were saying that this was a moral obligation on us.'

'Well, I suppose it's not exactly a moral *law*, but a moral *principle* that you can see from quite a lot of the laws.'

'So really it's not a question of separating out "moral laws" as such, but looking for moral principles that underlie any or all of the laws – whatever category we think they come into.'

'Something like that.'

A good deal of impatient puffing heralds the entry of an ecclesiastical heavyweight into the fray:

'All this talk of law is pointless. It can only lead us into legalism which is the bane of the church's life. What the church is called to is to be a prophetic voice in society. The really key figures in the Old Testament were the prophets. Think how much they had to say about the very issue we are discussing – social and economic justice for the poor and downtrodden. We should take our cue from Amos and proclaim the anger and judgment of God on our society and on the whole unjust system of trade and oppression that the wealthy nations of the world are guilty of.'

(Loud murmurs of agreement all round.)

'Well, of course we have to speak up, if we are to be like salt and light in the world,' ventures a bravely questioning voice. 'But the question is, what basis do we do it on? Amos and the other prophets were sent to Israel who were the people of God, with a covenant and the law of God. They appealed to the nation and its leaders on the basis of a relationship between them and God. But no modern secular state stands in the same relationship to God as Israel did. So surely we can't appeal to it, or denounce it, on the same grounds, as if it did, can we?'

'In fact,' nods a friend, 'if the Christian church is supposed to be the successor of Israel, then we need a "prophetic voice" to challenge the sins and inequalities within the church first, before we start firing Amos at society outside.'

Perhaps here would be the best point to step into the group, excuse our rude interruption, and politely introduce them to this book. For in it I hope they will find answers to some of the questions and problems they have come up against in their discussion.

It sets out first of all to outline the basic framework of belief that lies behind the moral teaching of the Old Testament. It is necessary that we see clearly the background, the context, in which all the multitude of details – laws, narratives, prophecy, liturgy – are set, so that we interpret and apply them in a valid way. We need a map to give us the important fixed points and to orientate our journey.

In the second part, we look at a selection of ethical issues to which the Old Testament makes an important contribution. As we work through them, we shall see that each of the approaches touched on in the discussion above – creation ordinances, the relevance of the law, the message of the prophets – have important and valid applications, but none is sufficient in itself or without its dangers. And we shall see that there are other ways of releasing the ethical relevance and power of the Old Testament.

It was the Old Testament that the apostle Paul had in mind when he spoke of the double purpose of the Scriptures. Not only are they able to bring people to saving faith ('to make you wise for salvation'), but they have a continuing ethical validity. They are 'useful for . . . training in righteousness, so that the man of God may be thoroughly equipped for every good work' (2 Tim. 3:15f.). This is a conviction I have always shared. The writing of this book has served only to deepen it. My prayer is that the reading of it will have the same effect.

PART ONE

THE FRAMEWORK OF OLD TESTAMENT ETHICS

Introduction:
The ethical triangle

We have seen that the way in to understanding and applying the Old Testament ethically is not by plunging in and seizing on whatever appears relevant. What we have to try to do is to put ourselves in Israel's position and understand how Israel perceived and experienced their relationship with God and how that experience affected their practical living as a community.

Theology and ethics are inseparable in the Bible. You cannot explain how and why they lived as they did until you see how and why they believed what they did. So our purpose in this part is to outline the ground-plan of principles that lie behind the wealth of laws and exhortation, as well as the moral values implicit or explicit in the narratives, worship and prophecy.

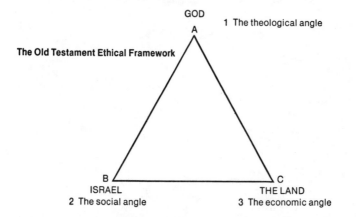

Old Testament ethics are built upon Israel's understanding of who and what they were as a people, of their relationship to God, and of their physical environment – their land. These were the three primary factors of their theology and ethics: God, Israel and the land, in a triangle of relationships, each of which affected the others. So we can take each 'corner' in turn and examine Old Testament ethical teaching from the theological angle, the social angle and the economic angle. As we shall see, this will provide a comprehensive framework which is both compatible with the shape of the canon of the Old Testament, and with the covenantal basis of Old Testament theology.

1
The theological angle

The history of human ethical systems shows that a great variety of moral axioms or assumptions can be taken as the starting point or goal of ethical imperatives. There have been, for example, the 'Golden Mean' of Aristotle, the 'greatest good of the greatest number' of the Utilitarians, and so on. In the Old Testament, however, ethics are fundamentally *theological.* That is, they are at every point related to God – to his character, his will, his actions and his purpose. We can expand this in four ways. Old Testament ethics are God-centred in origin, in history, in content and in motive.

GOD-CENTRED ORIGIN

God acts first and calls people to respond. This is the starting point for the moral teaching of the Old Testament. God takes the initiative in grace and redeeming action and then makes his ethical demand in the light of it. Ethics then becomes a matter of response and gratitude, not of blind obedience alone. This might not always appear so when we read the laws of the Old Testament by themselves. That is why it is important that we pay attention to the narrative framework in which they are set.

So let us look at the foundational story of the origin of Old Testament law, namely, the exodus and Sinai events described in Exodus 1 – 24. We find the Israelites oppressed and in slavery in Egypt, crying out under intolerable conditions. Their cry is heard by God (2:23–25) and he acts. In a series of mighty acts he delivers (redeems) them from Egypt (chs. 3 – 15), brings them to Sinai (16 – 19), gives them his law (20 – 23) and concludes a covenant with them (24). And all of this God does out of faithfulness to his own character and the promises he had made to the forefathers of the nation (2:24; 3:6–8):

> Moreover, I have heard the groaning of the Israelites, whom the Egyptians are enslaving, and I have remembered my covenant.
> Therefore, say to the Israelites: 'I am the LORD and I will bring you out from under the yoke of the Egyptians. I will free you from being slaves to them and will redeem you with an outstretched arm and with mighty acts of judgment. I will take you as my own people, and I will be your God. Then you will know that I am the LORD your God, who brought you out from under the yoke of the Egyptians. And I will bring you to the land I swore with uplifted hand to give to Abraham, to Isaac and to Jacob. I will give it to you as a possession. I am the LORD' (Ex. 6:5–8).

The sequence of events in the biblical story is very important. God did not send Moses down to Egypt with the law already tucked under his cloak to say to Israel in bondage, 'Here you are. This is God's law, and if you keep it fully from now on, God will rescue you out of this slavery.' Israel were not told they could deserve or hasten their own deliverance by keeping the law. No, God acted *first*. He redeemed them and then made his covenant with them, which included the law as their side, their response of grateful obedience to their saving God.

This point is seen clearly in the giving of the Ten Commandments at Sinai. Before anything happens at all, God reminds Israel of 'the story so far':

> You yourselves have seen what I did to Egypt, and how I carried you on eagles' wings and brought you to myself. Now if you obey me fully and keep my covenant . . . (Ex. 19:4f.).

And even the Decalogue itself does not begin with the first commandment. There is the vital preface: 'I am the LORD your God, who brought you out of Egypt, out of the land of slavery' (Ex. 20:2). Thus, God identifies himself and his redeeming activity, and then goes on, 'You shall have no other gods before me'. The command *follows* the statement, with an implied 'therefore'.

The relationship between God's command and his previous acts on behalf of Israel is even more clearly shown in Deuteronomy where the whole historical prologue, chapters 1 – 4, precedes the Decalogue in chapter 5.

Right from the start, then, Israel's keeping of God's law was meant to be a response to what God had already done. This is the foundation not only of Old Testament ethics, but is indeed the principle running through the moral teaching of the whole Bible. The same order is seen in the New Testament: 'Love each other *as I have loved you*' (Jn. 15:12); 'We love because he first loved us' (1 Jn. 4:19; *cf.* Rom. 12:1). Some people think that the Old Testament, in contrast to the New, taught that redemption was achieved by keeping the law. But it does not. There too, God's grace comes first, man's response second.

As we go further into the story of the book of Exodus, we find that not only was Israel's relationship with God founded on his *redeeming* grace, it was sustained by his *forgiving* grace. This is the point of chapters 32 – 34. While Moses is on the mountain, Israel rebels and makes the idol of the golden calf. God declares he will destroy them utterly. But Moses intervenes and pleads with God for the people. First of all he reminds God of his own reputation which would be lost if, having rescued Israel, he let them perish: 'Why should the Egyptians say. . . ?' (32:12). Then he reminds him of his earlier promise to Abraham (32:13). At that point God relents a little and says he will keep that particular promise: Israel may go and possess the land. But God himself will not go with them (33:3). However, that is not good enough for Moses. He presses on and reminds God of the covenant he has just made at Sinai, in which he had promised to be their God and take them as his people: 'Remember that this nation is *your* people' (33:13). But how would anyone know that, if God did not go with them (33:16)? That prayer goes right to the heart of God. In his mercy, he forgives the people and in chapter 34 the covenant is re-established.

From such beginnings, Israel knew that the survival of their relationship with God depended totally on his faithfulness and loyalty to his own character and promises, not on their own success in keeping the law. God was the origin of their very existence as a nation, and he was also the origin of the laws which were to govern their life as his people. Sheer gratitude should have compelled obedience.

GOD-CENTRED HISTORY

There is something dynamic about Old Testament ethics. It has a living relevance which matches the vitality of the faith of Old Testament Israel. That vitality was largely due to the way the Israelites' faith was *historically* generated, grounded and sustained. God was believed to have acted, and to be continuously active, in history; therefore events and sequences of events took on moral significance. Without this conviction of God's active involvement and interest in affairs, ethics becomes pragmatic and even dispensable. For who cares? But because it was such a live conviction in Israel, there developed a whole genre of literature which we tend, by familiarity, to take for granted – namely prophetic historical narrative.

The historians of the Old Testament are sometimes called 'moralistic' – as a reproach. Yet the ethical significance of their achievement is enormous. They performed the task of collecting, selecting, editing and commenting on the stories of Israel's past – centuries of it – with consistent theological and ethical criteria and assessment. They were prepared to evaluate boldly events and people in a way that affirmed the ethical significance of both. The Hebrew canon's own term for them was 'The Former *Prophets*', a fact that shows that these historians were regarded as making these ethical assessments from a divine perspective. Not that they are forever 'moralizing' – far from it. Indeed, the skill of the Hebrew historians often lies in the tantalizing way they present a story and refrain from comment, allowing the reader to draw his own ethical conclusions (which are not by any means always straightforward). But the ethical impact remains, precisely because God is at work within the narrative – explicitly or behind the scenes – initiating, reacting, controlling.

This conviction that God was in control of events did not, however, lead them into fatalism. They did not work with a mechanistic view of God's sovereignty which would have eliminated human ethical freedom and responsibility. The best illustration of this is provided by the cycle of Joseph stories. Indeed, it is probably part of the narrator's purpose to exploit this very enigma of divine sovereignty and human moral decisions. From a human point of view, the whole story is one of free choices, some evil, some good; at no point does anyone act other than as a free agent according to his own choice. That applies to all the characters – Jacob, Joseph and his brothers, Potiphar and his wife, Pharaoh and Joseph's fellow prisoners. Yet at the end of it all, Joseph acknowledges the sovereign control of God, whose redemptive purposes governed the whole story: 'You [his brothers] intended to harm me, but God intended it for good to accomplish what is now being done, the saving of many lives' (Gn. 50:20).

But neither, on the other hand, did their belief in human ethical freedom and responsibility lead them into relativism, as though everything were determined by the immediate situation, with no absolute or prior principles. The story of David's encounter with Saul in the cave illustrates this (1 Sa. 24). The circumstances presented him with a perfect opportunity for killing Saul. David knew he had already been anointed as the next king, and his men urged him to see the situation as divinely arranged for the very purpose of disposing of Saul (v. 4). Yet David refrained, checked by the higher principle of the sanctity of one anointed by the LORD, enemy or not (vv. 6f.). The situation by itself was insufficient, even though it was acknowledged as arranged by God (vv. 10, 18). The decision was guided by prior principle, derived from God's past action.

The two dimensions of Israel's sense of history which had the deepest ethical significance were, if we may be allowed to indulge in technical jargon, the redemptive and eschatological dimensions. The redemptive aspect signifies the belief that God had acted in the past with mighty acts of deliverance for his people and of judgment on his enemies. This feature of the Old Testament we have already looked at, noting how it affects ethics by stimulating the response of gratitude and obedience consistent with such undeserved favour. The eschatological aspect signifies the belief that in those redemptive acts God has a continuing purpose. This he will ultimately bring to complete fulfilment in the elimination of evil, the vindication of the righteous, the establishment of justice and peace, and the restoration of harmony between God, humanity and nature.

The combination of these two poles of Israel's historical faith gave immense ethical importance to the present. What I do here and now matters because of what God has done in the past and what he will do in the future. I am part of a people he has chosen, delivered and blessed beyond measure; therefore my deeds must display my gratitude. I look forward to the 'Day' of his final intervention and therefore wish to be sure of being found among the righteous.

It can be seen at once how similar this is to the twin ethical thrusts of the New Testament theology of the Kingdom of God. Christians live in the light of its historical inauguration in the earthly work of Christ, and also in the expectation of its ultimate establishment when he comes again. Without minimizing in any way the radical newness of the impact of Jesus, there is clearly a profound continuity between the Testaments in this theological and historical origin of biblical ethics.

GOD-CENTRED CONTENT

What shape, then, should Israel's obedience take? What was to be the substance and quality of their ethical behaviour? Here again, the answer is thoroughly theological: nothing less than the reflection of the character of God himself. What God is like is to be seen in what he does or has done. That was an axiom of Israel's belief about God's self-revelation. Therefore, history became something of an ethical 'copy-book', because it showed God in action. For example, God had just freed Israel from slavery. So that same justice and mercy of God was to be reflected in Israel's own treatment of slaves and other vulnerable people in their society: 'Do not oppress an alien; you yourselves know how it feels to be aliens, because you were aliens in Egypt' (Ex. 23:9; *cf.* Ex. 21:2–11, 20f., 26f.; Dt. 15:15). The most succinct expression of this principle is found in Leviticus: 'Be holy because I, the LORD your God, am holy' (Lv. 19:2).

We are inclined to think of 'holiness' as a matter of personal piety or, in Old Testament terms, of ritual cleanliness, proper sacrifices, clean and unclean foods, and the like. But the rest of Leviticus 19 shows us that the kind of holiness which reflects

God's own holiness is thoroughly practical. It includes
generosity to the poor at harvest time, justice for workers,
integrity in judicial processes, considerate behaviour to other
people, equality before the law for immigrants, honest trading
and other very 'earthy' social matters. And all through the
chapters runs the refrain: 'I am the LORD', as if to say, 'This is
what I require of you because it is what I myself would do'.

Holiness is the biblical 'shorthand' for the very essence of
God. This makes the command of Leviticus 19:2 quite breath-
taking. Your quality of life, it said to Israel, must reflect the
very heart of God's character. No less breath-taking, of course,
was Jesus' own echo of the verse to his disciples: 'Be perfect,
therefore, as your heavenly Father is perfect' (Mt. 5:48).

A favourite picture to describe this feature of Old Testament
ethics is that of *walking in God's way* – God's way, as distinct
from the ways of other gods, or of other nations, or one's own
way, or the way of sinners. You observe what God has done
and how, and then you try to follow suit. There is a strong
element of 'imitation of God' in Old Testament ethics as there
is in the New (*cf.* Eph. 5:1f.) A model passage for this is Deuteronomy 10:12–19. First of all the moral appeal is issued in
general terms:

> And now, O Israel, what does the LORD your God ask of you
> but to fear the LORD your God, to walk in all his ways, to
> love him, to serve the LORD your God with all your heart
> and with all your soul (v. 12).

And what are 'his ways'? The answer is given first in broad
terms. His was a way of condescending love in choosing
Abraham and his descendants to be the special vehicle of his
blessing.

> To the LORD your God belong the heavens, even the highest
> heavens, the earth and everything in it. Yet the LORD set his
> affection on your forefathers and loved them, and he chose
> you, their descendants (vv. 14f.).

That required an inward response of love and humility in
return: 'Circumcise your hearts, therefore, and do not be stiff-
necked any longer' (v. 16).

But what *specifically* were the 'ways' of God, in which Israel was to walk? This passage singles out a few:

[He] shows no partiality and accepts no bribes. He defends the cause of the fatherless and the widow, and loves the alien, giving him food and clothing. *And you are to love those who are aliens*, for you yourselves were aliens in Egypt (vv. 17–19).

It is not only in the law that 'imitation' of the way of God is seen. The Psalms contain repeated references to the character and deeds of God, in a way clearly designed to inculcate the same ethical values through repeated use in worship. This was certainly the desire of David in Psalm 25. Psalm 146:6–9 shows God in action; Psalm 72 prays that the king will do likewise.

Similarly in the Wisdom literature, if the motto of Proverbs is 'The fear of the LORD is the beginning [or, first principle] of wisdom' (Pr. 9:10), it would be appropriate to add, 'the imitation of the LORD is the application of wisdom'. This arises not only from specific passages where, for example, the reader is exhorted: 'Trust in the LORD with all your heart . . . in all your ways acknowledge him' (3:5f.), with the promise that 'the way of the LORD is a refuge for the righteous' (10:29); it emerges also in the way that so many of the little details of behaviour commended in the book do indeed reflect the character of God himself. There is emphasis on the virtues of faithfulness, kindness, work, compassion, social justice, especially for the poor and oppressed, generosity, impartiality and incorruptibility.

Finally, the same factor can be seen at work in the narratives. The characters who are most commended are those whose closeness and obedience to God lead them to reflect his nature in their actions and attitudes. We might think, for example, of Abraham and Moses reflecting God's compassionate love that 'desires not the death of a sinner' back, as it were, to God himself in their intercessions for iniquitous Sodom (Gn. 18:20–33) and rebellious Israel (Ex. 32:11–14); or of Samuel's uncompromising righteousness; or of David's kindness (2 Sa. 9:3).

GOD-CENTRED MOTIVATION

This aspect of Old Testament ethics is an expansion of the last. It is not simply that 'this is what God is like: follow his example'. Rather, 'this is what God has done *for you*. Therefore, out of gratitude you should do the same for others'. Personal experience of God is turned into motivation for consistent ethical behaviour. We have already seen above how the content of the slavery law in Exodus is affected by Israel's historical experience of deliverance from slavery. But in the related legislation in Leviticus and Deuteronomy the motive is even more explicitly stated.

In Leviticus 25:35–55 there are regulations concerning various degrees of impoverishment and the steps to be taken by the better-off kinsman. No less than three times the latter is reminded of the exodus as motivation for fair treatment of the poorer brother (vv. 38, 42, 55; *cf.* 26:13). Similarly in Deuteronomy 15 generosity is commanded for the poor in general and the debt-slave in particular. The motivation is clear in verse 15:

> Remember that you were slaves in Egypt and the LORD your God redeemed you. That is why I give you this command today.

This kind of 'motive clause' is one of the most characteristic features of the Deuteronomic laws, for the purpose of Deuteronomy was not just to state the law, but to persuade and motivate the Israelites to obey it. It has been described as 'preached law'.

The force of this motivation can also be felt in the warnings against *forgetting* the great acts of God. If Israel were to lose sight of what God had done for them, it would inevitably lead to failure to obey his law. They would lose both the model and the motive. So Deuteronomy devotes the first third of its bulk to sustained historical reminders. Chapter 8 gives the reason:

> Remember how the LORD your God led you . . . (v. 2)

> Be careful that you do not forget . . . (v. 11)

Otherwise, when you eat and are satisfied . . . then your
heart will become proud and you will forget the LORD your
God, who brought you out of Egypt, out of the land of slavery
(vv. 12–14).

The prophets attributed Israel's later moral decline and
outright disobedience to precisely this failing: they had forgotten God and were no longer motivated by the ethical implications of their own history. The ingratitude and inconsistency
of their rebellious ways was what so hurt and infuriated
these spokesmen for Israel's God. Hear Amos, after his scathing
accusations of 2:6–8, and Hosea and Micah:

> I brought you up out of Egypt,
>> and I led you for forty years in the desert
>> to give you the land of the Amorites (Am. 2:10).

> But I am the LORD your God,
>> who brought you out of Egypt. . .
> I cared for you in the desert. . .
> When I fed them, they were satisfied;
>> when they were satisfied, they became proud;
>> then they forgot me (Ho. 13:4–6).

> My people, what have I done to you?
>> How have I burdened you? Answer me.
> I brought you up out of Egypt
>> and redeemed you from the land of slavery. . . .
> Remember your journey from Shittim to Gilgal,[1]
>> that you may know the righteous acts of the LORD
>>>>>> (Mi. 6:3–5).

The same theme of ingratitude producing disobedience is to be
found in Isaiah 1:2–4; 5:1–7; Jeremiah 2:1–13; 7:21–26; Ezekiel
16; 20.

The same combination of positive and negative motivation in
ethical matters is found in the New Testament. There is Jesus'
parable of the unmerciful servant who, though himself
acquitted of a huge debt, ungratefully refuses to follow suit

---

[1] *i.e.* the crossing of the Jordan in conquest.

with a paltry debt owed to himself (Mt. 18:21–35). Jesus makes his own humility and self-sacrifice the model and motive for his disciples (Jn. 13:12–17; 15:12f.), something which is picked up and passed on by his apostles (1 Pet. 2:21; 1 Jn. 3:16f.). But the most extended moral argument of this sort is found in Romans 6:1 – 8:17, where Paul draws all his ethical motivation and appeal from the facts of our experience in Christ. In baptism we were identified with the historical events of Christ's death and resurrection, which, in the New Testament, correspond to the redemptive history of the exodus in the Old.

So the ethical teaching of the Old Testament is first and foremost God-centred. It presupposes God's initiative in grace and redemption; it is framed by what he has done and will do in history; it is shaped by his character and action; and it is motivated by personal experience of God's dealings with his people.

Two conclusions follow. First, this underlines for us the importance not only of the first commandment ('You shall have no *other* gods before me', for any *'other* god' would result in a different ethic) but also, more pertinently, of the second commandment ('You shall not make for yourself an idol . . .'). The prohibition on idols in Israel was not because they were material whereas God is spiritual, or because they were visible whereas he is invisible. It was primarily because they were lifeless, impotent and (especially) dumb, whereas the God of Israel was living, active and one who speaks. That is why the only image that was 'allowed' was the one God had designed and created himself – the image of God, man himself. It is man, as a thinking, living, choosing, speaking, moral agent, who alone reflects the living God of the Old Testament. Therefore any attempt to represent God in static or lifeless objects, even a human statue, reduces him and denies the most fundamental thing about him. This was not only a theological or religious issue. It was a deeply ethical command, for a false view of God would destroy the central foundation of ethics as well. Only the *living* God of history could initiate, shape and motivate the moral lives of his people.

Secondly, it underlines for us the importance of deriving our ethical teaching from the *whole* Old Testament. We have seen how the laws are not always sufficient in themselves; we need the narrative in which they are set to understand the principles on which they operate, and we need the later narratives, prophets, psalms and wisdom literature to see how they were taken up into the life of the nation. God has spoken in all the Scriptures 'in many and varied ways', and we must use them all in building up our picture of his character, acts and purpose. That overall picture will then control whatever interpretation we make of particular passages, so that we are not guilty of the short cuts or short circuits illustrated in the Prologue. We shall comment further on this point at the end of Part One, after we have looked at the other two angles.

2
The social angle

THE PATTERN OF REDEMPTION

The early chapters of Genesis relate the tragedy of mankind's fall into rebellion, disobedience and sin. Faced with the resulting catastrophe, God had, if we may so put it, several options. He could have destroyed man and abandoned his whole creation project. But he did not. He chose instead to redeem and restore.

Again, one could conceive of him redeeming people individually – saving a soul here, another there, and conveying them straight to heaven. But neither did he do that. God chose to put into operation a plan of redemption which would encompass the whole of the rest of human history and would involve, as part of that history, the choosing, creating and moulding of an entire nation. No doubt he was aware of the risk involved in such a long-term, massive project. One can imagine the sharp intake of breath among the heavenly hosts when the amazing scheme was unveiled!

Here again, as we saw in the last chapter, it is vital that we pay attention to the order of the Old Testament story. Genesis 11 brings us to the climax of the stories about mankind after the fall – the Tower of Babel. The nations were scattered and divided in order to prevent a unified rebellion against God. The effects of sin have reached 'global' proportions. What can God do now? It is against this background that the story of redemption begins in Genesis 12. God calls Abraham and promises to give him a land and to make his descendants into a nation through whom all the nations on earth would be blessed. The contrast between the curse at Babel and the promise to Abraham is very striking:

> That is why it was called Babel – because there the LORD confused the language of the whole world. From there the LORD scattered them over the face of the whole earth (Gn. 11:9).
>
> > . . . go to the Land I will show you.
> > I will make you into a great nation
> >   and I will bless you;
> > I will make your name great,
> >   and you will be a blessing . . .
> > and all peoples on earth
> >   will be blessed through you (Gn. 12:1–3).

From the land of Babel the curse of confusion, division and scattering spread to affect the whole world of the nations of man. But from the land to be given to Abraham, and through the nation he would become, blessing would spread to the same global extent. God's answer to the international blight of sin was a new community, a nation that would be the pattern and model of redemption, as well as the vehicle by which the blessing of redemption would eventually embrace the rest of mankind.

And so the story continues: Abraham, Isaac, Jacob, twelve tribes, oppression in Egypt, the exodus. And at last there they are, gathered before God at Mount Sinai, the people whom he will call his own – Israel. So when God entered into covenant with Israel and led them forward to take possession of the land of promise, it was with the full intention that they should be a nation in every normal sense of the word. They would inhabit a specific territory and have social, political, economic, military and judicial institutions. There would be critical differences, of course, from other nations, for they were to be a nation 'holy to the LORD', as we shall see below. But at a basic level they were a nation among the nations and therefore their laws and institutions reflect this.

The importance of this point for our ethical understanding of the Old Testament is that we must take account of the fact that so much of its ethical thrust is necessarily social. It is not simply a compendium of moral teaching to enable the individual to lead a privately upright life before God. Now, of course, this is not to deny that the Old Testament is deeply interested in the individual, as our final chapter will show. Indeed that is one of its major contributions to the fundamental principles of Christian ethics as a whole. Nor am I forgetting that many Old Testament laws, including the Ten Commandments, are framed in the second person singular, addressing the individual. But they are addressed to the individual as part of the community, and their purpose is not just individual purity but the moral and spiritual health of that whole community. For God's purpose, as we have seen, was not just righteous individuals, but a new community who in their social life would embody those qualities of righteousness, peace, justice and love which reflect God's own character and were his original purpose for mankind.

So the relevance of the 'social angle' is that when we seek to interpret an Old Testament text ethically we must not stop short at the question, 'what does this say to *me*?' We must study the passage within its own social context of life in Old Testament Israel and ask what it has to say within the present community of God's people, and then, further, what social implications it may have in human society at large. We shall see this method in operation in Part Two.

THE DISTINCTIVENESS OF ISRAEL

Israel, then, was a nation among the nations. But at the same time they were conscious of being different from the rest of the nations. In the first place, they believed in the uniqueness of their own *historical* origin as a nation – namely, the election of Abraham, the national deliverance from slavery in Egypt, the covenant at Sinai and the gift of the land.

Ask now about the former days, long before your time, from the day God created man on the earth; ask from one end of the heavens to the other. Has anything so great as this ever happened, or has anything like it ever been heard of? Has any other people heard the voice of God speaking out of fire, as you have, and lived? Has any god ever tried to take for himself one nation out of another nation, by testings, by miraculous signs and wonders, by war, by a mighty hand and an outstretched arm, or by great and awesome deeds, like all the things the LORD your God did for you in Egypt before your very eyes? (Dt. 4:32–34).

However, at least one prophet, Amos, saw that unless Israel lived out this historical privilege by obedience to the demands of the covenant, particularly in terms of social justice, then they were no better than other nations with a history of migration and settlement (Am. 9:7).

In the second place, they were repeatedly reminded of their strict *religious* distinctiveness. The basic covenant stipulations of the first and second commandments – no other gods but the LORD and no idols or images – were reinforced by a complete ban on any compromise with the religious practices of other nations, especially the Canaanites whose land they would possess.

Do not bow down before their gods or worship them or follow their practices. You must demolish them and break their sacred stones to pieces (Ex. 23:24; *cf.* Dt. 6:14; 7:5f.; 29:16–18).

But religious distinctiveness by itself was not enough either. Not all the prophets did battle with idolatrous worship of other gods as did Elijah (1 Ki. 18:20–46). There were those who saw that outwardly orthodox worship of the LORD could flourish alongside the most blatant social evils of oppression and injustice. It stung them to vehemently indignant language.

Stop bringing meaningless offerings!
    Your incense is detestable to me.
New Moons, Sabbaths and convocations –
    I cannot bear your evil assemblies.
Your New Moon festivals and your appointed feasts
    my soul hates.
They have become a burden to me;
    I am weary of bearing them.

And the reason?
    Your hands are full of blood;

> wash and make yourselves clean . . .
> Seek justice,
>   encourage the oppressed.
> Defend the cause of the fatherless,
>   plead the case of the widow (Is. 1:13–17; *cf.* Is. 58;
>   Mi. 3).

This drives us on to the third aspect of their distinctiveness which was *ethical*. The purpose of their historical experience and of their religious faith and observance was to nourish a national system of social life that was consistent with God's own character and in contrast to the ways of 'unredeemed' nations round about. Without such ethical distinctiveness, the mere facts of their history and features of their religion remained fruitless. Now, it is possible to study Israelite society in close detail and compare it with what is known of their contemporary neighbours to see if and how they actually were different. Recent sociological study of this sort has shown clearly both that Israel did have a consciously articulated sense of national distinctiveness and that this difference was expressed in social, economic and political, as well as religious, terms.[1]

For example, in contrast to pre-Israelite Canaanite society which was organized along 'feudal' lines, with power residing at the élite top of a highly stratified social pyramid, Israel was a 'tribal' society. It had a kinship structure based on a large number of 'extended-family', land-owning households. These units, which were largely self-sufficient economically, performed most of the socially important functions locally – judicial, economic, cultic, military. Israelite society was more broadly 'egalitarian' rather than 'hierarchical'.

The same contrast is seen in economic life in the forms of land tenure. In the Canaanite city-states, all land was owned by the king and there were feudal arrangements with those who lived and worked on it. In Israel the land was divided up as widely as possible into multiple ownership by extended-families. In order to preserve this system, it could not simply be bought and sold commercially, but had to be retained within the kinship groups. Furthermore, many of the Old Testament laws and institutions of land use (see chapter 4) indicate an

---

[1] See especially, N. K. Gottwald, *The Tribes of Yahweh*.

overriding concern to preserve this comparative equality of families on the land and to protect the poorer, the weaker and the economically threatened, and not to uphold the status and wealth of a small land-owning nobility.

Likewise, in political life, power in Israelite society was originally very decentralized and located in the wide network of local elders in each community. Although this was supplemented in times of emergency by figures of temporary 'charismatic' leadership (the judges), there was resistance for a long time to anything like a dynastic central monarchy. When one did eventually emerge, it was limited by the law that the king was to be 'one from among your brothers', who was not to 'consider himself better than his brothers' or copy the extravagances of the surrounding monarchies (Dt. 17:15–20).

> The result [of this sociological study] has been the emerging cross-section of Israel as an egalitarian, extended-family, segmentary tribal society with an agricultural-pastoral economic base . . . characterized by profound resistance and opposition to the forms of political domination and social stratification that had become normative in the chief cultural and political centers of the ancient Near East.[2]

Now the fact that in many respects and at different times Israel failed to maintain this socio-ethical distinctiveness does not destroy our point. Indeed, it is often the places of failure that show up more starkly what the ideals and standards were in this area. The most poignant illustration of this is the rejection of Samuel and his sons and the demand for a king in 1 Samuel 8.

There is great subtlety in the narrative. It begins with the miserable failure of Samuel's sons to emulate their father's integrity. They pervert the very thing they were appointed to uphold, justice (v. 3). The request of the elders for a king thus appears at first sight to be a laudable desire to have a strong figure who would fulfil one of the prime functions of public leadership in the ancient world, the administration of justice. However, their motive is more clearly betrayed at the end of their request: 'Appoint a king to lead us, *such as all the other nations have'* (v. 5; my italics).

Samuel may have been upset by the personal slight to his own leadership, but God showed him the true essence of the matter. Israel's desire for a king was a rejection of God himself as ruler. Hitherto they had 'by faith' accepted theocratic rule, that of God himself. But now they wanted a king like the other nations. Very well, they would have one. But had they thought through the *social* consequences? Samuel proceeds to show the people that if they become like other nations in having a king, then like them they will suffer all the social burdens of a costly monarchy:

> Samuel told all the words of the LORD to the people who were asking him for a king. He said, 'This is what the king who will reign over you will do: He will take your sons and make them serve with his chariots and horses, and they will run in front of his chariots. Some he will assign to be commanders of thousands and commanders of fifties, and others to plough his ground and reap his harvest, and still others to make weapons of war and equipment for his chariots. He will take your daughters to be perfumers and cooks and bakers. He will take the best of your fields and vineyards and olive groves, and give them to his attendants. He will take a tenth of your grain and of your vintage and give it to his officials and attendants. Your menservants and maidservants and the best of your cattle and donkeys he will take for his own use. He will take a tenth of your flocks, and you yourselves will become his slaves. When that day comes, you will cry out for relief from the king you have chosen, and the LORD will not answer you in that day.' (vv. 10–18).

His account of kingship is explicit and accurate, both as a description of contemporary non-Israelite monarchy and as a prediction of what Israelite monarchy actually came to entail from the reign of Solomon and increasingly thereafter. 'But the people refused to listen to Samuel. "No!" they said. "We want a king over us. *Then we shall be like all the other nations"* ' (vv. 19f.; my italics). And so one facet of their social distinctiveness was compromised.

ISRAEL AS GOD'S PARADIGM

The question might arise at this point: yes, but where does this get us in the task of Old Testament ethics? It may be interesting to take note of the social differences of Israel from other nations, but surely that is irrelevant to discovering and applying the message of the Old Testament text itself. Is not our authority 'what the Scriptures say', not, 'what Israel may have been like'?

Our answer to this is that so much of the Old Testament text is in fact taken up with precisely this matter of what Israel were supposed to be and do as a society, or, more often than not, what they were failing to be and do as such. One finds theological and ethical justification or critique of Israel's social life woven into every part of the Old Testament canon. Clearly it mattered very much indeed. The social shape of Israel was not an incidental freak of ancient history, nor was it just a temporary, material by-product of their spiritual message. It was an integral part of what God had called them into existence for. God's message of redemption through Israel was not just verbal; it was visible and tangible. They, the medium, were themselves part of the message.

This understanding of Israel's *raison d'être* is to be found in the words addressed to them in the preface to the foundational Sinai covenant.

> Now if you obey me fully and keep my covenant, then out of all nations you will be my treasured possession. Although the whole earth is mine, you will be for me a kingdom of priests and a holy nation (Ex. 19:5f.).

Common political terms are used here: 'kingdom' and 'nation', but they are placed, almost with a touch of irony, alongside words that were the opposite of 'common' – 'priestly' and 'holy'. The holiness of Israel we have already touched on, noting its dependence on, and imitation of, the holiness of God.

But what is meant by calling the whole nation 'priestly'? A priest, in Old Testament thought and practice, stood between God and the people, a mediator in both directions. He represented God to the people, both in his person and example (*cf.* Lv. 21 – 22), and especially in his role as *teacher* (Dt. 33:10; Ho.

4:6; Mal. 2:4–7). Through the priests, the word and will of God were to be made known to the rest of the people. Now if Israel as a nation were to be a priesthood, the implication is that they would represent God to the peoples of mankind in an analogous way. God's way would be made manifest in their life as a nation.

We have already seen that the holiness of Israel was not a merely spiritual matter but had very practical implications. Now we can see it was not an exclusive or inward-looking distinctiveness. Rather it was God-centred precisely in order that it should be directed to the benefit of the rest of mankind, for 'the whole earth is mine'. And in order for it to have that 'outward' orientation in an effective way, their holiness needed to be given social, community, 'flesh'. That is why the purpose of God for Israel expressed in Exodus 19:6 is so closely dependent on their obedience to the covenant law laid down in the preceding verse. It would be as they lived out the quality of national and social life demanded by the law they were about to receive, with its great chords of freedom, justice, love and compassion, that they would function as God's holy priesthood: as a nation, among the nations, for the nations (*cf.* Ps. 99:1–4).

Our introduction of the word 'flesh' raises overtones of 'incarnation'. This is deliberate, for there is indeed something 'incarnational' about the role of Israel in the Old Testament which points typically to Jesus Christ. The best place to focus this line of thought is in the Servant passages in Isaiah. There the identity of the Servant oscillates between the nation of Israel collectively (Is. 42:18–22; 44:1–5) and the individual figure portrayed by the prophet (42:1–7; 50:4–11; 52:13 – 53:12). Twice, the role assigned to the Servant is described as one of bringing the light of the knowledge of God and a covenant relationship with him to nations beyond the borders of Israel herself.

> I will keep you and will make you
> to be a covenant for the people
> and a light for the Gentiles (42:6).

> It is too small a thing for you to be my servant
> to restore the tribes of Jacob
> and bring back those of Israel I have kept.
> I will also make you a light for the Gentiles,

> that you may bring my salvation to the ends of
> the earth (49:6).

This second text links the world-wide work of the Servant to his role in relation to Israel precisely because he is the embodiment of what Israel was supposed to have been but had failed to be, namely a manifestation of God himself. Earlier in the same passage it is Israel who is addressed as the Servant:

> You are my servant,
> Israel, in whom I will display my splendour (49:3).

The work assigned to the individual Servant is necessitated by the failure of the nation as Servant to display this splendour.

> Who is blind but my servant,
> and deaf like the messenger I send?
> Who is blind like the one committed to me,
> blind like the servant of the LORD?
>
> It pleased the LORD
> for the sake of his righteousness
> to make his law great and glorious.
>
> [But] they would not follow his ways;
> they did not obey his law (42:19, 21, 24).

And significantly, the work assigned to the Servant, in fulfilment of the failed vocation of the nation, is to exemplify and generate all the *social* blessings that should have been displayed in the nation. This is patently clear in chapter 42 and is found also in 48:17–19; 49:8–10 and 51:4f.

> I will put my Spirit on him
> and he will bring justice to the nations.
>
> In faithfulness he will bring forth justice;
> he will not falter or be discouraged
> till he establishes justice on earth.
>
> . . . to open eyes that are blind,
> to free captives from prison
> and to release from the dungeon those who sit
> in darkness (42:1, 3f., 7).

The fact that Jesus applies these and other similar passages to himself shows that he regarded himself as assuming this Servant-role that Israel had failed to fulfil.[3] And since a major purpose of the incarnation of Christ was to reveal God, one can, by analogy and a legitimate typology, affirm that there was an 'incarnational' and revelational aspect to God's creation of Israel.[4] Their very existence and character as a society were to be a witness to God, a model or paradigm of his holiness expressed in the social life of a redeemed community.

The choice of the term 'paradigm' needs some explanation and justification. A paradigm is something used as a model or example for other cases where a basic principle remains unchanged, though details differ. It commonly refers, for example, to patterns in grammatical inflection – a verb, say, taken to exemplify the way endings or prefixes will go for other verbs of a similar type. A paradigm is not so much imitated as applied. It is assumed that cases will differ but, when necessary adjustments have been made, they will conform to the observable pattern of the paradigm.

In my view, the social relevance of Israel is to be seen as paradigmatic. Indeed, I would regard 'paradigm' as a useful category for ethically understanding and applying the Old Testament itself. This way of looking at the social life, institutions and laws of Israel protects us from two opposite dangers.

On the one hand it means that we do not think in terms of literal imitation of Israel. We cannot simply transpose the social laws of an ancient people into the modern world and try to make them work as written. That would be tantamount to taking the paradigms of a grammar book as the only words one could use in that particular language. The paradigms are there, not to be the sum of possible communication ever after, but to be applied to the infinite complexities of the rest of the language.

On the other hand, the social system of Israel cannot be dismissed as relevant only within the confines of historical Israel, and as totally inapplicable to either the Christian church or the rest of mankind. If Israel was meant to be a light to the

---

[3] *e.g.* Mt. 8:17; 12:18–21; Mk. 10:45; Lk. 4:18f.
[4] It is seen, for example, in the way Jerusalem and its temple are described as the place where God 'causes his name to dwell' – the name being tantamount to the presence and known revelation of God himself.

nations (*cf.* Is. 49:6), then that light must be allowed to illumin-
ate. The purpose of the chapters in Part Two is to show how
different aspects of Israel's social life can act as critique
and corrective to analogous aspects of our own age. I believe
this paradigmatic approach opens up the Old Testament most
fruitfully as a resource for Christian social ethics.

The comparison with Christ's incarnation is again helpful
here. The Gospels take very seriously the fact that Jesus was a
real man who lived, behaved, related, travelled and taught in
the way described in their account of his ministry. He called
his disciples to 'follow him' and we are commanded in various
ways in the New Testament to model our lives on his (*e.g.* Eph.
5:2; Phil. 2:5; 1 Pet. 2:21ff.). But rarely in the history of Christian
moral thought has that been taken in the sense of literal imitation down to detail (in the way that, for example, the details of
Mohammed's life and habits became obligatory on his
followers). We do not feel obliged to practise carpentry, wear
seamless clothing, pursue an itinerant and homeless lifestyle,
worship in synagogue or temple, eat with tax-collectors and
prostitutes, or teach by parables.

Yet neither, on the other hand, do we feel free to treat the
Gospel accounts of the life of Jesus as ethically irrelevant,
choosing to pay attention only to his teaching. For it was in
part the quality of Jesus' *life* which authenticated his teaching,
confounded his enemies and rendered his execution the trav-
esty of justice it was. Rather we tend, unconsciously or otherwise, to use the example of Jesus paradigmatically in our ethical
decisions, seeking to move from what we know Jesus *did* do to
what we might reasonably presume he *would* do in our changed
situation. The overall shape and character of his life – com-
prising his actions, attitudes and relationships as well as his
responses, parables and other teaching – becomes our pattern
or paradigm, by which we test the 'Christ-likeness' of the same
components of our own lives.

Similarly, we are to take Israel's social shape and characteristics, her institutions, laws and ideals (the latter so often clarified
by Israel's manifest failure to achieve them), as paradigmatic
when we are engaged in the social ethical task – both in theory
and in practice. They are not, of course, the exclusive paradigm
for social ethics; the Christian brings this, as he does every
other aspect of the Old Testament, into the light of the new age

of fulfilment and the Kingdom of God inaugurated by Christ. He therefore sets his Old Testament social paradigm alongside the paradigm of the social life of the early church as well as the explicit social teaching of Jesus and the apostles. Only then is he beginning to formulate a wholly biblical social ethic.

3
The economic angle

THE LAND IN ISRAEL'S STORY

The Bible's story of redemption begins with God's promises to Abraham. A fundamental constituent of that promise, as it is revealed and repeated in the patriarchal narrative, is that God would give to Abraham and his descendants a *land*. That land becomes one of the most prominent features of the entire sequel of the Old Testament story.

Once again it is important that we allow the Old Testament to speak to us, not in bits and pieces taken at random, nor from the perspective and in the technical terms of one systematic theology or another, but as a *narrative*. When we do so, it is at once very apparent that the overarching theme of the great history of the Pentateuch, on through the books of Joshua and Judges and up to the establishing of the territorial limits of the kingdom of David, is the promise and the possession of the land.

The Pentateuch generates tremendous suspense concerning the land. Genesis records the patriarchs wandering in the land with no secure footholds, except for the elaborately achieved purchase of a burial site (Gn. 23), and concludes with the whole family settling down in Egypt. The land was not lost sight of, however, for the book ends with the dying words of Joseph recalling the promise of God and trusting in its fulfilment.

Exodus is launched with God's 'awakened' intention to keep that promise. When, in the course of the momentous events of the first nineteen chapters, Israel has been freed, mobilized, organized and bound together and to God by covenant at Sinai, the reader would be inclined to think that occupation of the land was but a step away. First, however, he must grapple with a detailed description of the tabernacle and its furnishings, not once but twice! The lesson was as clear as the prayer of Moses in Exodus 33:15f.; the presence of God in the midst of his people was even more important than the gift of the land. And so the book ends with the glory of the presence of God settling on the 'Tent of Meeting' and accompanying the Israelites in all their forthcoming travels (Ex. 40:34–38).

Leviticus suspends the story still further as detailed laws are given. But in the latter section of the book, often called the 'Holiness Code', the land comes back into focus. For many of the laws are framed from the perspective of life in the land after the conquest. Indeed, the land is personified as the agent of God's blessing or curse, inasmuch as it is described as 'vomiting out' the present inhabitants for their wicked ways, and quite capable of repeating the performance on the Israelites if they imitate them (Lv. 18:24–28; 20:22–24). That is even foreseen in chapter 26, but not without another concluding reassurance of the permanence of the promise to the patriarchs (26:42–45).

Numbers brings the suspense to a climax with the stories of the spies, the people's failure of nerve, the abortive first attempt at invasion, and the dreary years of a whole generation spent in the wilderness (Nu. 13 – 14). Will this people ever capture Canaan? Can the promise really be fulfilled? Eventually, however, the painful journeys through hostile territories come to an end with the tribes encamped in the plains of Moab, and only the Jordan to cross. The oracles of Balaam reassure the reader of God's benevolent purpose. But the action of the Reubenites and Gadites again raises our suspense (Nu. 32). Will they seduce the whole people into accepting life on the wrong side of Jordan? That threat is averted diplomatically and the book ends optimistically with the map of Canaan already being redrawn to accommodate the victorious Israelites. But they are still not actually in.

Surely the new book must take us into the land. But no! Deuteronomy begins and ends in Moab. We are treated to a detailed recapitulation of the story so far, with sustained exhortation to obedient faithfulness to the covenant (Dt. 1 – 11). Then comes the major part of the book, devoted to the law – some old ones modified, some new ones introduced (12 – 26), but all based on life in the land they have *still* to occupy. As at the end of Leviticus, the land itself will be both the arena and agent of God's blessing or curse, depending on the people's obedience or otherwise (28 – 30). Finally, after the song and blessing of Moses, Deuteronomy brings to a close both itself and the whole magnificent structure of the Pentateuch, with the moving account of the death of Moses, who had led his people to within a day's march of the land of promise but would not himself set foot in it (34). So the story of God's people in the Pentateuch ends, as it began, with the promise of the land to Abraham (Dt. 34:4), but with that promise still unfulfilled.

Joshua begins with words the reader has begun to wonder if he would ever hear: 'Get ready to cross the Jordan River into the land I am about to give to them – to the Israelites' (Jos. 1:2). The rest of the book then has the land as its principal theme: its invasion, conquest and division. It ends in the same way as Deuteronomy with a renewal of the covenant, but with one of its promises now an accomplished fact, no longer a future hope.

The stage lights dim, however, as the book of Judges shows how incompletely the initial conquest had been effectively followed up. The land of promise becomes a land of struggle, where long periods of defeat are interspersed with hard-won, short-lived victories. Our suspense revives, no longer as to whether the people will enter the land, but whether they can survive within it. With the onslaught of the Philistines, the obstacles to secure possession of the whole land seem insuperable. The last and greatest of the judges, Samuel, achieves a victory that holds them at bay during his personal rule (1 Sa. 7). But Israel's first king, appointed for the very purpose of leading Israel against them (1 Sa. 8:20), witnesses at the point of his own death the Philistines achieving their deepest inroad into Canaan, virtually cutting Israel's land in half (1 Sa. 31). What has happened to the promised secure boundaries of the land (Gn. 15:18f.; Ex. 23:31; Nu. 34:1–12)? Not until the sustained victories and long rule of David does Israel eventually live at peace within secure borders embracing the territory actually promised (2 Sa. 8; 10). At last the promise is manifestly and effectively fulfilled.

But the land does not disappear from the continuing story of the Old Testament. The accumulated burden of oppression and injustice in the nation during the centuries after Solomon led to a fresh outburst of prophetic activity in the eighth century. The most shocking ingredient in the prophets' message was the threat and prediction of exile from the land. This new and jarring note had not been heard before. It had not been part of the message of the ninth-century prophets such as Elijah and Elisha. It may well have been the factor which precipitated the writing down of the prophetic oracles – beginning with the earliest of the written prophetic collections, Amos. Imagine the electrifying effect of oracles like these:

> 'Fallen is Virgin Israel,
>> never to rise again,
> deserted in her own land,
>> with no-one to lift her up.
> I will send you into exile beyond Damascus,'
>> says the LORD, whose name is God Almighty
>>> (Am. 5:2, 27).

In fact we need not imagine, for their effect on the religious and political establishment is vividly described in 7:10ff. Bluntly, Amos is told to shut up and get lost (7:12f.). The threat recoils on its bearer, however, for Amos makes a 'private' prediction for Amaziah the priest that he and his family will personally suffer the calamity that will overtake the nation (v. 17).

Such threats, when set against the cardinal tenets of Israel's faith in God's promise and gift of the land, cannot but have sounded like gross heresy. Yet they remained a constant feature of the message of all the pre-exilic prophets right up until the events which vindicated them – namely the destruction of the northern kingdom of Israel by Assyria in 721 BC, and the sack of Jerusalem and exile of the Judean kingdom to Babylon in 587 BC. In those events the warnings of the law (Lv. 26; Dt. 28) and the threats of the prophets came true, and another generation of Israelites learned what it was to live without their own land, under the hand of God's chastisement. The pain of the experience of exile can be felt in passages such as Psalm 137 and Lamentations. Life without the land was scarcely life as God's people at all.

Yet God's people they still were, for he had not abandoned them. Nor had he abandoned his promise to Abraham or relinquished his claim to the land. It was the great achievement of the prophets of this searing period, especially Jeremiah and Ezekiel, to reinforce this hope, with specific reference in both cases to the land. One of the most outstandingly courageous acts of any prophet, in practical demonstration of faith in his own prophetic word, was Jeremiah's purchase of land from his kinsman Hanamel, at a time when Jerusalem was in the last throes of its final siege and Jeremiah was cooped up in a dungeon (Je. 32). He would never set foot on it, nor, being unmarried, had he any family to pass it on to. But it was a tangible token of his faith in God's promise that, after the judgment of exile,

> Once more fields will be bought in this land of which you say, 'It is a desolate waste, without men or animals, for it has been handed over to the Babylonians.' . . . because I will restore their fortunes, declares the LORD (Je. 32:43f.).

And so he did. The restoration of the relationship between God and his people was sealed by the restoration of his people to their land – described in the visionary language of a new exodus (Is. 43:16–21; Je. 23:7f.). The wheel had turned full circle.

The point of this rapid review of the Old Testament story has been to show that the land is one of its dominant themes. It was *not* just a neutral stage where the drama unfolds (since, let's face it, people have to live somewhere!). The land, in all its dimensions – promise, conquest, shared possession, use and abuse, loss and recovery – was a fundamentally theological entity. The story of Israel is the story of redemption and we have seen that the social shape of Israel was part of the purpose and pattern of redemption. The same can now be said of the role of the land within the Old Testament story of Israel. The land was part of the pattern of redemption too, because the social shape of Israel was intimately bound up with the economic issues of the division, tenure and use of the land.

Now since, as we have already seen, Old Testament ethics are inseparably dependent on Old Testament theology, it follows that anything so important to its theology as the land must be correspondingly important to its ethics. This is indeed so, as we shall now proceed to discover.

THE LAND AS DIVINE GIFT

As we have now seen, the promise of land and its historical fulfilment in the gift of the land together form the major theme of the Pentateuch and early historical books. Israel had a land to live in because God, quite simply, had given it to them. This strong land-gift tradition had wide implications on Old Testament thinking and practice.

In the first place, it was *a declaration of Israel's dependency*. Right at the start Abram was called to leave his native land and go to a country which, in the event, was not specified until he got there. The patriarchal narratives emphasize the alien, 'sojourning' state of these ancestors of Israel. Israel, therefore, could make no 'natural' claim to any land. The only one they possessed they owed solely to God's election of and promise to Abraham – just as indeed they owed their very existence as a nation to these same two facts. These points were forcefully and unflatteringly impressed upon Israel in Deuteronomy's preparation for the conquest. They must not think they had any claim upon God's acts on their behalf: they had been, and always would be, utterly dependent on his love and faithfulness.

> The LORD did not set his affection on you and choose you because you were more numerous than other peoples, for you were the fewest of all peoples. But it was because the LORD loved you and kept the oath he swore to your forefathers . . . (7:7f.).

> You may say to yourself, 'My power and the strength of my hands have produced this wealth for me.' But remember the LORD your God, for it is he who gives you the ability to produce wealth, and so confirms his covenant, which he swore to your forefathers . . . (8:17f.).

> It is not because of your righteousness or your integrity that you are going in to take possession of their land; but on account of the wickedness of these nations, the LORD your God will drive them out before you, to accomplish what he swore to your fathers . . . (9:5).

Belief in the givenness of the land, then, preserved the right perspective in Israel's relationship with God. He could not be regarded in the same way as the gods of other nations – a figurehead for their nationalism or a merely functional protector of their territorial claims. Rather the reverse; without him they would have been no nation and had no land. His moral sovereignty was therefore absolute. As they were to discover, on account of their moral disobedience he would bring both nation and territory to the brink of extinction, were it not for the fact that his wider redemptive purpose was unshakeable.

Secondly, the land-gift was *a declaration of God's dependability*. Every harvest reminded Israel of this. This land whose produce they now enjoyed had not always been theirs. They had not always even desired it, as the traditions of their wilderness grumblings painfully reminded them. But here it was. God had kept his promise even in spite of their resistance. His dependability knew no limits: 'his steadfast love endures for ever'.

The strength of this proven article of faith is seen not only in worship, such as in the refrain just quoted (Ps. 136 RSV), but in the almost 'credal' statement placed on the lips of the farmer bringing the firstfruits of his harvest to the sanctuary. It is worth savouring to the full. Having been instructed to place his basket of harvest produce before the altar, he is told:

> Then you shall declare before the LORD your God: 'My father was a wandering Aramean, and he went down into Egypt with a few people and lived there and became a great nation, powerful and numerous. But the Egyptians ill-treated us and made us suffer, putting us to hard labour. Then we cried out to the LORD, the God of our fathers, and the LORD heard our voice and saw our misery, toil and oppression. So the LORD brought us out of Egypt with a mighty hand and an outstretched arm, with great terror and with miraculous signs and wonders. He brought us to this place and gave us this land, a land flowing with milk and honey; and now I bring the firstfruits of the soil that you, O LORD, have given me' (Dt. 26:5–10).

What is remarkable about this declaration is that although the occasion of it is the goodness of God in the fruitfulness of *nature*, its total emphasis is on the faithfulness and power of

God in control of *history*. And the focus and climax of the recitation is the gift of the land, for it was the monumental, tangible proof of God's dependability. Here in these few succinct verses an Israelite could recount a history that embraced several centuries, moved through several national and cultural 'zones', and yet was 'contemporized' in the harvest he had just reaped. And he could unify all of it under this one theme of the fulfilment of God's promise in the gift of the land. There was no greater visible proof of the qualities of the God of Israel. (Would that our own harvest festivals had such a sense of history and of the faithfulness of God's redemptive purpose!) Morally speaking, therefore, he was a God *worthy* of obedience; his response to human behaviour would be consistent and dependable, not a matter of arbitrary whim. He could be pleased, but not humoured.

Thirdly, in combination of both the above points, the land-gift functioned as *proof of the relationship between God and Israel*. Israel knew they were the people of God because he had given them his land, and that gift verified the relationship written into both the covenant with Abraham and the covenant made at Sinai with the whole people.

Another way in which this was expressed was by the use of the term *inheritance* to describe the land, implying as it does a relationship of sonship between Israel and God. It is interesting that in the Exodus narrative God refers to Israel as 'my firstborn son' (Ex. 4:22), for whom he demands release from captivity, with the intention of bringing him to the land of promise. The situation was intolerable. What was God's firstborn son doing languishing in a foreign country when his inheritance awaited him? The language of inheritance as such is not found often in Exodus (*cf.* 15:17; 32:13), but it comes to the fore in Deuteronomy. The word frequently used for 'to take possession of' or 'to give possession to' was commonly used in connection with inheritance. In some passages the land is explicitly called an inheritance (*e.g.* 4:21; 4:38; 12:9; 15:4; 19:10; 26:1), and in others Israel is called God's son or offspring (14:1; 32:5f., 18f. and, metaphorically, 8:5) – and thereby his heir.

Just as the gift of the land was God's act and owed nothing to Israel's greatness or merits, so with Israel's sonship. They belonged to God, not by their choice of him, but because he had brought them to birth. The bond between Israel's land theology (the 'economic angle') and their unique relationship with God is here seen at its closest. The one is, as it were, the tangible manifestation of the other.

One practical consequence of this was the unreserved enjoyment of the land as a blessing. Its praises are sung with luxuriant detail in Deuteronomy (*e.g.* 8:7–9; 11:8–12). There was no embarrassment over the prospect of abundant fruitfulness and prosperity. The land was the good gift of their bountiful God and was meant to bring joy, festivity and gratitude. Now of course, as we shall see in a moment, this was contained within a strong moral framework of responsibility to God for one another – especially those who would become poor as a result of corporate disobedience (*cf.* Dt. 15:4ff.). The answer to poverty was not the reduction of all to equivalent frugality, but rather, a return to repentant obedience to God that would raise all to renewed blessing and bounty.

Fourthly, it was the historical land-gift tradition which generated *individual property rights* in Israel. We have already caught a passing glimpse of this in the harvest declaration quoted above. The Israelite farmer speaks of 'the firstfruits of the soil that you, O Lord, have given me'. Not, we take note, 'to us', but 'to *me*'. The Israelite did not think only in terms of the whole land given to the whole nation. That concept could have been compatible with the whole land being held on the nation's behalf, as it were, by a king as their representative. That, in fact, was the Canaanite system. But such a notion was strongly resisted among the Israelites. The gift of land 'percolated', so to speak, down to the lowest social level, so that each individual household could claim that its right to the land it possessed was guaranteed by God himself. Thus, inheritance language was used of the small portions of land belonging to each household, as well as of the territory of whole tribes or the whole nation. They, too, were held as the gift of God.

This is what gives significance and importance to Numbers 26 and 34 and Joshua 13 – 19, which describe the division of the land. It is repeatedly referred to as a division 'according to their clans', *i.e.* the sub-groupings of families within the larger unit of the tribe. To us these detailed lists seem tedious and interminable, but for Israel they enshrined a fundamental principle: the land was intended to be equitably shared out, so that every household had its part in the national inheritance.

The strength of this belief is seen in Naboth's reaction to King Ahab's suggestion, which seems innocent enough to us. Ahab proposed that he should purchase, or exchange other land for, Naboth's vineyard. The response was vehement: 'The LORD forbid that I should give you the inheritance of my fathers!' (1 Ki. 21:1–3). It was not really Naboth's to give, sell or exchange. He held it on trust from the LORD for the benefit of his family. It was not a question of 'human rights', 'natural justice' or anything so abstract. It was a staunch upholding of the right of a member of God's people to maintain that part of the national inheritance which God had assigned to his personal household. Significantly, the only way Ahab could get the vineyard was by falsely convicting Naboth of blasphemy, an offence by which he forfeited his right to belong to God's people. He was stoned accordingly, and his land confiscated (1 Ki. 21:11–16). The whole incident shows how closely possession of a share in the land and personal belonging within the covenant relationship to God were bound together.

Fifthly, the sequel to the Naboth incident opens up our understanding of *the prophets' preoccupation with economic exploitation*. Scarcely had the dust of Naboth's stoning settled before Elijah was bearing down on Ahab as he inspected his ill-gotten possession. His message was blunt and simple: God is angry at your compound crime and will punish you in like manner (1 Ki. 21:17–22). But Naboth's fate became typical of what happened to large numbers of the ordinary populace, as royalty and its attendant wealthy nobility made ever-increasing incursions into the traditional Israelite system of inalienable family land tenure. More and more people were deprived of their ancestral land and forced, by debt-bondage and other means, into a state of virtual serfdom on land once their own but now in the hands of the wealthy, powerful few And it was the prophets who came to their defence, exposing the corruption and exploitation as mercilessly as it was being practised.

> Woe to those who plan iniquity,
> to those who plot evil on their beds! . . .
> They covet fields and seize them,
> and houses, and take them.
> They defraud a man of his home,
> a fellow-man of his inheritance (Mi. 2:1f.).

> Woe to you who add house to house
> and join field to field
> till no space is left
> and you live alone in the land (Is. 5:8).

Everywhere you look in the prophets, this vehement indignation at economic injustice is either evident or not far from the surface.

In the light of the principles outlined above we can see that this aspect of the prophetic message did not stem from a general concern for human rights, nor from an advancing ethical sensitivity. It was not even a merely economic issue. It was deeply spiritual. Anything which threatened a household's economic viability or drove them out of secure tenure of their portion of land was a threat to its secure membership of the covenant people. To lose one's land was more than economic disaster: it struck at one's very relationship with God. That is why the wealthy establishment was so appalled at the language of Amos, when he insisted on calling 'the righteous' those who were being oppressed and dispossessed. Popular thinking of his day would probably have 'excommunicated' them. Amos reverses the evaluation (2:6; 5:12).

But the other aspect of the matter which so hurt the prophets was that it was *Israelites* who were so viciously oppressing their fellow-Israelites, and that they were using the greatest token of God's common blessing on them all, the land, to do so. Here was a horrible perversion indeed. One section of God's people was depriving another of what was God's gift and every Israelite's right: freedom and land. Such internal exploitation had been forbidden in the law on the grounds of the equality of all Israelites as God's freed slaves (Lv. 25:42f., 53–55). But now the defenceless were being devoured by an enemy *within*.

> Lately my people have risen up
> like an enemy. . . .
> You drive the women of my people
> from their pleasant homes.
> You take away my blessing[1]
> from their children for ever (Mi. 2:8f.).

[1] Or, 'glory'.

Economic exploitation is a moral evil which could be condemned on the wide basis of common humanity and an ethic of stewardship (which we shall consider below in chapter 4). But when those who are the agents and victims of the exploitation are members of the people of God, and when the means of exploitation is a supreme and 'costly' gift of God to his own people, then the evil is seen in all its unnatural perversion, and the vehemence of the prophets' denunciations can be properly understood.

THE LAND UNDER DIVINE OWNERSHIP

A cynic might be tempted to shrug off the prophets' indignation by saying that surely, if the land had been given to Israel, they were free to use or abuse it as they pleased. The answer to this lies on the other side of the coin of Old Testament land theology: *the land was still God's land.* He retained the ultimate title of ownership and therefore also the ultimate right of moral authority over how it was used. This is hinted at in one of the earliest pieces of Israelite poetry, the song of Moses in Exodus 15. It celebrates the miracle of the exodus and looks forward to the entry into the land, which is described (addressing God) as 'your holy dwelling' (v. 13), 'the mountain of your inheritance' (v. 17) and 'the place, O LORD, you made for your dwelling' (v. 17). Another early poem refers to 'his land and people' (Dt. 32:43). The clearest statement, however, comes in Leviticus: 'the land is mine and you are but aliens and my tenants' (25:23).

The description of the Israelites' relationship to God in respect of the land in this verse is interesting. The terms 'resident aliens and tenants' ('strangers and sojourners', RSV) referred to a class of people within Israelite society who did not own any land, being descendants of the old Canaanite population or else immigrant workers; they were wholly dependent, therefore, on being able to reside within a landed Israelite household. As long as the host household retained its land and was economically viable, their position was secure. But without such protection they were very vulnerable indeed. God casts himself in the role of the landowner and the Israelites as his dependent tenants. As long as their relationship was maintained and his protection afforded, they were secure. But if they rebelled against his authority and his protection were withdrawn, they would have to face the consequences. The implication was clear: 'Be careful what you do on and with my land'. A socio-economic pheno-menon (dependent labourers in Israelite households) has been taken to describe figuratively a theological relationship (between Israel and God), in such a way that the ethical implication can be directed back into the socio-economic realm.

Another way of looking at the claim of divine ownership on the land is to compare it with the systems of land tenure in some contemporary cultures. In pre-Israelite Canaan, for example, the king held title to the whole of his land. His subjects lived on it and farmed it as his dependent tenants, usually with a heavy burden of taxation (*cf.* Samuel's description, 1 Sa. 8:11–17). That whole demand of human authority is now lifted out of the reach of any human individual or group, where it results in inequality and oppression, and claimed by God alone. The whole land belongs to him and therefore he alone has the right to lay claim to his people's dependency. Under a *human* land-owning king, people live in the equality of oppression. Under their land-owning *God*, Israel lives in the equality of freedom.

This equality of redeemed brothers, now slaves of God, is reiterated throughout Leviticus 25. If God alone ultimately owns the land, then no Israelite has the right either to treat his own land as if he 'owned' it, in the sense of being able to do as he liked with it, or to lay claim to the land of any other Israelite, except according to the laws of inheritance and kinship. Even a king is but a tenant in God's land! Ahab is only a fellow-tenant to Naboth.

So it emerges that just as, on the one hand, the concept of the land as divine *gift* generated a strong set of *rights* for both the nation and individuals, so, on the other hand, the concept of the land as under continuing divine *ownership* generated a wide range of *responsibilities*. These responsibilities can be clas-sified broadly under three heads: responsibility to God; to one's family; to one's neighbours.

Responsibility to God for the land included such things as tithes and firstfruits of the harvest, other harvest laws, and the sabbatical legislation as it affected the land – the fallow year and the release of debt-pledges. Responsibility to the family included the fundamental law of inalienability – that is, that land was not to be bought and sold commercially but preserved within a kinship framework. This principle was then buttressed by other kinship responsibilities that related directly or indirectly to land – redemption procedures, inheritance rules and levirate marriage. Responsibility towards one's neighbours included a host of civil laws and charitable exhortations concerning damage or negligence to property, safety precautions, respect for integrity of boundaries, generosity in leaving harvest gleanings, fair treatment of employees and, indeed, of working animals.[2]

So many of the detailed instructions of the law come into this category of responsibility in respect of the land, directly or indirectly, that it is easily the most comprehensive of the ethico-theological principles governing the law. It is the belief that *God owns the land and demands accountability in the use of it* from his 'tenants' that generates the literal 'earthiness' of Old Testament ethics. Nothing that you can do in, on or with the land is outside the sphere of God's moral inspection. From major issues of the defence of the national territory down to how you prune your fruit trees, every area of life is included. Based on such a principle, so simply stated, Old Testament ethics could be both comprehensive and yet deeply practical and particular.

THE LAND AS 'SPIRITUAL THERMOMETER'

Now that we have outlined the substance of the theology of the land in the Old Testament we must summarize the function it performed within our 'basic framework'. What is the role of this 'economic angle' in our overall understanding of Old Testament ethics? Its function can be described as a measure or gauge of the effectiveness of the other two angles.[3] That is to say, the economic sphere is like a thermometer which reveals both the spiritual temperature of the theological relationship between God and Israel (angle A), and also the extent to which Israel was conforming to the social shape required of her in consistency with her status as God's redeemed people (angle B).

[2] Details and references for all the above are provided in chapter 4.
[3] See again the diagram on p. 19.

As regards the first of these, the theological angle, there appears to have been a prolonged struggle in early Israel to bring them to realize that the LORD, the victorious God of their redemptive history, was also entirely competent in the matter of land use, rain, fertility, crops and herds. The tendency to regard the Baals of the previous occupants of the land as more likely to 'produce the goods' in the economic realm seemed ineradicable, from the conquest to the exile.

This issue is explicitly tackled by Hosea, though it can be seen as early as Elijah and as late as Jeremiah. Speaking of Israel's self-prostitution to the Baals as 'lovers', Hosea declares:

> She said, 'I will go after my lovers,
>> who give me my food and my water,
>>> my wool and my linen, my oil and my drink.'. . .
> She has not acknowledged that I was the one
>> who gave her the grain, the new wine and oil
>>>>> (Ho. 2:5, 8).

The irony was that Israel did not apparently perceive this as disloyalty to the LORD, for were they not still worshipping him with all his appointed festivals, sabbaths, *etc.* (v. 11)? But such worship was hollow. Indeed, it was abhorrent to God, inasmuch as it excluded him from the economic realities of daily life. The measure of the sincerity and integrity of the nation's acceptance of God's authority over them as his people was the extent to which they would acknowledge his sovereignty in the economic, as well as the religious, sphere. Looked at in terms of the geometry of our diagram, the 'theological angle' was not complete unless line AC and line AB converged under the sole authority of the LORD. Failure to honour God in the material realm cannot be compensated for by religiosity in the spiritual realm.

Not that there was any illusion in the Old Testament that such economic obedience to God was easy. It was one thing to celebrate the victories of God in *past* history. It was another to trust his ability to produce the *future* harvest. It was still another to trust his ability to provide you and your family with sustenance for a year if you obeyed the fallow or sabbatical year laws and did not sow a crop – or for two years if you had a double fallow at the jubilee! And could you afford to let your slave, an agricultural capital asset, go free after six years, still less with a generous endowment of your substance, animal and vegetable? Were you not entitled to extract maximum yield from your own fields and vineyards without leaving valuable remainders for others? How could you possibly cancel debts after six years? Would it not ruin your own family if you had to redeem and look after the land or personnel of some incompetent kinsman? The whole range of economic requirements in the Old Testament demanded trust in the providential sovereignty of God over nature and a readiness to obey him in spite of the sort of questions posed above (of which the Old Testament was well aware, Lv. 25:20; Dt. 15:9).

As regards the second angle, the social shape of Israel, this can be seen at its most distinctive in economic terms. We saw in the last chapter that the introduction of monarchy politically compromised that distinctiveness. But it was not utterly incompatible, inasmuch as the king could still live by and under the law of God and lead the nation in the way of God's righteousness. Indeed, theologically, the monarchy, although its human origins are seen as tainted with sin and apostasy, became a vehicle for a new set of ideas and expectations regarding God's kingly relationship to his people and his future messianic purpose for them (see chapter 5). It was the baleful effects of monarchy in the *economic* realm that so dangerously threatened the distinctive social shape of Israel, as was so perceptively foreseen by Samuel (1 Sa. 8:11–17).

We have already seen some of these and the prophets' reaction to them. Viewing the situation from God's standpoint, they realized the tragedy of what was happening to God's people. A nation which allowed itself to succumb to the same economic evils as the world around could not function as a 'light to the nations'. It was no paradigm of the social shape of a redeemed people if it was the same shape as the unredeemed Gentiles – worse still, if it descended below the level of those paradigms of wickedness, Sodom and Gomorrah. Yet that is the comparison drawn by more than one prophet. Ezekiel puts Judah and Sodom in the same family as sisters, and comments: 'Now this was the sin of your sister Sodom: She and her daughters were arrogant, overfed and unconcerned; they did not help the poor and needy' (Ezk. 16:49) – a thoroughly *socio-economic* analysis. He then goes on, breathtakingly, to say of Judah, 'You have done more detestable things than they, and have made your sisters seem righteous' (v. 51). The sisters, remember, include *Sodom*!

So we see that it was the content of the 'economic angle' which in large measure acted as a test of Israel's conformity to the social paradigm of redemption that was God's purpose in calling her into existence. The prophets simply would not allow Israel to get away with claiming the blessing and protection of the covenant relationship for their society while trampling on the socio-economic demands of that relationship (*cf.* Je. 7:1–11).

Conclusion:
Covenantal, canonical,
comprehensive

In the introduction to these first three chapters, we claimed that this basic framework of God, Israel and the land enables us to study Old Testament ethics in a way which is covenantal, canonical and comprehensive. It remains now to expand this claim a little more fully.

The pattern of relationships outlined in our framework includes all the essential features of that relationship between God and his people for which the term *covenant* was used – both the covenant of election and promise with Abraham and the national covenant and giving of the law at Sinai. The basis of the covenant was the sovereignty of God: his free choice, in love, of Abraham; his historical faithfulness in redemption from Egypt; his moral authority to stipulate the contents of his people's obedience in the giving of the law. The other side of the statement: 'I am the LORD your God' was 'You are Israel, my people'. This affirmation defined not only their identity but also their purpose in the world. They were to be, and also to live as befitted, the people of God. It was to fit them for this purpose that the host of vertical and horizontal obligations formed part of the covenantal relationship.

As token and proof of that relationship, there was the land of promise and gift, with all the rights and responsibilities we have examined. All of this was of the essence of the covenant. Whenever we seek to interpret any passage ethically, by locating it within this framework, seeing where it 'fits' and how it functions, we shall be seeing it in the light of the 'main beams' of Israel's spiritual constitution – namely the great themes of election, redemption, law and land.

In these three chapters we have noted how each of the three 'angles' forced us to pay attention to the *canonical* order of the Old Testament story. We have to see the whole sweep of Scripture, and ensure that our ethical constructs are consistent with the whole. Now there is a perfectly valid place for studying traditions underlying the finished books, for isolating, comparing and contrasting the varying ethical emphases of different authors, editors and schools within the living kaleidoscope of the Old Testament documents. Such a task would be appropriate in a large-scale analytical work on Old Testament ethics. But it is not only limitation of space and the pursuit of simplicity that keep us from that task here; it is also the conviction that if our aim is a coherent biblical ethic, then our final authority must be the completed text in its canonical form. And the broad framework we are working with keeps us aligned with the order and rationale of the canon itself.

Finally, this framework is *comprehensive*; it permits an inclusiveness that some of the approaches mentioned in the introduction actually hinder or destroy. It enables the student of the Bible to take seriously Paul's assertion that '*All* Scripture is . . . useful for teaching . . . and training in righteousness' (2 Tim. 3:16). He can take any particular text and seek to relate it to one or other of these 'angles', and then to interpret it in the light of the major principles embodied in that sector of Old Testament theology. This is simply a widening of the fundamental rule of interpretation, taking a text in its context.

But the reader can then go further, for each 'angle' is related to the other two, so that the text in question can be opened up by whatever light such inter-relations may shed. In this way the ethical relevance of the text is neither denied to it, *a priori*, nor is it imposed on it by non-biblical considerations. Rather it is evaluated from the function it has (which may be quite limited) within the wider framework of Old Testament life and thought. Thus, no text is dismissed just because 'it doesn't apply to us'. It is no longer a question of direct applicability of every text, but of seeing how it functioned within its Old Testament context, as part of a larger model, which then in its wholeness is to be interpreted and applied paradigmatically. During the course of the following chapters we shall see examples of this method at work.

PART TWO

THEMES IN OLD TESTAMENT ETHICS

4
Economics and the land

'Where there's muck there's money', goes the old country
saying. Its earthy simplicity contains the truth that all human
wealth depends ultimately on what God has entrusted to us in
the immeasurable riches of the earth's crust. In the end all the
complexities of economic science go back to what grows on,
feeds on or is dug out of the soil of our planet. (We have, of
course, scarcely begun to tap the resources of the oceans and
their floors.)

The Old Testament, with its foundation of creation faith and
its rich theology of the land which we sketched in chapter 3, is
therefore bound to have plenty to contribute to Christian economic ethics. In this chapter we shall look first at the economic
implications of the creation faith. Then we shall see how Israel's
experience of redemption deepened and amplified the creation
principles. Once again, we shall ask how these Old Testament
concepts apply within a Christian framework, illustrating our
proposals with an ethical interpretation of the jubilee
institution.

PERSPECTIVES FROM CREATION

DIVINE OWNERSHIP AND DIVINE GIFT
The creation narratives provide us with two complementary
aspects of the earth in relation to God and to man. On the one
hand, God, as Creator, is Lord and ultimate owner of all created
things. Therefore any claim of economic ownership by man

(collectively or individually) is secondary and subordinate to God's ownership, from which it derives. Man is himself part of God's total creation; he has no absolute ownership over the rest of it. On the other hand, God has given the earth to man as his trustee. Part of the implied purpose of making man in his own image was so that he would be capable of being entrusted with dominion over the rest of the created order. This seems a reasonable deduction from the way the two points about man's constitution are placed side by side in Genesis 1:26:

> Then God said, 'Let us make man in our image, in our likeness, and let them rule over the fish of the sea and the birds of the air, over the livestock, over all the earth, and over all the creatures that move along the ground.'

So within the context of this conferred dominion over a 'given' earth, man's exercise of subordinate ownership and use over the earth and its resources is theologically and morally legitimate.

This duality of relationships is expressed in the Psalms: 'The earth is the LORD's, and everything in it' (Ps. 24:1), but also: 'the earth he has given to man' (Ps. 115:16), and 'You made him ruler over the works of your hands' (Ps. 8:6).

Stewardship, then, is the key word in this creation perspective. God owns the earth but has entrusted it into the keeping of mankind whom he has equipped for the task and whom he holds accountable for his trusteeship. This concept of man's economic stewardship generates a number of derivative ethical principles which we can only outline here, though each is capable of much deeper discussion by Christian economists.

1. Shared resources

Since the earth was given to all mankind, access to and use of its resources were meant to be shared and available to all. The creation narratives cannot be used to justify privatized, individual ownership, since it is to mankind as a whole that the earth is entrusted. This is *not* to say that there can be no legitimate private ownership of material goods; we have already seen how in Israel legitimate property rights were grounded on the belief of God's gift of the land and its distribution to the household units. It *is* to say that such individual property rights, even when legitimate, always remain subordinate to the prior right of all men to have access to and use of the resources of the earth. In other words, the claim 'I (or we) own it' is never a final answer in the moral argument. For ultimately, God owns it and I (or we) only hold it in trust, and he may well hold me (or us) responsible to himself for others who might have greater need of it.[1] Ownership does not entail absolute right of disposal, but rather responsibility for administration and distribution. The right of all to *use* is prior to the right of any to *own*.

2. The responsibility of work

The command to 'fill the earth and subdue it' inescapably entailed work on man's part. Work itself is not a result of the fall, though it was certainly affected by it. Rather, it too is part of the image of God in mankind, for God, as he is presented to us in the creation narratives, is a worker. It is thus mankind's nature, as well as his responsibility and his right, to be engaged in productive economic work with the material resources of the world. This means that we not only have the duty to work ourselves, such that voluntary, deliberate idleness is a sin (*cf.* 2 Thes. 3:6–13), but also that we have a responsibility to enable or allow others to work. So to prevent another person working, or to deny or deprive him of work, is to offend against his humanity and the image of God in him, as well as failing in one's responsibility to God for him. Work, in this creation context, has the widest possible meaning, and certainly has to be distinguished from our modern tendency to limit its significance to paid employment.

3. The expectation of growth

The words, 'Be fruitful and increase' were, of course, spoken to mankind with reference to his own offspring and growing population. Growth in numbers, however, requires growth in material production and provision. God provided for that need both in the astounding and incalculable riches of the legacy he put at man's disposal in the earth's crust and in the equally

---

[1] An interesting illustration of the claimed exercise of this moral right was reported in the *New Internationalist*, 107, January 1982, as 'The Campesinos' Story'. Impoverished farmers in the hills of Honduras, frustrated by government delay in implementing the Agrarian Reform Bill under which they should have received land, peacefully 'invaded' unused parts of huge estates in the valleys, owned by absentee wealthy cattle owners, and claimed them by clearing and cultivating them. The case was presented that the moral claim of their need to use the land outweighed the legal claim of private ownership of unused land.

incalculable endowment of ingenuity and adaptability he gave to mankind himself. So although the greatest part of human labour – in the ancient world certainly and still in much of today's world – is geared to meeting subsistence needs, mankind had a built-in potential to produce material goods beyond immediate subsistence needs. Alongside this potential is the actual fact of the wide variety of the geographical location of resources, and of climate, vegetation and soil-type. If mankind was to 'fill the earth and subdue it', this was bound to lead to surplus of some products in some places, and scarcity of some in others, so that exchange and trade are natural consequences of human growth in all its dimensions. Being set within the context of creation commands, however, all such economic activity and relationship at every level comes within the sphere of God's active concern and moral scrutiny.

4. *Shared produce*

Just as the right of access to, and use of, the *resources* of the earth is a shared right which sets moral limitations to the right of private ownership of resources, so too the right to consume or enjoy *the end-product* of the economic process that uses the resources is limited by the needs of all. We are as responsible to God for what we do with what *we* produce, as we are for what *he* has given us 'raw'. There is no mandate in the creation material for private *exclusive* use, nor for hoarding or consuming at the expense of others. Private dominion over some of the material resources of the earth does not give a right to consume the entire product of those resources, because dominion always remains trusteeship under God and responsibility for others. There is no necessary or 'sacrosanct' link between what one owns or invests in the productive process and what one can claim an exclusive right to consume as income in return. The creation principle of stewardship, implying a mutual responsibility for the good of the whole human community, cuts across the idea that 'what's mine is mine and I am entitled to keep and consume whatever I can get out of it'.

Much more could be said on each of these points, of course, and needs to be when specific issues in the contemporary national and global economic scene are brought into Christian debate. But these principles and their implications form a basic framework within which a biblical Christian will want to work. They are the creative stage which supports the shifting sets and scenes of economic history. However, to continue the metaphor, the play has not proceeded as the author intended. We have to take account of the effect of the fall and the inroads of sin and evil in the economic sphere.

THE EFFECT OF THE FALL

The essence of the fall was man's arrogant desire for autonomy, a rebellion against the authority and benevolence of the Creator. The havoc caused by this attempted reversal of status and the curse it brought affected not only man's spiritual relationship with God and his personal and social relationships, but also his whole economic and material environment. Each of the four principles set out above was corrupted and violated, to man's own cost.

Thus, first, in place of shared access to and responsible stewardship of the earth's resources, *land and resources* have become the greatest single cause of strife and warfare between men. Some resources are hoarded by a few and denied to others. Some are squandered, polluted or abused. Possession of resources, instead of being used as an opportunity for mutual sharing, as of an unmerited gift, has become a matter of conquest and seizure, a tool of oppression, greed and power.

Then, secondly, *work* is corrupted. On the one hand this means that work in itself became toilsome and frustrating because of the curse on the earth, and the fact that work was no longer simply part of our human nature, but a necessity for survival: 'By the sweat of your brow you will eat your food' (Gn. 3:19). This feature of work in the fallen world has been aggravated by changes in the very nature of work in modern times, changes caused by factors which may not *in themselves* be sinful. Industrialization and technological advance may be regarded in some senses as inevitable and not intrinsically evil, except inasmuch as they share in the fallenness of all human enterprise. But the resulting mechanization of work, with fragmented specialization and dull repetition, simply intensifies, for those caught up in it, the actual experience of the curse of frustration which attaches to a greater or lesser degree to all human work in a fallen world.

On the other hand it also means that human relationships in

the sphere of economic work are corrupted. Work becomes a commodity to be bought and sold with little care or responsibility for the working human being. Work becomes a slave of greed, a tool of oppression, a means of replacing God with one's own ambition, even an idol in itself for some.

The book of Ecclesiastes has some of the sharpest insights in the Old Testament into the paradoxical nature of human work. On the one hand, it is still the gift of God, and there is no better alternative for a man than to find satisfaction in his work (Ec. 2:24f.; 5:18; 9:10). But on the other hand, it can be fruitless and frustrating (2:4–11), wasted in the end (2:18–23), riddled with evil motives (4:4), or empty of any purpose (4:8), and finally reduced to vanity by death (9:10). There is no more perceptive exposition of the outworking of God's curse upon the earth and the lot of fallen man upon it than these observations of Ecclesiastes.

Thirdly, *economic growth* becomes pathologically obsessive. For those who live in obedient relationship with God, increase of material goods is seen in the Old Testament as a blessing to be received as a gift and enjoyed responsibly; but never is it seen as a guaranteed 'reward', and indeed some of God's most faithful servants remained materially poor. For those who live in alienation from God, however, growth in prosperity becomes an end in itself.

Paul was not the first to teach that covetousness is tantamount to idolatry, which is as much as to say that to break the tenth commandment is to break the first. Deuteronomy is well aware of the danger that the very blessings of God, when they increase, can usurp his place so that he is forgotten. Deuteronomy 8 describes the abundant natural resources of the land (vv. 7–9). It then immediately describes the symptoms of complacent, growth-obsessed materialism:

> When you eat and are satisfied, when you build fine houses and settle down, and when your herds and flocks grow large and your silver and gold increase and all you have is multiplied (vv. 12f.).

This is followed by a warning against the obvious danger: 'Then your heart will become proud and you will forget the LORD your God' (v. 14).

But again, it is Ecclesiastes who observes the insatiable thirst for more, even though wealth is so fickle:

Whoever loves money never has money enough;
> whoever loves wealth is never satisfied with his income.
This too is meaningless.
As goods increase,
> so do those who consume them.
And what benefit are they to the owner
> except to feast his eyes on them?
>> (Ec. 5:10f.; *cf.* 5:13f.; 6:1f.).

Fourthly, *the end product* of the economic process is also manipulated unjustly. Claims of ownership are privatized and regarded as absolute, in the absence of any sense of transcendent responsibility for others. Grossly unfair trading arrangements prevent the poor of the world from enjoying even the fruit of resources they have got, as they are exported to countries already rich. The problem is now global; but it is not new, for it was observed by the sage of Proverbs,

A poor man's field may produce abundant food,
> but injustice sweeps it away (Pr. 13:23).

So evil has woven its way into every aspect of man's economic life. Furthermore the Old Testament hints at the extra dimension of the problem, namely that the whole realm of the material, economic order has become prey to demonic forces which both incite human sin and amplify and solidify its effects. The narrative of the fall portrays the personal force of evil approaching man by means of the material creation and using the same material creation as a means of enticement to unbelief, disobedience and rebellion. The struggle of the prophets with oppression and injustice was not merely economic but closely linked with their struggle against the spiritual power of Baal worship. For they saw clearly how rejection of the service of Yahweh led to the service of the 'gods' of selfish greed and cruel oppression. Conversely, the battle waged by such as Elijah and the choice he put before the people – the LORD or Baal (1 Ki. 18:21) – was not merely spiritual or religious. He was fighting on behalf of the victims of greedy *economic* callousness linked to religious apostasy. The tragic case of Naboth was to underline this. It was as true in Elijah's day as it was at the time Jesus said the words, and is now: 'You cannot *serve* both God and Money' (Mt. 6:24).

The Old Testament creation narratives, then, provide a framework of ideals and principles for economic life on the earth God has given us. These ideals are tempered, however, by the realism of its comprehensive doctrine of the fall but are also elevated by the transcendent dimension to which it relates the whole of life, including economics.

So the Christian involved in any branch of this vast sphere of human life needs to remember that the issues are not merely material or physical. Here, as elsewhere, 'our struggle is not against flesh and blood' (Eph. 6:12), nor merely against the 'sweat' and 'thistles' of a cursed creation groaning in frustration. It is against spiritual powers and forces which, by their invasion of and influence over human economic relationships and structures, can wield an oppressive tyranny over mankind in this sphere, just as they hold people in the slavery of mental and spiritual darkness. Thankfully, the redemptive acts of God also operate in this sphere of human life, and we now turn to examine the economic implications of the Old Testament's theology of redemption.

PERSPECTIVES FROM REDEMPTION

One outstanding feature of the redemption achieved at the exodus was its comprehensiveness. In that one sequence of events God gave to Israel a fourfold freedom: politically from the tyranny of a foreign autocratic power; socially from the intolerable interference in their family life; economically from the burden of enforced slave labour; spiritually from the realm of foreign gods into the unhindered worship of the LORD and covenant relationship with him.

Once again, it is very clear how closely bound together are the economic and the spiritual realms. The thing which awakens God's concern for his people is their outcry under economic oppression and injustice (Ex. 2:23–25). The purpose of his intention to deliver them is to fulfil his covenant promise to Abraham by giving them the economic blessing of a land of their own (Ex. 3:7f.; 6:4–8).

DIVINE OWNERSHIP AND DIVINE GIFT

When the promise was fulfilled and Israel had taken possession of the land, we discover that the same twin concepts of divine ownership and divine gift applied to the land of God's redeemed people that we saw applied to the whole earth in relation to mankind. In fact, there are passages where the creation themes of God's ownership or gift of the whole earth are explicitly linked with, or merge into, his redemptive relation to Israel and their land. Returning to the exodus, for example, we find that God emphasizes his claim to be Lord and owner of the whole earth, a claim which the plagues dramatically proved (Ex. 9:15f., 29). But it was a power exercised discriminatingly and redemptively in favour of his people Israel.

Israel is reminded of the point in Deuteronomy 10:14f. God's sovereign right of ownership over the whole creation is stated: 'To the LORD your God belong the heavens, even the highest heavens, the earth and everything in it', but only as a background which throws his loving acts of election and redemption into sharper relief: 'Yet the LORD set his affection on your forefathers and loved them, and he chose you, their descendants, above all the nations, as it is today'. The miracle of the exodus is also linked with God's universal ownership in Psalm 89:10f. (where Rahab is a nickname for Egypt).

Correspondingly, though Israel acknowledged the gift of the earth to mankind, any prayers for national or personal prosperity, or any rejoicing in such blessings, were based on the gift of their own land in the historical outworking of God's redemption and on God's covenant love. The themes are joined beautifully in Psalm 115. The Psalm begins with praise of the unique incomparability of the LORD, the only living God (vv. 2–8) and goes on to pray for blessing and prosperity not only on the grounds of his creatorhood and gift of the earth to mankind (vv. 15b, 16), but primarily because of his historical love and covenant faithfulness to Israel (vv. 1, 9–12: note the emphasis on the LORD, the covenant God of Israel; his 'love and faithfulness'; his 'help and shield').

Now we looked quite thoroughly in chapter 3 at the significance of the themes of divine gift and divine ownership of

Israel's land. The important point for us to recall at this juncture is the close correspondence between what the Old Testament has to say about Israel's land in the context of its *redemption* theology, and what it has to say about the whole earth and mankind in a *creation* context. Just as the election and redemption of Israel was God's answer to the fall of man and the global spread of evil, Israel in her social life becoming the prototype of redeemed humanity as well as the vehicle of God's complete redemption,[2] so also Israel's land became the prototype, or earnest, of a new creation, God's redemptive purpose for the whole earth. The land was now, as the whole earth had once been, the *place* of God's dwelling and presence and blessing, just as Israel was the *people* of his own special possession. Since the fall, God no longer dwells with mankind in the earth in the same intimate way as before the fall. But by his redemptive activity, he dwelt with Israel in their land, thus creating not only a social and economic model of a redeemed community which functions *paradigmatically*, but also a foreshadowing of the new creation, which functions *eschatologically*. For the Old Testament as well as the New looks forward to the complete redemption of *creation*, when God will once more dwell with mankind in a world freed from the curse of sin.

CREATION VALUES IN REDEMPTION CONTEXT
We shall work out some further implications of the paradigmatic and eschatological dimensions of Old Testament economics for social ethics in the next section. For the moment, we pause to reinforce the point that for Israel economics were governed not only by creation principles such as outlined in the last section, but in addition by their status as a redeemed people. Indeed, because of the effect of the fall, both on mankind and on the earth itself, Israel would be able to match up to creation principles economically only insofar as they obeyed the requirements God laid upon them as his redeemed people. Those requirements amounted to a call to costly love for one another, to the sacrifice of self-interest in favour of the needs of a fellow-Israelite, and to a preparedness to trust the Creator-Redeemer God, even in the face of economic 'common sense' (*cf.* above, pp. 60f.). We can see this in each of the four creation principles outlined

---

[2] All this we saw in chapter 2.

above. They provide a convenient and comprehensive structure on which to set out the economic laws and customs of Israel.

1. *Shared access to and use of the land and natural resources* of the earth was the first creation principle we noted. In Israel this was worked out in the first instance by a system of land division which was intended to be as equitable and widely spread as possible. Given the variety of Palestinian geography, this did not mean that everyone should have the *same*, but that every family should have *enough* for economic viability. Here is a creation principle operating in a redemption context.

However, the economic effects of sin, such as greed, dispossession, political displacement, coupled with natural disaster, warfare and others, resulted in large numbers of people existing without land of their own. Such people would survive by selling themselves into the service of landed households. The 'Hebrew slaves' of Exodus 21:2–6 and Deuteronomy 15:12–18 belonged to this landless class of people.[3] Israelite law, therefore, took a special interest in protecting them, as it did other groups of landless people, such as widows and orphans, immigrant aliens and Levites. Economic generosity to ease their plight was commanded, and reinforced by a mixture of theological and economic arguments in Deuteronomy 15:14f.; 18.

Ultimately, however, generosity was not enough in itself. The eschatological vision of the prophets looks forward to the day of God's redemptive transformation. Then *'Every* man will sit under his own vine and under his own fig-tree' (Mi. 4:4), and those who are now landless will have secure tenure and share in the 'land' of God's new creation (Ezk. 47:22f.). Here is the restoration by God's redemptive act of the first principle of 'creation economics'.

2. *The privilege and responsibility of work,* our second creation

---

[3] It is now widely agreed that the word 'Hebrew' is linked to the word *'apiru,* which is found in a wide range of Mesopotamian and Egyptian texts. The term described a certain social stratum that was common throughout the ancient Near East, namely a class of landless people, sometimes political refugees, displaced people, outlaws and others. The Israelites were appropriately called 'Hebrews' while in Egypt. The word later became an ethnic name equivalent to Israel. But in the early legal texts the term 'Hebrew slave' almost certainly refers, not to Israelites, but to landless people, the dispossessed Canaanites and immigrants, who survived by selling themselves and their labour into the service of landed Israelite households. Full technical details of the debate over the identity of the *'apiru/* Hebrews can be found in N. K. Gottwald, *Tribes of Yahweh,* and in M. Weippert, *The Settlement of the Israelite Tribes in Palestine, SBT,* 2nd series, 21 (SCM, 1971).

principle, applied as much to the redeemed community in the promised land as to mankind in the Garden of Eden. Even the idyllic descriptions of God's blessing on his people if they lived obediently in the land presupposed the normal work of agriculture. But in view of the corruption of work and of working relationships by sin, as we have noted, the law made certain explicit demands on the redeemed people in this sphere also.

(i) *Conditions*: 'Hebrew' slaves were to be given the opportunity of freedom (which in practice amounted to a change of employer) after six years, and the terms of their service and release were clearly laid down (Ex. 21:1–6). The owner of slaves was placed under clear legal restraint in his physical treatment of slaves (Ex. 21:20f., 26f.), while those who had voluntarily entered the service of a creditor because of inability to support themselves were not to be made to work in oppressively harsh conditions (Lv. 25:39f., 43).

(ii) *Payment*: The wages of hired workers were to be paid fully and promptly (Lv. 19:13; Dt. 24:14f.). The prophets condemn the oppression and exploitation of labourers, specifically on the matter of pay (Is. 58:3; Je. 22:13).

(iii) *Rest*: Sabbath rest, a principle and privilege since creation, was made mandatory on employer, employee and even working animals, not only on the basis of God's example in creation (Ex. 20:11), but also on the grounds of his redemptive act (Dt. 5:15). In addition to this regular weekly total rest, slaves and other residential and hired workers were to be allowed to enjoy all the benefits of the great festivals and cultic occasions, which added several days' break from work throughout the agricultural year (*cf*. Dt. 16:11, 14). In an agricultural life of long, hard, physical labour, such regular relief would have been invaluable.

Disastrously, however, the laws governing working life and conditions were ignored from the king downwards, from the time of Solomon and in increasing measure thereafter (*cf*. 1 Ki. 5:13–17; 9:20–23; 11:28; 12:3f., 10f.). This is one of the factors which lay behind the exile, which could only be interpreted as divine judgment in the light of Leviticus 26. In that chapter the judgment is repeatedly related to the people's failure to observe the sabbaths. Now, in the context of Leviticus 25, that includes the sabbatical legislation concerning the *land*, which included: the seventh year fallow (explicitly for the benefit of the poor);

the release of pledges taken for debt (*cf.* Dt. 15:1–3; 'pledges' probably included dependants of the debtor who were working off his debt by their labour); and the jubilee release of those whose land and labour were mortgaged to their creditors. All of these sabbatical institutions were concerned with the interests of *workers*, especially those whose *only* asset was their labour. Neglect of the 'sabbaths', in this sense, corresponds to the accusations of injustice and exploitation of the poor which is so common in the prophets. Similarly, economic exploitation is linked to violation of the sabbath day for greedy motives, by Amos (8:5f.), Isaiah (58:3–14) and Jeremiah (17:19–27; *cf.* 7:5–11).

So then, from the laws themselves and from the prophets' reaction to their neglect, we can see that there was a deep and detailed concern in the Old Testament with work and employment, in respect of conditions and terms of service, adequate rest, and fair pay. And this concern applied across the whole spectrum of the working population – employers, free hired workmen, slaves. Indeed, the principles of fairness and compassion extended even to working animals, such as the laden donkey and threshing ox (Ex. 23:4f.; Dt. 25:4; *cf.* Dt. 22:1–4).

This concern, while it falls within the context of Israel as God's redeemed people, has paradigmatic relevance to Christian ethical concern and action within this economic sphere of work and employment. Obviously, there is a vast difference between the nature of employment within a comparatively simple agricultural economy such as ancient Israel's and the complex industrialized economies of modern developed countries. But the constant quest for satisfactory and dignified conditions of work and fair pay shows no signs of receding. On the matter of 'rest', the problem in developed countries has been inverted, since the combination of endemic unemployment and the micro-chip revolution has made the pressing problem not one of a surplus of work, but of its absence or scarcity. We are being forced to realize afresh that 'work' is not synonymous with 'paid employment' and are having to rethink the meaning and uses of leisure.

Nevertheless, there are still vast areas of the developing world where the nature of human labour has changed little from the ancient patterns such as are found in biblical times. And there are societies where the conditions of allegedly 'free' employees are pitiably more harsh and oppressive than those of slaves in

Israel. In such situations, the paradigmatic relevance of the Old Testament economic laws concerning work and employment can be taken almost as they stand. To introduce statutory rest days and holidays, statutory terms and conditions of employment, statutory protection from infringement of personal rights and physical dignity, statutory provision for fair wages promptly paid, would revolutionize the face of economic life for multitudes of workers in some parts of our world. And all of these are drawn from the economic legislation of God's redeemed people, Israel.

Therefore, although we may rightly wish to advocate the simple principles and ideals inherent in the creation ordinance of work, the effect of the fall is such that we cannot do so adequately without reverting to the principles and concrete models provided in the redemption context of God's people. Incidentally, this remains the case if we choose also to bring the New Testament to bear on our ethic of work and employment; for the instructions to employers and their slave-employees and the warnings against deliberate idleness are clearly given within the 'redemptive context' of Paul's letters to Christian churches. In the one 'prophetic' blast against exploitive employers, who (presumably) stood outside the community of the redeemed whom he is addressing, James does precisely what we have seen cannot be avoided; he draws on the language and concepts of the covenant law of Old Testament Israel:

> Now listen, you rich people, weep and wail because of the misery that is coming upon you. . . . Look! The wages you failed to pay the workmen who mowed your fields are crying out against you. The cries of the harvesters have reached the ears of the Lord Almighty (Jas. 5:1–6; *cf.* Ex. 22:22ff.; Lv. 19:13; Dt. 24:14f.).

Furthermore, work has its place in the eschatological visions of the new creation. The removal of the curse on the earth and the abolition of human wickedness will not leave mankind in Elysian idleness. The prophets envisage redeemed man as man at work, but in the joy afforded by the absence of warfare, the reign of righteousness and peace, and the co-operation of nature.

'The days are coming,' declares the LORD,

> 'when the reaper will be overtaken by the ploughman
>   and the planter by the one treading grapes.
> New wine will drip from the mountains
>   and flow from all the hills' (Am. 9:13).

> They will beat their swords into ploughshares
>   and their spears into pruning hooks.[4]. . .
> Every man will sit under his own vine
>   and under his own fig-tree,
> and no-one will make them afraid
>   (Mi. 4:3f.; *cf.* Is. 11:1–9; Ho. 2:18–23).

Here again, the new creation restores God's original purpose for man. The eschatological vision, alongside the creation ordinance, is thus an incentive for our social ethic, while the redemption ordinances provide principles and models for the present which take account of our fallenness.

3. The third creation principle was the result of human economic work, namely, *economic growth* through exchange and trade and the increase of material goods as mankind spread and diversified his dominion over nature. The effect of the fall was that the desire for growth became obsessive and idolatrous, the scale of growth became excessive for some at the expense of others, and the means of growth became filled with greed, exploitation and injustice. A dilemma arose, therefore, in legislating economically in this matter for God's redeemed people. How were economic growth and material productiveness to be allowed for and encouraged in line with God's creative purpose and express desire to grant abundance as a blessing, while at the same time the evils of illegitimate growth were prevented or mitigated as far as possible?

It is in this area that Old Testament economic ethics and laws are, in my view, at their most radical and subtle. They are also at this point most vulnerable to the misinterpretation of two opposite extreme views. On the one hand there are those who press the texts which refer to material prosperity and increase

[4] *i.e.* for work!

of goods as God's blessing, into a virtually *carte blanche* benediction on all forms of private enterprise and capitalistic growth-orientated economics. On the other hand, some extend the legal and prophetic antipathy to excessive and unjust accumulation of wealth into a malediction on any form of private property or wealth creation. Both views are mistaken and miss the balance of the Old Testament.

The guiding ethos of Old Testament economics could be said to be summed up in the tenth commandment: 'You shall not covet'. Addressed in the second person singular to the individual, and including among its specific objects a neighbour's economic assets, this fundamental commandment locates the source of all sinful forms of economic growth where they truly originate – the greed of individual human hearts. The prophet Micah saw behind the socio-economic evils of his day to the private covetousness of individuals who 'plot evil on their beds!' (Mi. 2:1f.). The antidote to 'covetousness which is idolatry' (Col. 3:5 RSV) is that 'fear of the LORD' which engenders the wisdom of contentment. The Wisdom tradition certainly accepted growth and prosperity as divine gifts (*cf.* Pr. 3:9f.; 10:22). But it was as aware of the dangers of excessive wealth as of the temptation of acute poverty:

> give me neither poverty nor riches,
> but give me only my daily bread.
> Otherwise, I may have too much and disown you
> and say, 'Who is the LORD?'
> Or I may become poor and steal,
> and so dishonour the name of my God (Pr. 30:8f.).

When we come to actual laws and institutions designed to embody this principle, the most important are the regulations concerning the inalienability of family land, and the supporting procedures of redemption and jubilee, in Leviticus 25. The combined effect of these regulations was to take the land itself right off the market as a commodity. Speculation in land or amassing huge private estates by permanent land purchase were *technically* impossible in Israel. Land could not be sold permanently (v. 23). The seller himself could redeem his land later, or the sale could be pre-empted or redeemed by a kinsman (*cf.* Jeremiah's pre-emption of his kinsman Hanamel's sale of land, Je. 32:6–12). In any case, if neither happened, the land returned to its original owner or his descendants in the jubilee, *i.e.* within a generation at most. Any exchanges of land that did take place, therefore, were not really sales of *land* at all, but only of the 'usufruct', or expected yield of the land until the next jubilee. The price, therefore, actually *decreased* yearly as the jubilee approached (Lv. 25:14–17)! The purpose, to check the unscrupulous 'growth' of some at the expense of others, is made clear twice: 'Do not take advantage of each other' (vv. 14, 17).

The jubilee also functioned as a safeguard, against another kind of 'taking advantage', namely, abuse of the legal redemption procedure. A prospering kinsman by operating his right of pre-emption or redemption 'in the interests' of his poorer relatives within the clan, could end up possessing most of their land, with the poorer kinsmen reduced to virtual serfdom on his estate (vv. 39f.). The jubilee set a limit to that kind of charitably disguised expansionism by ordering the release and 'return' of all households to their original inheritance.

Thus, the combination of an originally widely spread, multiple division of the land to families, the inalienability principle, the redemption option and the jubilee statute, amounts to an economic system which started from a position of broad equality, but recognized the fallen reality that some would prosper while others fell into poverty. It tried accordingly to set limits and safeguards on the worst effects of that process by regulative and restorative economic measures. The Old Testament was well aware that such measures run counter to the 'natural' economic tendencies of fallen man. That is why in Leviticus 25 there is an insistent appeal to the experience of redemption from Egypt and the covenant relationship with the LORD as sanction and motivation for the economic demands being made (vv. 17f., 23b, 36, 38, 42f., 55).

Around this central core of Old Testament economics we might also list some other injunctions designed to prevent or limit the growth of private wealth at the cost of injustice or oppression.

Firstly, there was the prohibition on removing *boundary stones* that marked out family land (Dt. 19:14). The seriousness of this offence is registered in its inclusion among the curses of

Deuteronomy 27 (v. 17). It is used as a byword for injustice by Hosea (5:10) and was a concern to the wisdom tradition also (Jb. 24:2f.; Pr. 23:10).

Secondly, the taking of *interest* for loans was prohibited between Israelites (Ex. 22:25; Lv. 25:36f.; Dt. 23:19f.). This did not refer to interest as we understand it in a commercial investment. Deuteronomy's permission to charge interest to a 'foreigner' probably has that kind of commercial trading in mind. But the other laws clearly specify that the loan is required out of *need*, primarily for the annual necessities of agricultural life, *e.g.* the load of seed corn. The ban is thus not concerned with growth in itself, but with growth achieved by taking unscrupulous advantage of another's need.

Thirdly, there was control over the use of *pledges* taken in security for loans. This ranged from plain humanity and personal considerateness (*e.g.* the return of a cloak by night time, Ex. 22:26f.; not to take a millstone in pledge, Dt. 24:6; not to invade privacy for a pledge, Dt. 24:10f.) to major sabbatical legislation. The 'release' prescribed for the seventh year in Deuteronomy 15:1–3 probably meant that pledges taken as security for a loan were to be returned to the owner and the loan suspended for the year (or perhaps cancelled altogether). The pledge might be land mortgaged to the creditor, or it might be the dependants of the debtor working off his debts. The releasing of such pledges would bring substantial relief to the debtor and effectively check the rapacious expansion of unscrupulous creditors. Again, the law was well aware of the tendencies of the economic heart of man, and, like Nehemiah, appeals to the redeemed conscience (Dt. 15:9ff.; Ne. 5:1–13).

Fourthly, the law prohibits excessive economic aggrandizement to the one person who might be expected to be allowed it, *the king*. But no, whether horses, wives or gold and silver: 'He must not accumulate large amounts' of them (Dt. 17:16f.). The fact that from the example of Solomon onwards the law was ignored by kings and royal favourites does not modify the point that it was a standing rebuke to that accumulative urge that pursues growth by injustice and oppression, a rebuke that was delivered in less legally muted tones by the prophets.

Finally, as we might expect from the previous two sections, the eschatological vision of the new creation, when God's people dwell in a new and perfect relationship with him, includes the fulfilment of the creation ideal of productive growth and fruitful abundance. Jeremiah 31 – 33, chapters which include outstanding prophecies of the new covenant and the everlasting age of God's blessing and bounty, include imagery drawn from the economic realm of the restoration of economic trade, produce and prosperity after the exile. While the outworking of God's ultimate purposes of redemption will certainly include the judgment and destruction of economic oppression and injustice (*cf.* the oracles against Tyre and Babylon in Is. 13 – 14; 23, and their echo, economics included, in Rev. 18), it will not ignore the economic dimension of man's created purpose.

4. The fourth principle of creation economics held that we are also *stewards before God of what is produced* by the economic process. Our responsibility to him for one another means that we can claim no exclusive or unqualified right of disposal, even over what we have produced ourselves. The claim, 'It is wholly mine for I made it' can be attributed only to God (*cf.* Ps. 95:4f.). In any human mouth, such a claim is countered by the fact that both the resource and the power to use it are alike gifts of God.

> You may say to yourself, 'My power and the strength of my hands have produced this wealth for me.' But remember the LORD your God, for it is he who gives you the ability to produce wealth (Dt. 8:17f.).

Naturally, therefore, he holds us morally accountable to himself for just and generous sharing of the wealth he has enabled us to produce.

This principle generated within Israelite law a remarkable number of injunctions to material generosity and regular systematic sharing of produce. The principle was established first of all in a vertical dimension. God laid claim on the first born of man and beast and the first fruit of the field, thereby establishing his prior right over all that a man might call his own (Ex. 13:2; 23:19; 34:19f.). To this was added the requirement of *tithing*. The tithe was sacred to the LORD, but was in fact to be consumed by the offerer in a cultic context, and shared with the sanctuary personnel, the Levites (Dt. 14:22–27).

Every third year, however, the tithe was collected and stored for the use of the poor in general – Levites, aliens, widows and orphans (Dt. 14:28f.; 26:12ff.). On top of this triennial tithe, there was the sabbatical fallow year on the land in the seventh year. This too is explicitly said to be for the benefit of the poor (Ex. 23:11; Lv. 25:6f.), a characteristically Israelite addition to an institution that was not in itself unique to Israel. Indeed, Deuteronomy extends the principle of 'release' for the *land* into an institution of even greater benefit for the poor – release *for people*, in the form of remission of pledges for debt (Dt. 15:1–3). It is Deuteronomy, too, which characteristically extends the law of the seventh year release of 'Hebrew' slaves by stipulating that they be sent away with a generous endowment of material goods (15:13–15).

Furthermore, in addition to this provision every third and seventh year, there was the annual allowance of gleaning from crops, vineyards and olive trees. The instructions to the farmer in Leviticus 19:9f. and Deuteronomy 24:19–22 not to be zealously thorough in his harvesting sought to ensure that there would be something worth gleaning. Again, such advice runs counter to natural selfishness and so, again, the motivation of divine redemption is invoked. The story of Ruth's gleaning and especially the generosity of Boaz illustrates both the right of the poor as well as the quality of righteousness as understood in the Old Testament (Ru. 2). And at any time a person had the right to satisfy his immediate hunger from a neighbour's produce without transgressing the laws of trespass or theft (Dt. 23:24f.).

Mention of Boaz and Ruth, however, takes us into an area of sharing that was deeper yet than the provisions outlined above, namely the responsibility of kinship. Two socio-economic institutions appear to be combined in the story of Ruth – the redemption of an impoverished Israelite's land by the *gō'ēl* ('kinsman-redeemer'), and the responsibility of a kinsman to take the wife of a man who died childless in order to try to raise a son for the dead man's name and inheritance ('levirate marriage'). The first is described in Leviticus 25:25, the second in Deuteronomy 25:5f.

Both constituted major financial undertakings. They demanded a considerable degree of sacrifice of self-interest on the part of the kinsman. In the additional provisions on behalf of the completely destitute kinsman in Leviticus 25:35–43, the law requires complete support for such persons until the jubilee! The sequel to the levirate law recognizes that even the bond of kinship will sometimes not be enough to persuade a man to take responsibility for his kinsman's widow and estate until it passes back to an heir as yet unborn.

In Ruth 4 it is precisely these considerations which make the anonymous nearer kinsman decline to exercise his prior right of redeeming Elimelech's land and marrying Ruth. He was not willing to take the risk that 'I might endanger my own estate' (Ru. 4:6). Boaz, however, putting the obligation of kinship before his personal security and doubtless spurred by a love for Ruth which the story-teller's art implies without bluntly stating, makes the potential sacrifice of exercising his right and responsibility as *gō'ēl*. Understandably, the local people show their appreciation of his generosity by praying that he may have many children. The first would inherit the estate of Ruth's former husband Mahlon. Only later children would inherit in his own line.

The point of dwelling thus on this story and the customs that lie behind it is that the economic ethics of the redeemed community take us beyond the realm of simple *sharing* into the realm of *sacrifice*. In a perfect world devoid of selfishness, the creation principle of sharing the produce of God's bounty would be a relatively simple matter. But in a fallen world, where human greed, injustice and incompetence have already put chasms between the rich and the poor, that creation principle of sharing cannot be approached without the redemption principle of sacrifice and the costly waiving of self-interest.

There is, of course, another sphere in which we are very familiar with the notion of redemption requiring sacrifice – the sacrifice of One who, as our 'Kinsman-Redeemer', laid aside all self-interest on our behalf. Here again we find that that great spiritual realm has its material counterpart. As mankind cannot be restored to the harmony with God that was his created purpose without the redemptive act of God that includes sacrifice, neither can the creation pattern for his economic life be recovered without the experience, relationship and motivation of redemption which calls for economic sacrifice as evidence of practical gratitude to the Redeemer and of mutual, covenant commitment to one's fellow redeemed.

THE LAND IN CHRISTIAN ETHICS

In chapter 3 we saw how central the land is to the Old Testament story and also the major role that the theology of the land plays in the overall faith of Israel. In this chapter so far we have seen the ways in which this theological centrality worked out ethically in the form of economic laws and institutions. It remains for us to ask how these various threads can be drawn through into Christian ethics. What hermeneutical methods are available to enable us to apply our understanding of Old Testament economics validly?

Two ways of interpreting the Old Testament in this respect have already been noted, because they arise from within the Old Testament itself. They are the *paradigmatic* and *eschatological* interpretations. To these we must add a third, from a New Testament perspective, the *typological*. Let us summarize the first two, with the aid of our diagram, and then explain the third in more depth. It should be emphasized that these are three complementary ways of interpreting and applying Old Testament ethical material. They are not mutually exclusive, nor are they all relevant in every case. The land, however, does provide a particularly interesting example, because it can be taken up into Christian reflection and application in all three ways.

PARADIGMATIC INTERPRETATION

This approach rests on the belief that God's relation to Israel in their land was a deliberate reflection of his relation to mankind on the earth, or rather, a redemptive response to the fracturing of his creative purpose in the latter sphere. Mankind was fallen and lived on an earth that was cursed. Israel was redeemed and would live in a land God would bless. This can be expressed diagrammatically by extending the triangle we used to visualize the basic framework of Israel's theological self-understanding in Part One.

This is not just a case of squeezing the material into a convenient geometric pattern. We have already clearly seen in chapter 2 how Israel as a society was chosen as a nation for the sake of the nations of mankind and that her social system was intended to be a part of her theological message and significance. And

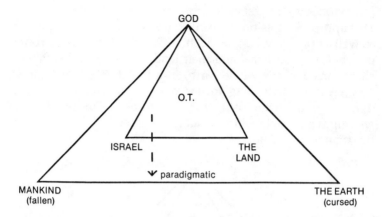

earlier in this chapter (pp. 75 and 76) we noted the correspondence between several themes associated with Israel's land and similar themes associated with the earth as a whole.

We are justified therefore in taking the social and economic laws and institutions of Israel and using them as models for our own ethical task in the wider world of modern-day secular society. In the economic sphere, the Old Testament paradigms provide us with *objectives* without requiring a *literal* transposition of ancient Israelite practice into twentieth-century society. But at the same time the paradigmatic approach compels us to wrestle seriously with the texts themselves in order fully to understand the models we are seeking to apply.

It also prevents us from taking this attitude, 'This was all given in the context of a redeemed community and is therefore irrelevant to secular, unregenerate society'. For we have clearly seen that the very purpose of the provisions given in the context of redemption was to restore a measure of conformity to the original economic purposes of God in creation. So if we believe that it is in the interests even of fallen human society to respect 'the Maker's instructions', as is the view of those who strongly uphold a 'creation ethic' approach, we shall advocate policies and values drawn from the ethics of that nation who knew God as both *Redeemer* and Maker. At the end of this chapter we shall suggest specific areas where Old Testament land law has paradigmatic relevance, using the jubilee as a model.

ESCHATOLOGICAL INTERPRETATION

This approach rests on the conviction, solidly based in the Old as well as the New Testament, that God's redemptive purpose, initiated through Israel and their land, will ultimately embrace all nations and the whole earth, in a transformed and perfect new creation. Returning to our diagram, if we can think in dynamic terms while using a static figure, this means that the redemptive triangle will ultimately 'transcend' (break through) the triangle of fallen creation.

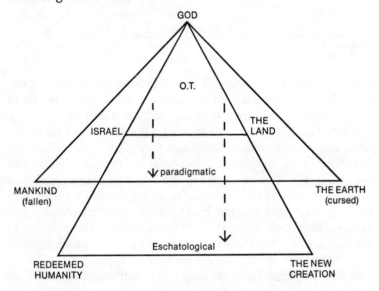

The Old Testament looks forward not only to the world of nations turning to acknowledge the God of Israel and living at peace under his rule (see chapter 5), but also to the world of nature being transformed by God's miraculous power. There is a serious 'earthiness' about the Old Testament hope. God will not just abandon his creation, but will redeem it. And the land of Israel functioned as a prototype of that redeemed earth. Hints of this are to be found in the descriptions of the land which contrast starkly with the cursed earth. It is the land of promise, whereas the earth was the arena of threat and judgment. It abounds in milk and honey (Ex. 3:8, *etc.*), not thorns and thistles (Gn. 3:18).

The descriptions in Deuteronomy recall some of the paradisical features of Eden: a 'good land' (8:7ff.), well watered, full of vegetation and rich in resources (*cf.* Gn. 2:8ff.). In short,

> It is a land the LORD your God cares for; the eyes of the LORD
> your God are continually on it from the beginning of the year
> to its end (Dt. 11:12).

Indeed, if only his redeemed people would wholly obey him,
it would be a land of such blessing as to be a veritable 'paradise
restored' (Dt. 28:1–14). The same theme is echoed in Leviticus
26:12, where God promises to 'walk among' his people, using
the same unusual form of the verb as is used to describe his
walking with the couple in the Garden of Eden.

Israel, however, though redeemed, was still part of fallen
humanity and their land was still part of the cursed earth. The
historical people and land were part of the *process* of God's
redemptive purpose, not its final, perfected product. The theological function of both is therefore that of a prototype, a fore-
taste. So naturally, as Israel looked to the future completion of
God's redemptive purpose, they did so in terms drawn from
their experience of the past and the present. Thus, just as
they could not conceive of the new covenant without *law*, even
though it would be law that transcended the reach of any legis-
lator, for it would be written on the *hearts* of God's people (Je.
31:33), so they could not conceive of God's future, worldwide,
'multi-national' redeemed people without *land*, even though it
would be land that transcended the imagination of any geogra-
pher or even zoologist! The transformation of nature in passages
such as Isaiah 2:2; 11:6–9; 35:1–10; Jeremiah 31:1–14 and Hosea
2:18–23 is clearly not intended literally. Yet neither should it
be utterly spiritualized or taken as *merely* metaphorical. God's
redemptive purpose for his creation may be beyond our imagination, but not beyond the eye of faith.

This, then, is another important function of the land of Israel
within the total sweep of biblical theology. It points eschatologically to that 'new heaven and new earth' in which righteousness
will dwell, because God will dwell there with his people (2 Pet.
3:13; Rev. 21:1–3). The identification is explicitly made in the
New Testament with the use of 'the new Jerusalem' as a figure
for the new creation to come (*cf.* Rev. 21:4f.; Heb. 12:22).

The biblical vision of the future, however, is not to be
regarded as psychological escapism from the problems of the

present. The prophets' use of their future vision, just as their use of the historical past, was designed to effect response and change *in the present*. Biblical eschatology is not just a utopian dream of what *might* be, 'if only. . .', which can lead to despair and cynicism regarding the present; it is a vision of what *will* be, because God will do it. Therefore it is frequently coupled with urgent moral challenge and the incentive of positive expectation (*cf.* Ps. 97:10; Is. 2:5; Mi. 4:5; Mt. 25; Rev. 21:8, 27; 22:11). Thus, an eschatological interpretation of any Old Testament theme, such as the land in this case, rebounds back into the present world with an ethical thrust.

This eschatological dimension of biblical ethics does not add materially to the specific *content* of our ethical imperatives in social or personal terms, in either Testament. That content is already present in the known commands of God and in the examples, paradigms and teaching provided through his revelation. What it does do is lend urgency and incentive to those imperatives on the one hand (as is the case in Rom. 13:11f.; 2 Pet. 3:11–14; 1 Jn. 3:2f.), and on the other hand give us the confident certainty that the vision of fulfilling those imperatives will be achieved. Our work will ultimately be 'not in vain in the Lord' (1 Cor. 15:58), as Paul concluded his affirmation of our future hope of the resurrection of the body.

TYPOLOGICAL INTERPRETATION

One important question remains. What happens to the land in the New Testament? There can be no doubt that the New Testament writers regarded Jesus as the Messiah who fulfilled and embodied the mission of Israel. Consequently the Christian church, as the Messianic community of those 'in Christ', stood in spiritually organic continuity with Old Testament Israel. Gentile or Jew, the believer in Christ was the spiritual seed of Abraham, and heir to the covenant and promise. But now, that promise had had the land as a major constituent. If all the great themes of Old Testament faith and cult converge typologically on Christ, where does the land fit in?

In one sense it is completely absent. The *physical territory* of Jewish Palestine is nowhere referred to with any theological significance in the New Testament. The land as a holy *place* has ceased to have relevance, partly because Christianity rapidly spread beyond its borders to the rest of the 'profane' world,

but more importantly because its holiness was transferred to
Christ himself. The spiritual presence of the living Christ
sanctifies any place where believers are present. This transference of the holiness of the land to Christ is well presented by
W. D. Davies, who points out how Christianity reacted to all
the concrete details of Judaism, including the land, 'in terms of
Christ, to whom all places and all space, like all things else, are
subordinated. In sum, for the holiness of place, Christianity has
fundamentally . . . substituted the holiness of the Person: it has
Christified holy space'.[5]

Furthermore, the geographical land of Israel has no place in
New Testament teaching regarding the ultimate future of God's
people. Even in key passages where the relation between Jew
and Gentile Christians is discussed, and especially in Romans
9 – 11 where Paul speaks of the future of the Jewish nation, no
mention whatever is made of the land. There is no indication
either that Paul, himself a 'converted' Christian Jew, believed
that the land, as physical territory, still had *theological* importance for the *Jewish* Christians. No doubt he would have included
the land among the 'gifts' which he said were 'irrevocable'
(Rom. 11:29), and the 'advantages' which the Jews enjoyed
(3:1f.); but the whole context and drift of his argument shows
that he regarded all that Israel had received from God as being
focused, fulfilled and surpassed in the person of the Messiah,
Jesus (*cf.* Rom. 9:4f.; 10:4).

That, indeed, was his personal creed when he compared all
he had had in Judaism with what he now had 'in the Messiah'
(Phil. 3:3–11). An argument from silence, which this is, can
never of course be the firm basis for dogmatic views. But my
own feeling (I put it no stronger than that) is that if Paul had
been faced with questions over the land as he was over the
matter of circumcision, he would have handled them in a similar
way. We know that he would not allow that physical circumcision had any further *theological* significance within God's
redemptive work, but once that point was conceded, he
regarded it as a matter of moral neutrality: it was of no theological importance whether you chose to circumcise or not (Gal.
5:6; 6:15). He had no objection to Jewish Christians continuing
the practice as a cultural custom, and indeed had Timothy

[5] *The Gospel and the Land*, p. 368.

circumcised because of the cultural environment of his work (Acts 16:3).

Similarly, he might have argued that, while the land as territory had no further theological significance in God's redemptive purpose, since that was now totally focused in the Messiah, there was no reason why Jews and Jewish Christians should not continue to feel an emotional and cultural bond with the land of their ancestors. But their faith and their worship must no longer be localized there, but on Christ alone. The Messiah himself had taught this when he had directed the attention of the Samaritan woman away from the debate over the proper territorial *place* for worshipping God, to recognize him as the Messiah in *person*, the focus of the spiritual worship of God (Jn. 4:20–26).

The New Testament, then, gives no theological significance to the territorial land of Palestine as such. However, in the Old Testament, the land is not merely a piece of territory, any more than the temple is merely a building or Jerusalem merely a city. Like them, it was the focus of major theological and ethical traditions. These traditions can hardly have just vanished from sight in the New Testament, especially since they were connected with the covenant with Abraham, which had a prominent place in Paul's theology. Elsewhere we can see how themes and symbols connected with the temple and Jerusalem are taken up and used spiritually in the New Testament. So again we ask, what has become of the land in the New Testament?

To answer that question we must first recall the *function* of the land in *Israel's* life and faith, and then ask what aspect of *Christian* life and faith has absorbed or fulfilled that function in the New Testament. What did the land signify for an Israelite? What bears a corresponding significance for the Christian?

We have already seen that, for an Israelite, the land was above all else *God's gift*, given in fulfilment of his promise to Abraham, and received in the course of their redemptive history. It was therefore a huge, symbolic, tangible proof to every Israelite that he and his people had a special relationship with God. Deuteronomy links it repeatedly with the assurance of their election in Abraham. They were the LORD's people because they lived in the LORD's land which he had given to them. The individual enjoyed his personal share in the land through the kinship network and his inalienable family inheritance.

Thus, to belong to an Israelite household living in God's land was to experience secure inclusion within the covenant relationship: it was the place of *life* with God. But it also meant to accept the demands of that covenant relationship, so it was also the place of a specific *life-style* before God. To possess the land was to share in the inheritance of all God's people. The land, in short, meant security, inclusion, blessing, corporate sharing and practical responsibility.

Alongside all this, however, there was also in the Old Testament an awareness that Israel's relationship with God, while undoubtedly grounded in and experienced through this socio-economic realm of land and kinship, transcended that realm, and was not permanently or exclusively bound to it. God had called them his 'first-born son' while they were still in Egypt (Ex. 4:22), and sealed his covenant with them before they actually entered the land. Likewise, they remained God's people even while undergoing the punishment of exile from the land.

More significant, as we move towards the New Testament, is the fact that in the eschatological visions of the prophets we can discern a loosening of, almost a dispensing with, the ancient land-kinship basis of the covenant, in visions of the future constitution of the relationship between God and his people. The new people of God will have an all-inclusiveness, in which categories of people who, on the old land-kinship criterion, would have been excluded or in a very uncertain position, will be brought into a full and assured relationship with God as an integral part of 'Israel'.

Thus, for example, in Isaiah 56:3–8, the doubts of the foreigner (who had no stake in the *land*) and of the eunuch (who could have no *family* or posterity) are alike allayed by the promise of permanent security in the new covenant. And in Ezekiel 47:22f., the idealized picture of the future 'land tenure' of Israel makes a point of explicitly including those who had previously been excluded or only tolerated as dependants – the *gērîm*, the alien, immigrant sojourners who previously had no permission to own a share in the land. In this vision of the future, their share in the inheritance of God's people will no longer depend on charity or good fortune but will be permanently guaranteed. In other words, the theological themes of security, inclusion, sharing and responsibility, which were once linked to the land, remain valid; but they are loosened from their literal, territorial moorings as the scope of salvation is widened to include non-Jews.

The New Testament sees this eschatological vision of the extension of redemption beyond the nation of Israel as being fulfilled in the inclusion of the Gentiles in the people of God, through the work of the Messiah, Jesus. Ephesians 2:11 – 3:6, Paul's classic exposition of this new, all-inclusive dimension of the Christian gospel, is significantly rich in Old Testament imagery.

He begins by summarizing the previous position of the Gentiles *outside* Christ in terms equivalent to the position of those who had had no share in the land-kinship membership of Israel: 'excluded from citizenship, foreigners to the covenants of promise' (2:12). Then, having described the work of Christ on the cross as breaking down that barrier, making peace and providing access to God for the believing Jew and Gentile alike, he returns to Old Testament imagery to describe the new position of the Gentiles *in* Christ: 'Consequently, you are no longer foreigners and aliens [words which translate *gērîm* and *tôšāḇîm* – the landless dependants in Israel's economy], but fellow-citizens with God's people and members of God's household' (2:19). This speaks of permanence, security, inclusion and, as he soon points out, practical responsibility. As the climax of this outline of 'his gospel', Paul sums up the new position of the Gentiles in the three words of 3:6. They are now joint-heirs (*synklēronoma*), a joint-body (*synsōma*) and joint-sharers (*synmetocha*) with Israel in the promise, in the Messiah-Jesus, through the gospel. The language of inheritance strongly evokes the pattern of relationships between God, Israel and their land within which the Israelites of old had found their security.

Thus, by incorporation into the Messiah, people from all nations are enabled to enter into the privileges and responsibilities of God's people which, in the Old Testament, were focused on life in the land. Now Christ himself takes over the significance and function of the old land-kinship qualification. To be 'in Christ', just as to be 'in the land', denotes a status and a relationship which have been *given* by God, a position of inclusion and security, and a commitment to live 'worthily' by fulfilling the practical responsibilities to those who share the relationship with you. This is what is meant by the *typological* understanding of the significance of Israel's land. It is simply treating the land as we do other great features and themes of the Old Testament, by relating it to the person and work of the Messiah and through him to the nature of the community of those 'in Christ', Messianic Israel.[6]

But what has become of the *socio-economic* dimension of the land, which we found to be of such importance to Old Testament Israel? Has it all just been transcended, spiritualized and forgotten? By no means! It feeds through precisely into that realm of the corporate sharing and practical responsibility which is just as much a feature of the New as of the Old Testament.

Before glancing at what that meant in practice, let us return to the passage we have just considered, Ephesians 2. Twice in that context, Paul refers to the role of the Holy Spirit in the incorporation of Jew and Gentile together into God's new community in Christ (2:18, 22). Elsewhere, indeed, Paul regards the gift of the Holy Spirit as itself the fulfilment of the promise to Abraham, also in the context of the extension of salvation to the Gentiles (Gal. 3:14). In the same context he also relates the *oneness* of believers in Christ to their status as seed and heirs of Abraham (Gal. 3:28f.).

Now this oneness of believers in Christ and their shared experience of Christ through the Holy Spirit is no mere abstract, 'spiritual' concept. On the contrary, it has far-reaching practical implications in both the social *and* economic realms. Both realms are included in the New Testament understanding and practice of 'fellowship', and both have deep roots in the soil of Old Testament land ethics.

Fellowship is the usual translation of the Greek *koinōnia*, which is itself part of a rich complex of words. A study of the root *koinōn-* in the New Testament reveals that a substantial number of the occurrences of words formed or compounded from it either signify, or are in contexts which relate to, actual social and economic relationships between Christians. They denote a practical, often costly, sharing, which is a far cry from that watery 'togetherness' which commonly passes as 'fellowship'.

Some examples will make the point. The first consequences of the outpouring of the Spirit at Pentecost was a new community who, in 'devoting themselves to . . . the fellowship'

---

[6] The Christian significance of the land theme is handled in a broadly similar way by E. A. Martens, *Plot and Purpose in the Old Testament*, pp. 242–248, 258–260.

(*tē koinōnia*), shared everything in common (Acts 2:42, 44) and ensured that nobody was in need (Acts 4:34). In Romans 12:13, believers are urged to share hospitality with the saints (*koinōnountes*). In 1 Timothy 6:18, the rich are to be commanded to be 'generous' (*koinōnikous*). The same duty is laid on all Christians in Hebrews 13:16. Paul refers to his financial collection among the Greek churches for the aid of the Judaean Christians as 'an act of fellowship' (*koinōnian tina*, Rom. 15:26), which he justifies on the grounds that if the Gentiles have shared (*ekoinōnēsan*) *spiritual* blessings from the Jews, they owe it to them to share *material* blessings (v. 27). The same reciprocal principle applies in the relationship between the teacher and the taught in Galatians 6:6 (*koinōneitō*). Indeed, in commending the Corinthians for their eagerness to share in the financial *koinōnia* collection (2 Cor. 8:4; 9:13), Paul describes it as proof of their *obedience to the gospel*, implying that such concrete economic evidence of fellowship was of the essence of a genuine Christian profession.

Is it then coincidental that when Paul's own gospel was accepted as authentic in Jerusalem by means of 'the right hand of *koinōnia*', he was immediately asked 'to remember the poor' – as if in proof (Gal. 2:9f.)? His Gentile collection did indeed bear out his professed eagerness to honour that gospel-fellowship. Likewise, when he thanks God for the Philippians' 'fellowship in the gospel' (Phil. 1:5), the rest of the letter makes it clear that he is thinking concretely, not just spiritually. They had been partners (*synkoinōnoi*) with Paul (1:7) in practical financial support (4:15ff.).

The extent of this kind of language in the New Testament understanding of fellowship leads me to the view that it has deep roots in the socio-economic ethics of the Old Testament. There are so many similarities which show that the experience of *fellowship*, in its full, rich, 'concrete', New Testament sense, fulfils analogous theological and ethical functions for the Christian as the possession of *land* did for Old Testament Israelites. Both must be seen as part of the purpose and pattern of redemption, not just as accidental or incidental to it. The explicit purpose of the exodus was the enjoyment of the rich blessing of God in his 'good land'; the goal of redemption through Christ is 'sincere love for your brothers' (1 Pet. 1:22), with all its practical implications. Both are linked to the status of sonship and the related themes of inheritance and promise. Both thereby constitute a proof of an authentic relationship with God as part of his redeemed community. For fellowship, like the land, has its limits; so that the person who departs permanently from it or refuses to accept it shows that he has no real part in God's people (*cf.* Mt. 18:15–17; 1 Jn. 2:19).

Above all, both are *shared* experiences: the land, by the nature of the Israelite economic system as we have outlined it; fellowship, by very definition of the word *koinōnia*. This gives to both that deeply practical mutual responsibility that pervades both Old and New Testament ethics. There is the same concern for the poor and needy (*cf.* 1 Jn. 3:17), the same ideal of equality among God's people, both economically (*cf.* 2 Cor. 8:13–15 with its Old Testament allusion) and socially (*cf.* Jas. 2:1–7). There is even the same prophetic indignation at those whose sin deprives or defrauds fellow members of God's people of their rightful share in what God has given for the enjoyment of all his people. The Old Testament prophets condemned the unjust oppressors who drove fellow Israelites off their land; compare with that Jesus' strictures on those who refuse to forgive a brother (Mt. 18:21–35), Paul's horror at the factionalism and lack of love at Corinth and the priority he gives in his various lists of sins to those that harm the fellowship (*e.g.* Eph. 4:25ff.; Phil. 2:1–4, 14; Col. 3:8ff.), and John's refusal to accept the man who hates his brother as a child of God at all (1 Jn. 2:9–11; 4:7ff.).

So then, the typological interpretation of the land, which relates it to the person and work of Jesus the Messiah, does not come to a 'dead end' with Jesus himself. Rather, it carries the social and economic thrust of Old Testament ethics into the New Testament ethics of practical relationships within the new Israel, the Messianic community. Citizenship of the kingdom of God most certainly has a social and economic dimension, which has transcended the land and kinship structure of Old Testament Israel, but not in such a way as to make that original structure irrelevant. This transference of the socio-economic bond of Old Testament society to the Christ-centred bond of the New Testament is recognized by the Jewish scholar, R. Loewe: 'The sociological basis on which Christianity rests is not the tie of kinship, as in the case of Judaism, but that of fellowship – fellowship in Christ'.[7] In this, as in so many other ways,

---

[7] R. Loewe, *The Position of Women in Judaism* (SPCK, 1966), p. 52.

Christ and the kingdom he proclaimed and inaugurated 'fulfil' the Old Testament, taking up its socio-economic pattern and transforming it into something that can be the experience, not just of a single nation in a small slice of territory, but of anyone, anywhere, in Christ.

Our diagram, then, must acquire yet another triangle, indicating the Christian church as the spiritual heir and continuation of Old Testament Israel; Christian fellowship, in its fullest, practical New Testament sense, as fulfilling similar theological and ethical functions to the land of Israel; and both together as the context of a typological interpretation of Old Testament ethics.

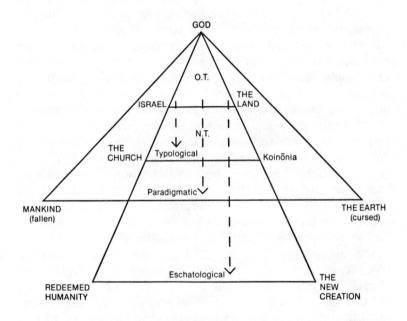

This threefold framework of interpretation, typological, paradigmatic and eschatological, releases the potential and power of Old Testament ethics into the whole range of Christian concerns – for the church, for the world and for the ultimate future of both. It is a framework that we have arrived at in our study of Old Testament economics in particular, but it is valid, I believe, for the whole range of ethical principles operating in and from the Old Testament, as we shall see in the following chapters.

As a concluding illustration, let us pass the *jubilee* and its associated sabbatical institutions through the prism of this threefold method of interpretation. The *typological* relevance is immediately clear, inasmuch as Jesus took up the major jubilee themes of release and restoration, as well as the sabbatical concept of 'rest' in its deeper senses, and applied them to the whole range of his own ministry and mission (Lk. 4:18f.; Mt. 11:28–30). Furthermore, the early church sought to apply jubilary principles to its socio-economic life; indeed, Luke seems deliberately to describe its achievement in terms that echo the sabbatical promise in Deuteronomy 15 that God would richly bless an obedient people:

There will be no poor among you (Dt. 15:4 RSV)

There were no needy persons among them (Acts 4:34).

The paradigmatic relevance of the jubilee and related land laws in the Old Testament is particularly applicable to situations where land tenure and land reform are pressing issues of social and political dispute. The jubilee was designed to prevent the accumulation of the bulk of the land in the hands of a few. It protected a system of land tenure that was intended to be broadly equitable, with the ownership of land widely spread throughout the population. It was an attempt to impede, and indeed periodically to reverse, the relentless economic forces that lead to a downward spiral of debt, poverty, dispossession and bondage. Its major focus of concern was for the economic viability of the smallest economic units, namely the household with its land: it was a 'family-orientated' economic law. Within the limits of primitive agriculture, its sabbatical fallow embodied a concern for the 'health' of the soil itself.

All of these are far from being dead or irrelevant issues. They can still furnish principles, objectives, paradigms, for a wide variety of Christian socio-economic involvement in the modern world, perhaps especially in the field of development. As is the nature of paradigms, they can be outlined succinctly and with a perhaps deceptive simplicity. Of course, the application of them to the infinite variety of human socio-economic life and environments will be a complex matter (as is the application of paradigms to the complexity of a spoken language), which can be effectively undertaken only by those who live in the midst of given situations, 'on the ground'.

But our interpretation of the jubilee will be incomplete unless we also allow it to give content to our future hope. Even for Israel it had a built-in *eschatological* dimension. Anticipation of it affected all present economic values and set a limit on unjust social relations. It was proclaimed with a blast on the trumpet (the *yōbel*, from which its name derives), an instrument associated with decisive acts of God (*cf.* Is. 27:13; 1 Cor. 15:52). And its two central concepts, *restoration* and *release*, became symbolic, even in the Old Testament, of the new age of salvation when God would intervene to establish his kingdom of peace and justice. Then there would be the restoration of all things to their intended purpose, the release of God's people from sin and all that oppresses and binds and enslaves.

This is the vision and hope that inspired prophetic passages such as Isaiah 35 and 61, with their beautiful integration of personal, social, physical, economic, political, international and spiritual realms. Our use of the jubilee must preserve a like balance and integration, preventing us from keeping asunder what God will ultimately join together. And in all our endeavours, the Old Testament jubilee holds before us the light of its own, as yet future, perfect fulfilment. For the day has yet to come when

> the ransomed of the Lord will return.
> They will enter Zion with singing;
> everlasting joy will crown their heads.
> Gladness and joy will overtake them,
> and sorrow and sighing will flee away
> (Is. 35:10).

5
Politics and the world of nations

Israel lived as a nation among the nations in the centre of the international stage. Accordingly, substantial portions of the Old Testament are concerned with politics – both internal politics of Israel and the political relations between her contemporary neighbours. An important part of any treatment of Old Testament ethics, therefore, must be to examine this theme and assess its relevance to the political dimension of Christian ethics.

In this chapter I have adopted a similar method to that used for the treatment of economics in the previous chapter. First we set the subject in the light of the creation and of the fall. Then we look at some of the historical features of the political life of Israel, which may be termed a 'redemption perspective'. Finally we reflect on some features of Israel's relationship with other 'secular' powers and their relevance to the life of God's people in the midst of the world.

'EVERY NATION OF MEN'

SOCIAL DIVERSITY

The rich diversity of the economic resources of the earth, with which we began the last chapter, have their counterpart in the wide ethnic diversity of mankind and its ever-changing kaleidoscope of national, cultural, and political variations. The Bible enables us to see the one as just as much part of God's creative purpose as the other. Speaking as a Jew to Gentiles in an evangelistic context, Paul takes for granted the diversity of nations within the unity of humanity, and attributes it to the Creator.

> From one man he made every nation of men, that they should inhabit the whole earth; and he determined the times set for them and the exact places where they should live (Acts 17:26).

Although he goes on to quote from Greek writers, his language in this verse is drawn from the Old Testament, from the ancient song of Moses in Deuteronomy 32:

> When the Most High gave the nations their inheritance,
> when he divided all mankind,
> he set up boundaries for the peoples (Dt. 32:8).

So the equality and ordering of relationships between the different groupings of mankind forms part of man's accountability to his Creator God, as much as the accountability of one man for another, as the story of Cain and Abel shows. The same can be said of the structuring of social relationships within any such group, whether it is a small local community or a whole nation. This social nature of man and the socio-political organization that flows from it is a part of God's creative purpose for man, linked to the creation of man in God's own image. For God himself is 'social'. The decision to create man is introduced as a sudden, contrasting, switch to the plural: 'Let *us* make man in *our* image, in *our* likeness' (Gn. 1:26). And the first fact about this 'image of God' is sexuality, that complementary duality in unity, from which flows the rest of man's social nature: marriage, parenthood, family, kinship, and outwards in widening circles.

Now, of course, the human author of Genesis 1:26 can scarcely have had in mind what we, with the broader light of the whole biblical revelation, refer to as the doctrine of the Trinity. Nevertheless, in the light of that wider teaching, we can legitimately discern in the plural forms he used a deeper meaning which goes beyond the conscious meaning of the author (a *sensus plenior*). Genesis 1:2 had already spoken of the Spirit of God involved in creation (though, again, we cannot assert that the author would have understood that term in the developed sense of a distinct person in the Godhead, but more likely as just the dynamic, effective 'breath' of God), and the New Testament emphatically exalts Jesus Christ as the agent and goal of creation (Jn. 1:1–3; Col. 1:15–17; Heb. 1:1–3).

God himself, therefore, in the mystery of the Trinity, subsists in the harmonious relationship of equal Persons, each of whom possesses his proper function and authority. Man, his image, was created to live in the harmony of personal equality but with social organization that required functional structures of authority. The ordering of social relationships and structures, locally, nationally and globally, is of direct concern to our Creator God, then. But that is precisely the stuff of politics. The Bible, therefore, makes no unnatural separation between 'politics' and 'religion', though neither does it identify them. Both are essential dimensions of what it is to be human. Man the worshipper is also man the political animal, for God made him so.

SINFUL DIVISION
The fall, however, has wrought its evil havoc in this, as in every, sphere of human life. The Genesis narratives rapidly disclose the corrupting of the social relationships around which the life of mankind is structured. The fundamental structure of the relationship in marriage is twisted. Instead of man and wife finding the fulfilment of their own created function and purpose in enabling the other to fulfil theirs (Gn. 2:18–24), the relationship degenerates into one of harsh domination and lust (Gn. 3:16b). All derivative relationships are correspondingly debased, by spirals of jealousy, anger, violence and vengeance (Gn. 4), until the whole race is characterized by wickedness and evil (Gn. 6:5).

1. Babel
The effects of the fall upon the international sphere are summed up in the deceptively simple tale of the tower of Babel. There we see that there is a double cause behind the divisions, barriers and misunderstandings between men, summed up in the confusion of language, as well as behind the alienation and the sense of being mutually foreign, summed up in the scattering over the earth. Humanly, they are the result of arrogance and presumptuous ambition. But they are also portrayed as the divine response to the threat of mankind's unified rebellion in sin.

It is worth emphasizing this latter point. God's deliberation before acting is not about punishment but about prevention: 'If as one people speaking the same language they have begun to do this, then nothing they plan to do will be impossible for them' (Gn. 11:6f.). It is the limitless possibilities of a *unified* and fallen mankind's potential for evil which stirs God to 'divisive' action.

Something of the paradox of the mystery of evil and God's sovereignty is contained here. The same proud sin which prevents mankind from living in unity for good also prevents mankind from uniting in evil. Thus behind the sin, which has turned God's created diversity into man's strife-ridden divisiveness, one can see the mercy and grace of God which uses that very effect of sin as a dyke to save the human race from being totally engulfed in the self-destruction of unified evil. Indeed, it is the outworking of the combination of judgment and hidden grace in God's response to Babel which enables human history to continue, so that in the midst of the ebb and flow of its socio-political tides God can pursue his redemptive purpose. And when that purpose is complete, Revelation shows the dyke removed and mankind allowed to create a horrific global unity of deception and rebellion, an apocalyptic Babel, which will be the precursor of the final judgment.

2. Sodom and Gomorrah

At the more local or national level, the effect of sin on political life is seen in the lust for power. Like wealth, it becomes something to be grasped, defended, selfishly used and accorded that absolute status that is due to God alone. The first Middle East war that the Bible brings to our attention was caused by political subjugation and its inevitable violent backlash (Gn. 14:1–4).

The most spectacular divine judgment since the flood fell on Sodom and Gomorrah in response to the 'outcry' that was raised against them. The word 'outcry' (*tṣe'āqāh*), which is emphasized several times in the story (Gn. 18:20f.; 19:13), is the word used of the Israelites groaning under the socio-political oppression of Egypt, and under later foreign oppressors. This suggests that the wickedness of Sodom and Gomorrah was not confined to the perverted sexual assault upon Lot's visitors, with which we commonly associate these cities, but was an intolerable level of social injustice. Certainly, as noted in the previous chapter, this was how the prophets understood their sin. We have already referred to Ezekiel 16:49. Isaiah, in accusing the political rulers of Judah of oppression and injustice, twice drew comparisons with Sodom and Gomorrah (Is. 1:9f.). Amos, who had a similarly socio-political accusation against Israel, likewise compared God's previous partial judgment to that of Sodom and Gomorrah (Am. 4:11).

POLITICAL GEOGRAPHY

These early chapters of Genesis thus present us with God's passionate concern for, and sometimes direct involvement in, the political life of mankind, from the sphere of international relationships to the local politics of petty kingdoms in the Jordan valley. So it is no surprise, when the story of redemption gets under way in Genesis 12, that it takes place on the stage of the real human world of political geography and history, and not in some supra-terrestrial, mythological realm. Again we must pay attention to the order of the biblical narrative and its theological significance. Both the Babel event, with its implications for fallen, alienated, scattered man upon a cursed earth, in Genesis 11, and the call of Abraham, with its promise of redemption and blessing for man starting from a new land, in Genesis 12, are set against the background of the table of nations in Genesis 10. What is the purpose of this slab of ethnic geography?

Whatever the purpose for which it was originally recorded, its inclusion at this crucial point between the flood and the beginning of the redemptive history leaves the reader in no doubt about the nature of narrative. This is not a mythical, prehistorical world of gods and monsters, but the sober 'classifiable' world of nations, territories, cities, kingdoms and languages – a thoroughly recognizable, political, human world. Both the outworking of the baleful effects of the fall and the redemptive activity of God take place side by side in the real world of men and nations, and not only *in* it, but through and by means of the totality of their acts and relationships, including those we deem political. To borrow a picture from Jesus, the weeds and the wheat are in the same field, and 'the field is the world'.

SPIRITUAL POWERS

This is not at all to overlook the Bible's teaching on the spiritual battle that lies behind the historical work of redemption, the conflict between the rule of God and the usurped rule of Satan, 'the Prince of this world' and the demonic forces at his command. Indeed, there are hints in the Old Testament of an awareness that there is a 'personal' world of spiritual, invisible powers that lies behind the institutions and 'personifications' of states, the overwhelming force of political power, the distinctive 'character' of different social systems. It is not a question of polytheism or dualism, for these powers, though sometimes called 'gods', are known to be 'no-gods', but, if anything, created beings. Hence Isaiah's stinging debunking of the astral 'gods' of Mesopotamia: 'Who *created* all these?' (Is. 40:26). Whatever they are, they are subject, like men, including men who have exercised unbridled power under their influence, to the final judgment of God:

> In that day the LORD will punish
> the powers in the heavens above
> and the kings on the earth below (Is. 24:21).

Above all, the existence and activity of such spiritual forces in no way reduced the political freedom of choice that human beings must exercise, nor their moral responsibility for their political choices and their consequences. This was equally true of predictive prophecy. In his subtle study of 2 Kings,[1] Jacques Ellul shows clearly how men make their political decisions and actions in freedom, and bear responsibility for them, even though in doing so they fulfil the word of God, sometimes consciously, more often unwittingly.

THE REDEEMED NATION

'A CHOSEN PEOPLE'

As we saw in chapter 2, God chose to achieve the redemption of his fallen creation by a historical process which included the

---

[1] *The Politics of God and the Politics of Man.*

choice of a particular nation. Before we look at some of the political implications of that redemptive act and relationship, we should pause to take note that some people find difficulty with this idea of a 'chosen people'. Is it not favouritism on God's part, and a *carte blanche* religious justification for élitist claims of racial superiority? Several points may be made in answer.

1. 'People' not 'race'
It is better to use the term 'people' and avoid the phrase 'chosen race'. There are two relevant words in Hebrew: *'am*, used normally of a people considered as a community, large or small; and *gōy*, used of a nation in the politico-geographical sense. Israel is usually referred to as the *'am* of God, the community created by and belonging to Yahweh. *Gōy* is generally used of surrounding nations and races. The Old Testament concept of election is not, therefore, simply a matter of God arbitrarily picking out one nation or race from the rest. Rather, he called into being a community of people who would then live among the nations to serve his purpose.

2. A mixed multitude
There was an awareness that Israel was not a particularly 'pure' people, in the racial sense. Two of the tribes, Manasseh and Ephraim, were descended from Joseph's Egyptian wife (Gn. 41:50–52), and there were other mixed elements in the Israelite camp (Ex. 12:38; Lv. 24:10; Ezk. 16:3). So the Old Testament can never justify theories of a chosen, pure *race*.

3. Only by grace
Israel were repeatedly warned against attributing their chosen status to any racial superiority. God had chosen them as an act of free love, to which no human factor was to be added (Dt. 7:6–8; 9:4–6). Indeed, apart from God's grace, Israel were no different from other migrant nations (Am. 9:7).

4. Divine realism
The fact that God chose a people as his means of bringing redemption should not be regarded as endorsing any racial claim or privilege, but only as God's characteristic habit of engaging with real man in the real world of his own creation. He

would act through men to redeem men; but men exist in nations. Therefore he would use a nation as the vehicle of his purpose. This is not embarrassing favouritism, but divine realism taking seriously the totality of our human life as he himself designed it. As we pointed out in chapter 2, the election and mission of Israel has an incarnational aspect – God at work within our corporate humanity, just as, in Jesus, he entered our individual humanity.

5. *One for all*
God chose and called Israel, not at the expense of the rest, but for the sake of the rest. Right from their establishment as a 'kingdom of priests' (Ex. 19:3–6) at Sinai, there was an awareness that they existed to bring blessing and redemption to mankind (*cf.* Ps. 67; Je. 4:2; and the Servant passages discussed in chapter 2). Even their national history of redemption was 'made available' to the rest of the nations in the eschatological vision of the Psalms which celebrate the universal kingship of the God of Israel (Pss. 47:1–4, 9; 98:1–4; 99:1–4). This strain of universalism in the mission of Israel prevents the concept of a 'chosen people' being taken as mere chauvinism or national pride. That is true, at any rate, theologically; in practice, of course, Israel often fell into the trap of exclusive nationalism.

FROM SLAVERY TO FREEDOM
The events by which Israel were redeemed from Egypt and moulded into a nation, like the death of Christ and the birth of the church, which they prefigured, took place on the stage of international politics. Some salient features of the story, therefore, have political as well as spiritual significances.

1. *Pharaoh defeated*
God's intervention in Egypt for the sake of his oppressed people brought out into the open the totalitarian, absolutist claims of the Egyptian ruler. His refusal to acknowledge the LORD (Ex. 5:2) is understandable, since not only did Egypt have gods of its own, but the pharaoh was numbered among them. The purpose of God's engagement with him was both to unmask his arrogance and to humble him before the God of all the earth (*cf.* Ex. 9:13–17; 10:3). The lesson to be observed by his own people, the beneficiaries of the conflict, was that all the political

might of a great imperial nation was paltry in comparison with the 'mighty hand and outstretched arm' of Yahweh.

The spiritual contest that was bound up with the political events was in principle the same as the final conflict and victory of Christ. So it is not surprising that when Moses and Jesus were discussing the coming saving work of Jesus, they should speak of it as his 'exodus' (Lk. 9:31) – a victory which recalled, even as it surpassed, Moses' victory over Pharaoh. 'Having disarmed the powers and authorities, he made a public spectacle of them, triumphing over them by the cross' (Col. 2:15). All human political authority, then, as well as whatever spiritual forces are behind or within it, is subject and accountable to God, and resists him at its own peril (*cf.* Ex. 15).

2. The covenant pattern

The next stage of the story underlines the last point further. God established his relationship with his people using terms and forms drawn from the world of international politics – namely, the covenant. 'Covenant' (*berît* in Hebrew), of course, is a kind of solemn, contractually formalized relationship applied literally or figuratively to a range of human acts and relationships. The same word was used for international treaties. During the era of the exodus and settlement, a particular treaty form had already been common for some time between imperial sovereigns (such as the Hittites and Egyptians) and their dependent vassal kingdoms. The treaty would begin by identifying the two parties, emphasizing the sovereignty of the imperial king, recount the historical events leading up to the treaty, and then lay down stipulations on the vassal, sanctioned by blessings and curses.

The *form* of the covenant established between the LORD and Israel seems clearly to have made use of this protocol of international politics. It identified the LORD as the great king ('I am the LORD your God'), recounting his deeds ('who brought you up out of Egypt'), and recording the stipulations of the commandments and laws he laid upon his 'vassal' people.

There is more in this than just the intrinsically interesting fact that a political model should be used to convey the status and responsibilities of the redeemed people. The main significance lies in the effect that such a view of God's position has on all horizontal relationships within the covenant people. By attributing to Yahweh an infinite sovereignty *over* the whole nation, Israel greatly reduced the relative importance of all kinds of human authority structures *within* the nation. We might compare the effect of a telephoto lens. The longer its focal 'reach', the more it appears to reduce the distance between objects in the foreground. Giving to God his due position of authority reduced the claims of any human authority to their proper, subordinate perspective.

This shows us that the idea and ideal of 'theocracy' in Israel was not just an abstract religious notion. Properly applied, it had the socio-political levelling effect of reducing the differentials between individuals, groups, offices and functions. It did not, however, abolish them. Kings, judges, elders, masters, fathers and others all had their proper roles and appropriate authority. But the king was still a 'vassal' king, as much subject to the covenant law of God as any of his own subjects. The judge and the offender both stood before the bar of God's justice. The landlord was only a tenant in God's land. The slave owner and slave alike were slaves of the LORD. The father was one of a nation of sons of God.

There is, then, a strong link between Israel's theocratic monotheism (the central arch of her faith) and her tendency towards her own brand of socio-political and economic 'egalitarianism'. This did not obliterate differentials, but attempted to confine them within the proper limits of functional necessity for the harmony and peace of society. Faith and obedience rendered to an absolute God militated against allowing absolute power or prestige to any human authority. The sociological outworking of this link between covenant faith and socio-political and economic structures has been very thoroughly analysed by N. K. Gottwald, *The Tribes of Yahweh*, especially in Part Ten. In effect it resulted in Israelite society exhibiting clear and probably deliberate contrasts with their contemporary neighbours, politically and economically, on a scale which makes them possibly unique in the ancient world.

3. Freedom in framework

It was pointed out in chapter 2 how God did not impose the law upon Israel in Egypt as a pre-condition of redemption as if by keeping the law they could achieve or deserve their deliverance. Conversely, having redeemed them, he did not leave them without a framework of law. They were not set loose in the world in the hope that a redeemed people would know how to live harmoniously without the need for laws, institutions, and structures of social and political authority. The deliverance from the autocratic oppression of Egypt was not inspired by the anarchist's vision. On the contrary, the very freedoms and values that the exodus deliverance achieved were at once set within a protective framework of mutual responsibilities. The Ten Commandments particularly can be interpreted in that way (see below, chapter 6, pp. 142f.).

We saw at the start of this chapter that God's creation of man in his own image implied a human society that would exhibit diversity of relationship, function, structure and authority. Whether, if man had remained unfallen, the creation pattern of society would have included laws and institutions and all the apparatus of politics as we know them, must remain a hypothetical question. Certainly, in the context of fallen society, such structures of socio-political life are necessary in the case of unredeemed, 'secular' societies, in order to preserve society from the destructive snowballing of individual and collective wickedness. But they were necessary also in the case of the redeemed society of Israel, in order to enable them to embody *creation* principles in their socio-political life. This corresponds to the parallel purpose of their economic institutions as we saw in the last chapter.

G. R. Dunstan argues strongly for the importance of moral insights and values being embodied in social institutions and conventions if they are to survive and have lasting practical effect.[2] By 'conventions' he means the sort of moral controls which operate within the fabric of social life in a community. Sometimes these have the force of actual law, but they are more often a matter of non-enforceable mutual expectations and felt obligations, just as many of the injunctions of the *tôrāh* are not enforceable legislation, but demands based on the presupposition of covenant obligation to the LORD and to one's neighbour. He makes a double point about conventions in the context of Christian ethics which is equally applicable to the place of moral conventions and socio-political institutions in the Old Testament:

[2] *The Artifice of Ethics* (SCM, 1974), particularly chapter 1, 'Community and convention', pp. 1–17.

Conventions are *possible* because men are capable of moral insight, of agreeing in the recognition of moral insight, and of committing themselves to maintain it; they rest on a presupposition of fidelity to a common interest and purpose. Conventions are *necessary* because men fail conspicuously to follow their moral insights and are capable of ruthlessly exploiting one another in the pursuit of self-interest; they rest on a presupposition of infidelity to the community purpose. And in this double statement, of possibility and necessity, stands the realism of ethics – and, incidentally, the realism of Christian theology which sees man as both fallen and free, turned in upon self while still ordained by nature and grace towards community and reconciliation with God (p. 7).

Therein also stands the realism of God, as we have already commented. Having purposed to create a nation as the model and vehicle of his redemption, but set within and still part of fallen humanity, he gave to that nation a framework of social, economic and political institutions designed to preserve the freedom and moral values implicit in their redemption.

The goal of redemption is freedom. In Israel's case, not only freedom *from* the socio-political oppression of Egypt, but freedom *to be* the people of God, a 'priestly kingdom', a 'light to the nations'. And again, it is the power of conventions, in the above sense, that preserves such purposive freedom. Dunstan writes further:

Conventions . . . result in liberation – liberation for the individual and the conditions of freedom for the community. Assurance itself is a liberating force. Where there is a convention of honesty and fair dealing, buyer and seller can negotiate together without crippling suspicion or fear. . . . As in personal behaviour, so also on the social level: it is worth reflecting how much more constricted social and economic life would be – how much less free – were not so much of it governed by an extensive conventionalized morality . . . Convention is thus society's strongest preservative against both anarchy and the tyranny of an all-prevailing punitive and coercive law.

But convention makes great demands, for it stems from belief. It embodies in institutional form what the community

believes to be of worth – specific beliefs about the worth of
people, whether rich or poor, clever or simple . . . beliefs
about the value of human relationships and the common
interest in the truths upon which they stand (pp. 14–16).

For Israel, the beliefs which their institutions embodied, the
'truths upon which they stand', were governed by the powerful
vertical dimension of the covenant relationship. Once again we
see how pervasive and practical was the effect of the theocratic
constitution of the nation.

Deuteronomy displays the pattern at its clearest. Covenantal
in its very form, it sets the whole nation in the position of a
dependent vassal people, bound to their sovereign Lord. From
that perspective it builds up both the solid skeleton of actual
legislation and institutions, from kings to slaves, and also the
moral muscle and fibre of repeated exhortation, motivation,
promise and threat. That is, it is concerned not only to legislate
and politicize, but also to inculcate a whole ethos of 'conventional' morality that would be distinctly Israelite, fit for the
people of God. 'To read the Deuteronomic law is to feel oneself
living with a closely-knit, brotherly, godly and civilized society,
however far the vision was from the reality' (Dunstan, p. 24).

It is no surprise at all, therefore, that the prophets felt their
deepest concern over, and directed their most vehement protest
at, the breakdown of moral conventions in the political and
economic life of the nation (*cf.* especially Ho. 4:1–13). Without
their protective framework, the freedom that was the hallmark
of the redeemed people was being destroyed internally. Israel
was becoming socio-politically no less oppressive and unjust
than her unredeemed neighbours.

The implications for Christian social ethics of this aspect of
the way of Israel are clear enough. We must heed Dunstan's
plea to pay more serious attention to the institutions and
conventions of our society than we are accustomed to in the
insulation of our 'religious' concerns. This not only means that
we cease to take for granted the social structures of which we
broadly approve and which enshrine our freedoms and values;
but we must also actively protect them from erosion and that
false radicalism which suspects and 'uproots' *any* kind of
conventional morality.

It also means that in the constant struggle against social structures and conventions which embody evil and injustice we cease to be content with criticism alone. It means further that we go beyond merely purveying fresh moral insights and visions. Man does not live by visions alone, however exalted. Christians must struggle alongside those who shape, modify, and continually recreate the conventions and institutions of society, in order to give 'incarnational' bone and muscle to their ethical convictions.

> The moralist has his moment of vision; he may utter what he sees, in a word of compelling force; and he may be listened to or not, but his work is not done until he has transcribed his vision into the structure of a social institution, to last when his words are no longer heard but forgotten . . . [he] must weave his insight into the fabric of society (Dunstan, p. 4).

This is a task to which the Old Testament, with its record of the institutional, political and 'conventional' life of Israel, gives its approval.

THE MONARCHY

The scope of this book does not extend to detailed analysis of all Israel's political institutions – the role of elders, the military and judicial judges, the administrative and defensive bureaucracy of David and Solomon, the role of the army and its generals, the conduct of international affairs, wars and alliances, *etc.* We shall, however, turn our attention to the monarchy. For this emerged as the major political force in Israel during the central centuries of Old Testament history, and from our study we shall draw out a few noteworthy features for our own political ethics.

1. *Human origins*

One thing that stands out clearly in the emergence of monarchy in Israel is how characteristically human, ambivalent, even squalid at times, were the factors that gave rise to it. There was no divine command or initiating sanction to monarchy. The law in Deuteronomy refers to 'the king the LORD your God chooses', but only as the secondary, limiting, condition to a situation brought about by the people's desire: 'Let us set a king over us' (Dt. 17:14f.). And this is certainly the way the deuteronomic historian records the story in 1 Samuel 8 – 12. As we noted in chapter 3, the demand for a king sprang from a mixture of motives, some apparently good (the desire for justice and incorrupt leadership), others unquestionably retrograde (the desire to be like the rest of the nations). And the story unfolds with the continuing ambiguity of Saul, chosen yet rejected by God; raised to power in a wave of popularity, but enraged to jealousy and self-destruction by the fickle shift of that popularity; starting with promise, ending in tragedy.

This utter humanness of the story of Saul is very important precisely because of the glory of his successor David. David generated in Israel a whole new thread of theology, a new way of expressing the link between God's kingship and the king of Israel, a new eschatology of a coming Messianic king descended from David. But the memory of Saul kept both the political institution of monarchy itself and its human occupant at any one time firmly in perspective. Monarchy in Israel was not in itself sacred or divine. Kings in Israel could not trace their ancestry back to legendary gods or heroes of the prehistoric past. The historical, human origins of the institution and the all too human failings of its first holder, and indeed of his illustrious successors, were of great significance; for they kept Israel free of that kind of royal mythology which in neighbouring cultures gave unchallengeable sacrosanctity to social stratification and 'pyramid' power-politics.

A further effect of this human origin is that monarchy as a political institution was provisional, and, seen within the total sweep of the history of Israel in the Old Testament period, transient. Israel had lived for several centuries in the land before opting for a king, and survived without one from the exile onwards. Furthermore, if the beneficial effects of the monarchy were weighed against its detrimental effects, the scales would almost certainly come down on the debit side.

It was kings who split the nation, who infringed the traditional pattern of the land tenure and accelerated the economic forces of oppression and inequality, whose pride cost the nations dear in the game of political alliances and wars, who introduced, or did little to prevent, recurring popular apostasy and idolatry. There were, of course, notable exceptions. But in broad terms it can be said that the course of monarchy in Israel ran closer to the fears and warnings of Samuel (1 Sa. 8:10–18) than to the hopes of the people. The fallen humanity of even the redeemed people was nowhere more evident than in these upper levels of their political life.

2. *Divine involvement*

Yet the remarkable fact is that it is on this stage, crowded with the often sordid scenery and personnel of Israel's royal politics, that the major Old Testament historical narratives describe God at work. The great paradox of the monarchy is that, though human in origin and infected from the very conception of the idea by tendencies to apostasy and corruption, God nevertheless took it up and wove it into the very heart of his redemptive purposes. The king became the focus of new dimensions of God's self-revelation. He represented God's rule among his people in the present and became the symbol of the future hope of God's ultimate perfect, Messianic rule among men. Such is the wonder of the interplay between human freedom and divine sovereignty.

There is an interesting tension here between the theocratic ideal and the attributes and functions accorded to human kingship. As we noted above, the practical effect of theocracy was to reduce the differentials within Israelite society, socially, politically and economically. But the desire for a king was really an expression of dissatisfaction with theocracy, as the LORD himself warned: 'it is not you they have rejected as their king, but me' (1 Sa. 8:7). It was entirely reasonable, therefore, for Samuel to argue that this would lead to a social and economic stratification in Israelite society that would be unjust, burdensome and irreversible (1 Sa. 8:18). And, in the course of history, so it did.

Thus the very existence of the king was in one sense a denial of theocracy. Indeed, the earliest attempt to establish a royal house had foundered on this very point. Gideon refused a crown, saying, 'I will not rule over you, nor will my son rule over you. The LORD will rule over you' (Jdg. 8:23). Yet, in another sense, the king became the focal point of theocracy. He was certainly not regarded as divine in himself, but he was called upon to manifest divine qualities as a paragon of that 'imitation of God' which we saw in chapter 1 to be the heart of Old Testament ethics. He was not to be a 'super-Israelite', revelling in the prestige of status (Dt. 17:20), but the 'model Israelite', setting the highest standard of adherence to the law (Dt. 17:19). For his task he received special gifts of God's grace. He was anointed, which symbolized a special mission for God and the power of God's spirit. He was 'adopted' as God's son (2 Sa. 7:14; Ps. 2:7), thus uniting in his person both the status of sonship and the responsibility of obedience it entailed, a status and responsibility which belonged to the whole nation.

The high expectations that were placed on the Israelite kings are summed up in the term 'shepherd' that was applied to them, a term also applied to God, as we know (Ps. 23:1, *etc.*). At the human level, shepherds had very responsible and arduous jobs but a comparatively lowly status. Applied to kings, the comparison was a powerful reminder of the duties, not the glories, of kingship. The king was to see that justice was done among his people – God's idea of justice at that (*cf.* Ps. 72:1 and below, chapter 6, pp. 144), which operated especially on behalf of the poor and downtrodden. It was their failure precisely in this area that brought Israel's 'shepherd-kings' under the wrath of the prophets.

> Woe to the shepherds of Israel who only take care of themselves! Should not shepherds take care of the flock? . . . You have not strengthened the weak or healed the sick or bound up the injured. . . . You have ruled them harshly and brutally (Ezk. 34:2–4; *cf.* Je. 22:1–5; 23:1–4).

Interestingly, Ezekiel sees the ultimate solution to the problem of wicked and callous rulers as a reassertion of theocracy: 'I myself will search for my sheep and look after them . . . I myself will tend my sheep . . . I will shepherd the flock with justice' (34:11–16). Yet it remains a mediated theocracy; the Zion-David theology cannot be jettisoned: 'I will place over them one shepherd, my servant David, and he will tend them' (34:23f.). Only the advent of the Messianic king who was son both of David and of the LORD God himself enabled both aspects of the vision to be united. Not that Israelite kings failed wholly in their duty to mediate and reflect the character of God. Some of them at least achieved a reputation for being merciful beyond the usual standards of their age (1 Ki. 20:31ff.).

If the king was genuinely to pursue justice among his people, 'defending the afflicted, saving the children of the needy, crushing the oppressor' (*cf*. Ps. 72:4), then he had to be available and approachable, again just as a shepherd is to his sheep. And this indeed is a noteworthy feature of Israelite monarchy, at least in its early period. The king could be approached and implored by ordinary individuals or by prophets on their behalf. Examples include Nathan's parable on behalf of Uriah (2 Sa. 12:1–10), Joab and the wise woman of Tekoa's parable on behalf of Absalom (2 Sa. 14:1–24), the prostitute's appeal to Solomon (1 Ki. 3:16–28) and the Shunammite woman's appeal to King Joram (2 Ki. 8:1–6).

Again, this feature has its theocratic counterpart. A people who cherished the privilege of 'drawing near' to God in worship and prayer could hardly accept an unapproachable human king. If God, who inhabited eternity, condescended to dwell with the humble and hear the request of a Hannah, it was not for human political authority to exalt itself beyond approach or criticism. Even when later kings of Judah and Israel grew increasingly autocratic, the vital voice of prophecy could not be silenced. In political terms, the prophets fulfilled a role comparable with 'His Majesty's opposition', compelling political authority to listen to criticism, holding before it its inescapable accountability to God and to the people.

The parabolic approach of Nathan and Joab is interesting and suggestive as a means of confronting political authority. The first was provoked by blatant injustice, the second by an unpopular policy, but both had a similar effect. They gained the attention and involvement of the king as one who *ought* to act: morally and politically they implicated him. Both were practical, *ad hoc* interventions in immediate events, not abstract political theory. Both were successful in their intended effect, to bring about a change of heart and mind in the king. They required, in fact, repentance, moral in the first case, political in the second.

These parabolic appeals to authority serve as a motive and model for Christian involvement in politics. As 'salt' and 'light' Christians should persistently present to authority moral arguments with persuasive force and practical relevance. This should characteristically be on behalf of the weak, powerless and those wronged by injustice or callous neglect, as in Nathan's and Joab's action. And it is most likely to be effective at the level of specific issues and achievable, limited objectives.

3. *Double failure*

The importance, indeed the necessity, of such constant moral challenge and critique of the holders of political authority is highlighted by the remarkably candid history of the monarchy in the Old Testament. Jeroboam I, the first king of the seceding, northern kingdom of Israel, is remembered repeatedly as 'Jeroboam, son of Nebat, who made Israel to sin' (*e.g.* 2 Ki. 14:24, AV). But his rebellion was in protest against the oppressive policy of Rehoboam, successor to Solomon. So we could label the two kinds of political failure to which the kings of Judah and Israel both succumbed as 'the sin of Rehoboam' and the 'sin of Jeroboam'.

The *sin of Rehoboam* was the abuse of power for personal wealth and prestige. He inherited, of course, from his father, Solomon, an already overloaded empire that depended on an oppressive burden of taxation and forced labour. But Rehoboam *deliberately* chose the path of oppression and rule by force as a declared policy of state (1 Ki. 12:1–14). In doing so he rejected the advice of the elders who reminded him of the authentic Israelite concept of political leadership – mutual servanthood: 'If today you will be a servant to these people and serve them . . . they will always be your servants' (1 Ki. 12:7). Rejecting that advice cost him more than half his kingdom but did not deter him or his royal successors, north or south, from exploiting the temptations of power. The shepherds plundered their own flocks.

The *sin of Jeroboam* was to subordinate religious observance and traditions to political ends. His reign typified the ambiguity that surrounded Israelite monarchy. It began and it ended with a word of prophecy from Ahijah, first of all predicting his successful revolt against Rehoboam and promising an enduring dynasty on condition of his obedience (1 Ki. 11:27–39), but finally pronouncing his doom in punishment for his policy of religious pragmatism (14:1–16). It seems that Jeroboam took the first prediction as a virtual *carte blanche* to harness existing religious traditions to his political ambition, and to create new ones wherever the interests of his new, independent kingdom required it. He turned the faith of Israel into a tool of royal policy, and thereby rendered it idolatrous – the classic weakness of 'established' religion. The details are given in 1 Kings 12:26–33 and 13:33f.: golden calves at the northern and southern ends of his kingdom, Dan and Bethel; royally appointed shrines and priests; surrogate festivals, a mixture of the original and the innovative; a personal, royally attended and controlled shrine at Bethel.

With all outward forms of religion thus under royal control, the voice of prophetic criticism became increasingly unpopular. The experience of the anonymous Judean prophet, who protested in Jeroboam's presence at the Bethel shrine (1 Ki. 13:1–5), was repeated more emphatically in the experience of his fellow Judean, Amos, who found himself also sent by God to Bethel a century later, during the reign of Jeroboam II. He brought on himself the wrath of the royal priest, Amaziah, whose words are utterly revealing as to the extent of royal control of religion:

> Then Amaziah said to Amos, 'Get out, you seer! . . . Don't prophesy any more at Bethel, because *this is the king's sanctuary and the temple of the kingdom'* (Am. 7:12f.).

But political power, which seeks so to manipulate state religion as to exclude all criticism or challenge, exposes itself to the only other option, direct divine judgment. Such was the fate of monarchy in both kingdoms of Israel. Ironically, the last great prophet of the monarchy period, Jeremiah, was imprisoned in an attempt to silence his lonely challenge to the last reigning king of Judah, Zedekiah, who presided over the final destruction of Jerusalem and the demise of monarchy in Israel (Je. 32:3).

ISRAEL AND THE NATIONS

With the exile and the ending of monarchy, Israel found herself again in the position of being no longer a free nation-state, but rather a dependent, dispersed, vassal people. The new issues that they had to wrestle with at that time included how to cope with the experience of judgment, how to preserve the traditions of their faith in the absence of its external symbols and institutions, how to survive as a distinct people and keep alive a hope for the future. But above all they faced again the question of the relationship between themselves as the redeemed people of God and the external political authority of a sovereign, 'secular' state.

'Again' is used, because although the question had a poignant immediacy for the generation of the exile, it was not a new issue in the overall history of Israel. The fathers of the nation, the patriarchs, had been sojourners in a land not their own. The exodus had been preceded by centuries of foreign subjection which burned deep in the subconscious national memory.

So whatever else the 'holiness' of God's people meant, it did not entail living in unworldly isolation from the rest of humanity. The nation chosen among the nations for the sake of the nations was throughout her history fully aware of, and deeply engaged in, the affairs of the international world around them.

INTERNATIONAL AWARENESS

Even when Israel was a free and independent nation-state, there was no shortage of international awareness. Solomon, of course, was the great internationalist figure of the Old Testament, who opened up Israel to outside influence on an unprecedented scale. Some of that influence was beneficially absorbed, such as the wisdom schools which he patronized. Others, such as the influx of trading wealth and the spoils of empire and the religio-political alliances sealed by foreign marriage, were fundamentally detrimental.

The prophetic movement in Israel was, from a very early period, international in its scope. The ministries of Elijah and Elisha crossed the borders of Israel, both in the territorial field of their operations and also in their influence on events in countries other than Israel. Amos, the first of the prophets whose oracles were collected in a book of the prophet's own name, begins the book (and probably his prophetic ministry began in the same way) with an astonishingly comprehensive chain of oracles against the neighbour states of Israel, at every point of the compass (Am. 1:1 – 2:5). The rhetorical effect, which was surely deliberate, was to throw a kind of geographical noose around Israel and thus to make the climactic accusation against her even more devastatingly powerful. But the oracles against the surrounding nations have their own intrinsic importance, quite apart from showing how well informed was this Judean farmer.

The nations are accused by the God of Israel on the basis of moral criteria of universal human validity. They are not judged only for wickedness committed against Israel, God's people, but for wrongs done among themselves. Treaties had been broken, communities pillaged, captured and sold, atrocities committed, inhumanities perpetrated. And the LORD, *Israel's* God, had seen it and held these other nations accountable for their mutual behaviour. This is of considerable importance, for it shows us that the prophetic voice and ministry of the people of God is addressed not just internally to that people themselves, though that is certainly its primary purpose; it also conveys the challenge and reminder of God's moral sovereignty over the rest of humanity, including the world of international relationships.

This international dimension remained a prominent feature of Israelite prophecy and came to fullest expression in the detailed and expanded oracles of Isaiah, Jeremiah and Ezekiel. These much neglected parts of the prophetic books, the 'oracles concerning the nations', repay study within this context. Not only do they show Israel's unshakeable conviction of the incomparable superiority and sovereignty of their God, even in the face of apparently contradictory evidence, and her indomitable hope in the moral purpose of God to destroy the wicked and vindicate the righteous. They also show an awareness of international affairs and insight into realities that lie behind them.

Isaiah 15 – 16 focuses on a universal by-product of warfare, the streams of *refugees* after invasion, clutching the remains of their possessions (15:5–7), and pleading for succour in a strange land (16:1f.). If 16:3–5 are to be understood as God's instructions to Jerusalem in response to the Moabites' request, they show a compassion for the victims of the catastrophe, even though the catastrophe itself is seen as God's punitive judgment.

The subtle and seductive nature of *economic expansionism* and oppression is well portrayed in various oracles concerning Tyre (Is. 23; Ezk. 26 – 28). Likewise, *political arrogance* and exorbitant pretensions are disclosed and deflated, especially with reference to Egypt and its king. In a parody of the creation Psalms, the words are put in his mouth,

You say, 'The Nile is mine;
I made it for myself' (Ezk. 29:3).

He is even compared to a tree that tries to lord it even higher than the trees of the Garden of Eden (Ezk. 31). Similar accusations of political absolutism and pride are made against the king of Tyre and related to the obsessive delusion of economic power (Ezk. 28). Again, imagery from the Garden of Eden suggests the satanic nature of such politico-economic arrogance (Ezk. 28:12–19).

The course of events and underlying causes of the total *collapse of a society* are seen in the description of the judgment of Egypt in Isaiah 19: religious and moral impotence (v. 1); civil strife (v. 2); panic leading to the irrational and the occult (v. 3); external tyranny (v. 4); economic collapse and demoralization of the working population (vv. 5–10); political incompetence and confusion (vv. 11–15).

This international awareness of Israel, then, forms a starting point for working out an Old Testament perspective on the relationship between the people of God and the external state. The subject can be viewed from three further angles.

PRIESTLY SERVICE

'A royal priesthood' was one of the descriptions of Israel (Ex. 19:6). This we have seen meant they existed for the sake of others, as an intermediary between God and other nations. There are several incidents in the Old Testament where this priestly function is apparent.

The first antedates the above description, but shows a practical demonstration of it by the father of the nation, Abraham. Faced with the knowledge that God intended to launch an investigation of Sodom and Gomorrah, whose wickedness was notorious, Abraham rightly concluded that the outcome of such an enquiry could mean only destructive judgment. So he set about the task of intercession, in which he was as persistent as he was humble (Gn. 18:16ff.). The narrative gives the impression that such intercession was the very purpose of God's decision to reveal to Abraham what he was doing, for the decision is explained by reference to Abraham's calling on behalf of the nations (v. 18).

Now, of course, Abraham's nephew, Lot, was in Sodom. We

might be inclined, therefore, to say that Abraham's intercession was more than somewhat dictated by blood loyalty, and was not really for the sake of Sodom itself. However, we must note two factors that contradict such a view of his motives. First, he made no specific mention of Lot and his family. His prayer arose on behalf of the whole wicked population, for the sake of any handful of righteous that were there. Did he know for certain that Lot and his family could be still counted among the righteous? Secondly, he did *not* pray that the righteous be rescued and the wicked destroyed. In the event, that is actually what God did (Gn. 19), but it was not what Abraham prayed for. He had not said, 'Go ahead; blast the wicked as they deserve, but please rescue my family and keep them safe'. Rather, he had prayed for the whole place to be spared for the sake of the righteous.

The compassionate quality of Abraham's 'priestly' intercession, with its outcome not precisely what he had asked, contrasts strongly with the prophetic mission of Jonah. In his case the outcome was precisely what he had not wanted but had shrewdly suspected. The comparison is interesting because Nineveh was as notorious for wickedness and oppression as Sodom and Gomorrah. There the similarity ends. Abraham jumped unbidden to intercession; Jonah, though bidden, jumped the other way. Abraham failed to win a reprieve for the cities of the plain; Jonah, reluctantly, brought Nineveh to repentance and suspended judgment. Abraham interceded because he knew God to be righteous; Jonah tried to escape his mission because he knew God to be compassionate – embarrassingly so!

Together, the stories set before us the priestly duty of the people of God in a wicked world. We are to intercede even for those we know are facing God's judgment. We are also to proclaim that judgment, but in the hope of repentance and reprieve, in the spirit of Abraham and not of Jonah.

One other example of such priestly service on behalf of external nations and political authority is the notable letter of Jeremiah to the exiles in Babylon. In the circumstances it is quite astonishing.

Seek the peace and prosperity (*shālôm*) of the city to which I have carried you into exile. Pray to the LORD for it, because if it prospers, you too will prosper[3] (Je. 29:7).

Surely there is more in this than a prudential, pragmatic policy for survival. It rings true to the authentic mission of the priestly people of God, to exist in order to be the vehicle of God's blessing, God's *shālôm*, for those outside, even the oppressor himself.

This note finds its equally authentic echo in the New Testament injunctions that Christians fulfil the priestly duty of prayer for rulers. The grounds are the same, namely the redemptive desire and purpose of God.

> I urge, then, first of all, that requests, prayers, intercession and thanksgiving be made for everyone – for kings and all those in authority, that we may live peaceful and quiet lives in all godliness and holiness. This is good, and pleases God our Saviour, who wants all men to be saved and to come to a knowledge of the truth (1 Tim. 2:1–4).

Even more unmistakable is the Old Testament background to Peter's similar instructions to those whom he has likened to the exiles of Israel, and explicitly designated as heirs to the title 'royal priesthood' (1 Pet. 2:9–17). Also significant in this context is the fact that Paul's only use of the expression '*priestly* service', as a function of the Christian or the church, refers precisely to his evangelistic work *among the Gentiles* (Rom. 15:16).

POLITICAL SERVICE

There are wider possibilities, however, for the people of God in relation to external state authority than the priestly duty of intercession and proclamation. The Old Testament also furnishes us with illustrations of people who were able to serve and co-operate with state authorities in a political capacity without compromising their own faith, moral standards, or allegiance to the people of God. The two most interesting examples stand at opposite ends of Old Testament history, Joseph and Daniel.

Joseph and *Daniel* have added interest because they served respectively in Egypt and Babylon, the two nations most associated with imperial might and the oppression of God's people

---

[3] Literally, 'in its *shālôm* shall you find *shālôm*'.

and most frequently the target of oracles of doom and judgment. Each of these men attained to the highest level of political office and both carried very heavy administrative responsibility (Gn. 41:41–46; Dn. 2:48f.). This they did while still comparatively young. Both were tested severely. Joseph suffered moral temptation and the pressures of misunderstanding, unjust imprisonment and isolation; Daniel underwent questioning of his Jewish food scruples and the much more severe persecution that later threatened his life. Both survived by conscious acknowledgment of the presence of God with them.

Most important of all, both were able through their political office not only to serve the interests, and work for the good of, the states who employed them, gaining trust and approval for their wisdom and justice, but also in the process to benefit the minority interests of the people of God, to whom they belonged. Thus, Joseph, by his prudent policy on Egypt's behalf, ensured the physical survival of his family. Indeed, he had not advocated the storage policy for that conscious purpose, but in retrospect he saw that survival as God's real purpose behind his own changing fortunes in Egypt. Similarly, the uncompromising stand against idolatry taken by Daniel and his three friends resulted in freedom from religious persecution for everyone who worshipped Israel's God (Dn. 3:28ff.; 6:26ff.).

The careers of Joseph and Daniel repay study from this angle, for the insights they bring on the way that loyal servants of the living God can be called to cope with the vicissitudes of political service in a state which does not acknowledge God and is alien and potentially or overtly hostile to God's people.

There are other examples to mention briefly. *Moses* stands as the counterpart to Joseph. Joseph led his people *into* Egypt to ensure their survival. Moses led them *out* for the same reason. To Moses, also, God gave a thorough grounding in political service in the Egyptian imperial court, so that when in due course he was called to challenge it, he could do so with inside knowledge and political understanding.

From the settlement to the exile, the redeemed people of God was, in theory, identical and co-extensive with the nation-state of Israel (even though split into two kingdoms). But since the ruling authorities frequently flouted the covenant and introduced or tolerated other gods, the matter was never quite so simple. From the time of Elijah, at least, the idea existed of a faithful minority within an otherwise apostate nation. Certainly, with kings like Ahab, the issue of the relationship between loyal followers of the LORD and state authorities who were anything but loyal to him became critical and costly.

Elijah himself represents one response: implacable opposition and a declared position of allegiance to God above and beyond the state authority. That was the significance of his remark in the very presence of Ahab, 'As the LORD, the God of Israel, lives, whom I serve' – *i.e.*, 'I serve him, not you, Ahab' (1 Ki. 17:1). But another response in the same circumstances is represented by *Obadiah*. We are told that he was a 'devout believer in the LORD' (1 Ki. 18:3). Yet he chose to remain in high political office in the court of Ahab and Jezebel, and to use the access of his position to preserve the lives of a hundred other loyal prophets in the midst of fierce persecution (18:4).

Both responses took great courage. But it could be argued that Obadiah's was the more difficult in the long term. And the hundred prophets owed their lives to Obadiah's courage 'on the inside', not to Elijah's stand 'on the outside', of the political lion's den. Later, Jeremiah owed his life to another 'inside' official, Ebed-Melech (Je. 38:6–13).

Yet another response was that of *Jehu*, the way of violent, ruthless and very bloody revolution (2 Ki. 9 – 10). Jehu gets an ambivalent press in the Old Testament. Undoubtedly he was the instrument of God's retribution on the evil of Ahab and Jezebel and their successors. But he began his revolution spurred by a messenger prophet who went beyond the simple word of Elisha (9:3, 7–10), and Jehu went on to add some gory embellishments out of his own unlovely character. The eradication of Baal worship which he achieved was temporary, perhaps because it was a revolution of force and not a reformation of heart. Although it was commended in guarded and qualified terms (10:28–31), the final prophetic verdict on Jehu is one of condemnation and retribution (Ho. 1:4). So Jehu's *methods*, as a response to religio-political oppression, receive no commendation in the Old Testament.

In the exilic and post-exilic period, we have already noted the letter of Jeremiah to the exiles in Babylon. The story of *Esther* provides further illustration of how the interests of God's people are served by those with the courage and qualifications to stand close to the centre of political power in a hostile environment.

Likewise, *Nehemiah*, having risen to a position of ultimate trust in the king's service, did not hesitate to make full use of what civic resources he could call on, as well as a good measure of personal political leadership, diplomatic skill, and public courage, for the good of God's people. Significantly, like Daniel, his public and civic work was undertaken against the background of a devout life of prayer.

There is then, in the Old Testament, no single 'doctrine of the state', but a variety of responses to an ever-changing human institution. External political authority is to be respected, and can be served legitimately, but Joseph and Daniel show that there are limits beyond which compromise becomes impossible. For the state is not absolute; the king is not divine. But they have a tendency to regard themselves so, and those of God's people who enter the political service of such human authorities must accept the possibility of persecution and suffering. The God of Shadrach, Meshach and Abednego is still certainly able to deliver from the fiery furnace and the lion's den, but he is not bound to, as those stalwarts acknowledged: 'Even if he does not, we want you to know, O king, that we will not serve your gods' (Dn. 3:18).

Ultimately, even the most autocratic and seemingly invincible empires are subject to the control of the God of Israel. He raises and abases them according to his own will and purpose, and to him they will all eventually yield sovereignty. This brings us to our last point.

UNIVERSAL VISION

We began our chapter with the diversity of nations as part of God's *creative* order, and we return to it in conclusion. For the Old Testament has the ultimate vision of the inclusion of all nations in God's *redemptive* purpose. What was an implicit reversal of the scattering and confusion of Babel, in the call of Abraham, becomes explicit in the prophetic vision of Zephaniah. For after the consuming judgment of God's anger on the wickedness of the nations,

> Then will I purify the lips of the peoples,
> that all of them may call on the name of the LORD
> and serve him shoulder to shoulder (Zp. 3:9).

But this eschatological unity in the worship of God will not mean the dissolving of diverse national identities. Rather, the glory of the future reign of God will be the influx of the rich variety of all peoples. This is the throbbing joy of Isaiah 60, and the more sober warnings of Zechariah 14:16ff. Furthermore, not just the peoples, but all their achievement, wealth and glory will be brought, purified, into the new Jerusalem of God's reign. This Old Testament vision is found in Isaiah 60:5–11, Haggai 2:6–8, and in the astonishing conclusion of the oracle against Tyre, Isaiah 23:18, where it is envisaged that all the profits of that archetypal trading empire will be 'set apart for the LORD', for the benefit of his people.

This is not some kind of Zionist covetousness, but the realization that, since God's ultimate purpose is the creation of a people for himself, a new humanity in a new earth, then all that mankind does and achieves can only, in the end, under God's providential transformation, contribute to the glory of that new order. The same vision is taken up in Revelation, when 'the kingdom of the world has become the kingdom of our Lord and of his Christ', and 'the kings of the earth will bring their splendour into it' (Rev. 11:15; 21:24).

The final prophetic word must come from Isaiah. There can be few more breath-taking passages in the Old Testament than the conclusion of Isaiah 19. Hard on the heels of the oracle of total judgment on Egypt comes a message of restoration and blessing, in which terms recalling Israel's exodus are applied to *Egypt* herself, and she turns in repentance to acknowledge God and to find pardon and healing. Before we can recover from the surprise, there is more. *Assyria too!* Assyria will join Egypt in worshipping God, and on equal terms with Israel! All three will be 'a blessing on the earth', God's people, God's handiwork, God's inheritance. Egypt and Assyria – the arch-enemies of Israel, crushing her on both sides, historically and geographically, as hammer and anvil!

No vision could convey more confidence in the infinite power of God's transforming purpose for humanity than this incredible passage. Perhaps only Paul could comprehend its vastness. For if the grace of God could transform the arch-persecutor of the church into its foremost apostle, then he could do the same with the global oppressors of the people of God, human or spiritual. Such will be the ultimate power and final victory of the cross of Christ. For it is God's purpose 'to bring all things in heaven and on earth together under one head, even Christ' (Eph. 1:10), and 'through him to reconcile to himself all things, whether things on earth or things in heaven, by making peace through his blood, shed on the cross' (Col. 1:20).

6
Righteousness and justice

A discussion of Old Testament ethics must eventually enter the field of Old Testament law. But behind the detailed laws of Israel stands a more fundamental theological and ethical truth concerning the character of God himself – his justice.

> He is the Rock, his works are perfect,
> and all his ways are just.
> A faithful God who does no wrong,
> upright and just is he (Dt. 32:4).

> For I, the LORD, love justice (Is. 61:8).

No idea is more all-pervasive in the Old Testament than that God is a God of righteousness and justice. Yet these are words easily misunderstood, as young Luther discovered. Likewise, Jews can use the term 'the law' to include all their Scriptures, as well as of the Pentateuch proper. Again, the term is easily misunderstood, as Saul of Tarsus discovered. Our purpose in this and the following chapter is to outline an understanding of justice and law in their own Old Testament context, and then, as before, to reflect on some underlying principles that are relevant to these crucial areas of our own age.

THE VOCABULARY OF JUSTICE

The language of justice in the Old Testament has two major 'notes' with several 'harmonics'. The two primary words, *right-*

eousness and *justice*, come from two Hebrew words that are worth knowing.

The first is the root *tsdq*, which is found in two common forms, *tseḏeq* and *tseḏāqāh*, usually translated 'righteousness'. The root meaning is probably 'straight': something which is fixed and fully what it should be and so matches a 'norm'. It is used literally of actual objects when they are, or do, what they are supposed to: for example, accurate weights and measures (Lv. 19:36; Dt. 25:15) and straight paths (Ps. 23:3). So it comes to mean rightness, that which ought to be so, that which matches up to the standard – 'righteousness' in a very wide sense.

The second is the root *šp̄t*, which has to do with judicial activity at every level. A common verb and noun are derived from it. The verb *shāphat* refers to legal action over a wide range. It can mean: to act as a lawgiver; to act as a judge by arbitrating between parties in a dispute; to pronounce judgment, declaring guilty and innocent respectively; to execute judgment in carrying out the legal consequences of such a verdict. The noun *mishpat* can describe the whole process of litigation, or its end result of verdict and its execution; it can mean a legal ordinance, usually case law, based on past precedents (Ex. 21 – 23, known as the Covenant Code, or Book of the Covenant, is called in Hebrew, simply, the *mishpatîm*); it can also be used in a more personal sense as one's legal right, the cause or case one is bringing as a plaintiff. It is from this last sense in particular that *mishpat* comes to have the wider sense of 'justice' in the somewhat subjective sense, whereas *tseḏeq* has a more objective flavour. *Mishpat* is what needs to be done in a given situation if people and circumstances are to be restored to conformity with *tseḏeq/tseḏāqāh*.

There are certain other words which are closely related to these and are frequently found with them, especially when the character and activity of God are in view. First comes *holiness* (*qōḏesh*), the essential character of God as transcendently 'other' and separate. This absoluteness and perfection pervades all the qualities and acts of God, of course; but it is particularly 'visible' in his righteousness and justice, inasmuch as he is in his very nature both the ultimate standard of 'straightness' and the one who ultimately decides and executes what is 'straight'. Isaiah puts it succinctly:

The LORD Almighty will be exalted by his justice,
and the holy God will show himself holy by his righteousness (Is. 5:16).

Then there is the idea of *faithfulness*. This comprises a rich
trio of words, of which the richest is *hesed*. It is often translated
'kindness' or 'love', but it is more 'solid' than those words
suggest in common English. It means his abiding loyalty to his
covenant, his unshakeable will to keep his gracious promise.
What he has decided and established in his righteousness, he
stands by with fixed purpose. The translation *'steadfast* love'
(RSV) gets nearer the true meaning. Frequently, *hesed* and
tsedāqāh are paired off as parallels, both as qualities of God's
action (Ps. 36:10), and as requirements of human ethical
response (Ho. 10:12; Mi. 6:8). The other two members of the
trio are *emeth* (truth), which includes the idea of stability and
dependability, and *emûnāh* (faithfulness), a word that describes
what is firm, unchangeable and trustworthy (from which we
get 'Amen'). No wonder a favourite and very early description
of God in Israel was 'our *Rock*'!

Finally there is the beautiful Hebrew word *shālôm*, peace.
Coming from a root which means 'to be complete', this has a
deeper sense than absence of strife. It includes wholeness, total
welfare, that state of soundness and harmony that God desires.
It is thus closely related to the *tsedeq* concept of 'properness':
things and people as they ought to be. The connection comes
out literally in the references to accurate weights and measures
in Leviticus 19:36 and Deuteronomy 25:15, where the two roots
are used side by side. Socially and nationally (and internation-
ally, as we saw in chapter 5), peace is the fruit of righteousness.
The intimacy of the relationship is delightfully portrayed in
Psalm 85:10,

Love and faithfulness meet together;
righteousness and peace kiss each other.

What this merest sketch of a word study makes abundantly
clear is that righteousness and justice in Old Testament thought
are not abstract ideas. They are highly personal and relational
terms. Theologically, they characterize God in action in relationship with men – men at large, and especially his own people.

Socially, they are required of people in their relationship with one another. So we turn now to each of these spheres, the theological and the social. In this context, the latter includes the economic angle, since that is where justice or its opposite are most clearly visible.

THE THEOLOGICAL CONTEXT

As already noted, God himself is the ultimate standard of righteousness and justice for they are part of his intrinsic character. Theologians call them 'divine attributes'. The Old Testament, happily more poetic, expresses it thus:

> Righteousness and justice are the foundation of your throne;
> love and faithfulness go before you (Ps. 89:14).

Likewise, the verse from Deuteronomy quoted at the start of the chapter is from one of the oldest poems in the Old Testament. We need to make, however, a conceptual distinction between God's exercise of his righteousness and justice in *general providence* and his exercise of them in *redemption*.

RIGHTEOUSNESS AND JUSTICE IN PROVIDENCE

God reveals what he is by what he does. His righteousness is known to us because he rules the world in righteousness and justice. Whatever God does is, by definition, righteous. This was the boundless confidence of Israel: 'Will not the Judge of all the earth do right?' (Gn. 18:25).

> The Lord of all the earth does justice. . . . It is an unrelinquishable affirmation of biblical faith – an affirmation that brings all parts of the Old Testament with its many streams of tradition into a unity – that it is he who determines the right, upholds and establishes it, and rules the world of history by it. He is the Lord of the right.[1]

This providential rule of righteousness is not because he is

---

[1] J. Muilenburg, *The Way of Israel*, p. 65.

bound by some law of justice over and above or external to himself, but only because it is he, God, who is at work. It is simply unthinkable that God should act otherwise (*cf.* Jb. 34:12; Pss. 9:7f.; 96:10, 13).

Indeed, it is precisely the firmness of this belief which produces such consternation when God *appears* to act otherwise. The mental agonies of Jeremiah (12:1), of Habakkuk (1:12f.), of Job (*e.g.* ch. 10), and of the psalmist (Ps. 73) are shared down through the ages by all men of faith who are perplexed with the 'Why?' of God's deeds. Yet the faith in his ultimate justice prevails and sustains, because the only alternative is moral chaos and futility.[2]

The fact that God is righteous and exercises his justice especially on behalf of the weak and oppressed is closely linked with his providential care for the whole of creation. The connection is very clear in Psalms 145:9–18; 146:6–9 and 147:4–6. The importance of this is that although the *major* motivation within Israel for social justice was the fact of their equality as God's redeemed people, there was also the awareness that men are responsible to God for one another simply on the grounds of our common, created humanity. This creation-providence basis for social responsibility is found in the wisdom literature particularly.

> He who oppresses the poor shows contempt for their Maker,
> but whoever is kind to the needy honours God
> > (Pr. 14:31; *cf.* 17:5; Jb. 31:13–15).

But it is also implicit in the early narratives of Genesis, where, for example, Cain is held accountable for his treatment of Abel (Gn. 4:9f.) and the 'outcry' against Sodom and Gomorrah is duly investigated by the 'Judge of all the earth' (Gn. 18:20f.).

RIGHTEOUSNESS AND JUSTICE IN REDEMPTION

When God acts in his righteousness to establish justice, it is both to condemn the wrongdoer and to vindicate the one wronged. His verdict (*mishpat*) pronounces one party guilty or

---

[2] I am well aware that there are many other arguments besides this in the complex subject of 'theodicy' – *i.e.*, vindication of the justice of God's acts; but since our business here is with the great affirmatives of Old Testament faith and ethics, we must avoid being sidetracked into that minefield.

'wicked', and the other party in the right, 'righteous' (*tsaddîq*). These terms crop up again and again in the Psalms where the singer longs for God to act precisely in this way against wrongdoers.

Now, from the point of view of the first group, the wicked, God's righteousness is experienced as wrath and judgment. But for the second group, the righteous, it is an act of vindication and restoration. If the latter party were under legal attack or threat, then the verdict was a form of deliverance or salvation. This was what the psalmist prayed for:

> Vindicate me in your righteousness, O Lord my God;
> do not let them gloat over me (Ps. 35:24).
> Rescue me and deliver me in your righteousness;
> turn your ear to me and save me (Ps. 71:2).

If the prayer were answered, then God's righteousness *and* salvation would be praised in the same breath for, in the worshipper's experience, they were the same thing.

> My mouth will tell of your righteousness,
> of your salvation all day long (Ps. 71:15).

In the same manner, God's greater, national acts of salvation, deliverance, or redemption were also acts of righteousness. That, indeed, is how they are often described in the Old Testament. This is true, first because they are consistent with God's own character (as are all his acts); second, because they justly discriminate between the respectively guilty and innocent, the wrongdoer and the wronged, the oppressor and the oppressed, and the like; and third, because they establish, restore, or promote situations of justice. So Israel can speak of the great occasions of national deliverance or military victory in her history as 'the righteousnesses' (*i.e.* righteous acts) of the Lord. Deborah's victory is described thus (Jdg. 5:11) and so is the edict of Cyrus by which the Jews were freed from exile in Babylon (Is. 41:2; 45:8; 46:13). In short, God is 'a righteous God *and* a Saviour' (Is. 45:21).

Naturally, therefore, as Israel looked forward to the 'day' of God's ultimate intervention to establish his justice, this combination of righteousness and salvation characterizes that eschatological hope – especially as related to the Messianic king who would rule over the new age of peace and justice. In Jeremiah 23:6, a context where righteousness is both ethical (there will be sound judgment and social justice) and redemptive ('Judah will be saved'), Jeremiah names the coming figure:

> This is the name by which he will be called:
> The LORD Our Righteousness.

In the event, they called his name Jesus; that is, in Hebrew, Joshua, which means 'The LORD is salvation'. One can picture Jeremiah happily nodding his assent to what he would have regarded as a perfectly satisfactory, indeed equivalent, fulfilment of his prophecy.

THE SIGNIFICANCE OF THE DISTINCTION FOR SOCIAL ETHICS
It seems to me important that we should preserve this conceptual distinction between God's righteousness and justice in general providence and in his purpose of redemption. Every act of redemption is an act of righteousness, but not every act of righteousness is part of his redemptive purpose. What occurs within God's overall, providential ordering of human affairs, as sovereign Lord of the whole of creation, is wider than the scope of his redemptive activity at any one point in history. Therefore when the oppressed are liberated, or certain wrongs righted, or justice executed, we should not regard any or every such event or process in and of itself as part of God's *redemption*. We should, however, certainly want to affirm such things as part of the *providential* will and ordering of God the Creator and righteous Judge of all men.

I believe there is biblical support for making this distinction. Take the events surrounding the release of the Jews from exile in Babylon after the edict of Cyrus. At one level, this was purely a military and political event. A deeply oppressive and unjust empire, Babylon, was conquered by Cyrus of Persia, who, by the standards of his age, was a liberal and enlightened ruler. By his edict, liberty was granted to many 'gods' and peoples who had been captured and displaced by the Babylonians. This liberation was welcomed by many more than just the Jews. For large numbers of human beings the edict of Cyrus was a restoration of justice, and as such we can locate it, theologically, in the framework of God's providential world-rule. But only for Israel was it an act of righteousness-salvation as part of God's specific purpose of redemption. And for them there was also the requirement of repentance and a spiritual returning to God, as well as the vicarious work of the 'suffering Servant of the LORD'. The prophet sees both aspects of the achievements of Cyrus as the work of God. On the one hand, his victory over many nations,

> Who has stirred up one from the east,
>   calling him in righteousness to his service?[3]
> He hands nations over to him
>   and subdues kings before him (Is. 41:2; *cf.* 42:25; 45:1);

but on the other hand, the redemptive purpose in Israel's case,

> I will raise up Cyrus in my righteousness:
>   I will make all his ways straight.
> He will rebuild my city
>   and set my exiles free (Is. 45:13).

Another example of the distinction is implied when Amos, holding Israel up before God's judgment, puts them on the same level as other nations in one respect.

> 'Are not you Israelites
>   the same to me as the Cushites?'
>   declares the LORD.
> 'Did I not bring Israel up from Egypt,
>   the Philistines from Caphtor
>   and the Arameans from Kir?' (Am. 9:7).

In their national origins, Israel were no different from other nations who had a migratory past. God had been at work in his providence on the chess board of more nations than only Israel. Nevertheless, the same prophet emphatically reminds Israel of their unique redemptive-covenant relationship with God, who says:

---

[3] There is here the characteristic ambiguity over 'righteousness'; *cf.* NIV margin, 'whom *victory* meets at every step' (my italics).

'You only have I known
of all the families of the earth' (3:2, RSV).

The specific operation of God's redemptive righteousness,
which in this context includes his threat of punitive justice on
his own people,[4] is worked out within the wider sphere of the
world-wide rule of his righteous providence.

Armed with this distinction, we avoid regarding every current
event incorporating some degree of justice, such as a just ruling
of a court of law or the overthrow or liberalization of some
corrupt and oppressive regime, as an act of *redemption* in its
own right. But we do not thereby devalue the importance of
such events theologically or ethically, for we can still regard
them as falling within the providential sovereignty of God.
Furthermore, we may well discern that such events and
processes serve the furtherance of God's redemptive purposes,
just as the military victories and political edict of Cyrus facilitated the return of the Jews, and just as the political stability of
the Roman Empire facilitated the spread of the gospel. Nor do
we reduce our ethical obligation to work for justice in the world
by having this dual location. The distinction is conceptual: the
reality is only one God, both sovereign Lord of the world, and
covenant Lord of his people. The motivation and model for
our endeavour derive from the facts of our redemption and
our membership of God's people, consciously living under his
kingship. But the God we are thus committed to serve by the
obligations of our relationship to him is also Creator of all
men. He 'sends his rain on the just and on the unjust', and
holds all men accountable to himself for their treatment of one
another.[5]

THE SOCIAL CONTEXT

RIGHTEOUSNESS AS THE SOCIAL FOUNDATION OF ISRAEL

In turning now to justice as it was to be exercised and experienced within Israel, we have to take as a necessary starting

[4] The verse from Amos continues: 'therefore I will punish you for all your sins'.
[5] On the subject of responsibility before God and its relation to human rights, see further:
C. J. H. Wright, *Human Rights*.

point the fact that, for Israel as a social entity, righteousness and justice were something 'given'. They were foundational to their very existence as a nation, inasmuch as the exodus was an act of righteousness *par excellence* in both senses – judgment and salvation.

On the one hand the Egyptians were guilty of violating the rights of Israel – their right to freedom, to the product of their own labour, to worship their own ancestral God, even to unhampered reproduction and family life. The events preceding and accompanying the exodus, therefore, were an act of righteous judgment upon Egypt (Ex. 9:27), just as the conquest of the land was an act of judgment (for different reasons) on Canaan (Lv. 20:23). On the other hand, it all happened because God saw and heard the 'wronged' state of Israel under oppression, and in the exodus he gave actual freedom to a captive people, rescuing them out of actual injustice, restoring them to a situation of 'right' or justice, which eventually issued in secure possession of the land as a place to enjoy and protect that 'right'. For Israel it was vindication and salvation of the most direct and tangible kind.

However, righteousness was the social foundation of Israel not only because the initiative of God's redeeming power was an act of righteousness, but also because, as we saw in chapter 1, it called forth a response of imitative righteousness and justice among the Israelites themselves. Having been put 'right', so to speak, they were to maintain righteousness. Having experienced justice, they were to 'do justice'.

THE TEN COMMANDMENTS: RESPONSIBLE FREEDOM
It will help us to focus this point more clearly if we look at the Ten Commandments in this light, taking them as the foundational charter or policy statement of the rest of the covenant law. The Ten Commandments can be seen as given in order to preserve the rights and freedoms gained by the exodus, by translating them into responsibilities. Let us take them more or less in order from this point of view.

God had given them the right and freedom to worship him. This had been the express purpose of the demand for release from Egypt (Ex. 4:23); so now they must worship him exclusively (First Commandment). By his mighty act, God had shown himself to be a living and incomparable (jealous) God; therefore any lifeless image or idol was an insult (Second). The exodus had involved a powerful demonstration of the meaning of his personal name, Yahweh, the LORD; so they must not use that name selfishly, maliciously or foolishly (Third). God had freed them from relentless forced labour, enabling them now to work as free men; so they must preserve the right of regular sabbath rest for themselves, their families, employees and even their animals (Fourth). God had freed them from Pharaoh's intolerable violence against their family life; so they must protect the family as regards its parental authority (Fifth) and sexual integrity (Seventh, *cf.* chapter 8). Freed from the infanticide and murdering terror of Egyptian oppression, they must respect life and not tolerate murder in their own society, even of slaves (Sixth). Now that they would no longer be aliens in a foreign country, but possess a land of their own, they were not to steal or covet what was God's gift to all (Eighth and Tenth). With the example of God's justice before them they were not to betray one another by the malicious injustice of perverted testimony (Ninth).

When we look at the Decalogue from that perspective we can see it as a kind of 'Bill of Rights', human and divine, expressed in the form of responsibilities necessary to preserve and enjoy their freedom as a redeemed people.

MAINTAINING JUSTICE:
THE FUNCTION OF THE LAWS AND THE LEADERS

What was true of the Decalogue supremely was also true of the rest of the law. God had established Israel in righteousness and bound her to himself by covenant. The laws, then, were the stipulations to regulate and frame her response to his grace and righteous acts. To fulfil the law was to maintain that righteousness which was Israel's redemption gift. But the law allows for the fact that mankind is fallen and will disrupt and fracture that *shālôm* which should be the fruit of righteousness. Therefore another major function of many of the provisions in the law is to restore *shālôm* by 'making good' the loss or debt incurred by the wrongdoer, both by punishment and by compensation to the injured party, where applicable. Thus, to 'do justice' by keeping the law was, in Israel, for the purpose of maintaining or restoring a 'given' righteousness, not for the purpose of achieving or deserving it.

This is clearly seen in the way leaders in Israel, at all levels, were charged with the primary function of maintaining or restoring righteousness and justice, in their various senses. Those who were called 'judges' in pre-monarchic Israel were not only involved in judicial arbitration (*i.e.* 'judging' in our legal sense) like Samuel, the prototype circuit judge (1 Sa. 7:15–17). Indeed, some of them appear to have had no such function, but were, perhaps solely, military deliverers. But inasmuch as that entailed restoring Israel again from oppression and setting her back 'in the right' with God, it was an exercise of dynamic righteousness as Israel understood it. The military judges 'earthed' the righteous acts of God in the form of actual salvation. Such is the combined exultation of Deborah, the judicial judge (Jdg. 4:5), and Barak, the military leader, after the great victory of Megiddo.

> They recite the righteous acts of the LORD,
> the righteous acts of his warriors in Israel (Jdg. 5:10).

The duty of maintaining justice is even more clearly laid on the shoulders of kings. In some of the regal Psalms, their military and judicial roles are closely linked. The expectation was that if the king was faithful in his duty of executing justice and imitating God's own protection of the weak and the poor (*cf.* Dt. 17:18–20), then God would grant him success and prosperity in the other sphere. The best example of this is Psalm 72. It is a prayer for the king which begins by acknowledging the true source of all righteousness and justice.

> Endow the king with *your* justice, O God,
> the royal son with *your* righteousness (v. 1, my italics).

It then mingles descriptions of his practical execution of justice with the expectation of material blessing on the land. A stirring account of his international military prestige in verses 8–11 is linked by an explanatory 'for' to a further reference to his judicial activity – specifically in deliverance of the weak, needy and oppressed in verses 12–14 (*cf.* Ps. 45:4–6; and in contrast Ps. 58).

There is a similar emphasis on the requirement of social justice on the part of kings in the Wisdom literature (*cf.* Pr.

16:12; 29:4, 14), such that King Lemuel's mother warned him against drunkenness for this very reason:

> It is not for kings, O Lemuel –
> not for kings to drink wine,
> not for rulers to crave beer,
> lest they drink and forget what the law decrees,
> and deprive all the oppressed of their rights.

On the contrary, it is the duty of the king as the *most* powerful to champion the cause of the *least* powerful:

> Speak up for those who cannot speak for themselves,
> for the rights of all who are destitute.
> Speak up and judge fairly;
> defend the rights of the poor and needy
> (Pr. 31:4f., 8f.).

Ideals, of course, are one thing; the reality is usually different. A more pessimistic voice in Israel, also from the wisdom tradition, has this very modern-sounding observation to make on the oppressive results of hierarchy and bureaucracy:

> If you see the poor oppressed in a district, and justice and rights denied, do not be surprised at such things; for one official is eyed by a higher one, and over them both are others higher still (Ec. 5:8).

'SEEK JUSTICE': THE MESSAGE OF THE PROPHETS
The prophets observed the same social evils as Ecclesiastes. But they responded not with the shrug of pessimism, but with the shout of anger. Justice was being trampled on, turned upside down, turned to wormwood, denied. Such was their assessment. The most effective play on words was Isaiah's:

> And he looked for justice (*mishpat*), but saw bloodshed
> (*mishpach*);
> for righteousness (*tsedāqāh*), but heard cries of distress
> (*tse'āqāh*) (Is. 5:7).

In view of what has been said about righteousness being the

social foundation of Israel from the beginning, it is obvious that the prophets were not promoting some new, higher ethical ideal. They were not radical innovators, as they were once considered by some scholars. Rather they were radical reformers in the strict sense of calling Israel back to the foundations, the roots, of her own nationhood – namely her relationship with God and the demands it laid upon her. In its social living the nation was betraying the righteousness that gave it birth.

The passages in the prophets concerned with social justice are extensive and probably familiar to anyone interested in reading a book on biblical ethics. Nevertheless, it would be worth while pausing to read through the passages listed in the footnote in order to feel again the passion of the prophetic eloquence.[6]

Two features of the prophets' message stand out sufficiently for us to emphasize. First, *its theological basis*. For the prophets, God is the axiom and presupposition of all they say. Since God is the source of all righteousness and justice, knowledge of God is prior to the practice of justice. Therefore, they can confidently link the failure and tragedy in the realm of social injustice and general wickedness to failure to 'know' God (Is. 1:3ff.; Ho. 4:1ff.). Likewise, their call for justice was not grounded in an appeal to recognize some inherent quality or desert in the other man as a man, but rather in the inescapable demand of God in respect of him. It was *God* who asked the question of Cain, 'Where is your brother?' Both sides of justice – responsibility and right – are located in God.[7] The wicked might face no resistance from their victims, no hindrance from the courts (Am. 5:10–13), but the last word lay with neither of those human parties: 'prepare to meet your *God*, O Israel' (Am. 4:12).

Second, *its social bias*. The bias of the prophets in favour of the poor, the weak, the oppressed, the dispossessed and the victimized, is obvious. Even before the great writing prophets, we find Nathan confronting David on behalf of Uriah, and Elijah confronting Ahab on behalf of Naboth. This is as true of courtly prophets like Isaiah who stood close to the pulse of regal power, as it is of rustic outsiders like Amos. In this aspect,

---

[6] Is. 1:15–17, 23; 5:1–8, 22f.; 10:1f.; 58:3–7; Je. 7:5–11; 22:3, 13–17; Ezk. 16:49–52; 18; 22:6–12; Ho. 4:1f.; 12:6f.; Am. 2:6–8; 5:7, 10–15, 21–24; 6:12; 8:4–6; Mi. 2:1f., 8f.; 3:1–3, 8–11; 6:8–12; 7:2f.; Zc. 7:9–14; Mal. 3:5.
[7] See further on this, C. J. H. Wright, *Human Rights.*

of course, the prophetic representation of God is wholly in line with the voice of the law itself (*cf.* Ex. 22:22–24, 26f.; Dt. 10:18f.), with the worshipping voice of the Psalms (*e.g.* Ps. 146:7–9), and with the voice of wisdom (*e.g.* Pr. 14:31; 22:22f.).

However, this undoubted fact of God's active concern for the weak and the poor needs to be expressed carefully. It is not a case of biased or arbitrary partiality on God's part, such as the expression, 'God is on the side of the poor', rather implies. Nor is it that he turns a blind eye to the sins of the poor, as if poverty and oppression in themselves rendered their victims spotless and innocent. Indeed, Isaiah 9:14–17 includes even the fatherless and the widow, stock epitomes of the poor and powerless, in its detailed description of the total corruption of the nation. Rather, this group in society receives God's special attention because they are on the 'wronged' side of a situation of chronic injustice which God abhors and wishes to have redressed. For God's righteous will to be done requires the execution of justice on their behalf.

In proclaiming this fact so vehemently, the prophets in fact vindicate the *impartiality* of God. For in championing the cause of the oppressed in this way, they exonerate God from the suspicion of being actually on the side of the wealthy and powerful, who could point to their wealth and power as apparent evidence of God's blessing on them and their activities. Amos's device of reversing the popular assessment by attaching the judicial verdict 'righteous' (*i.e.* in the right) to the poor and dispossessed, but applying 'wicked' (*i.e.* in the wrong) to the wealthy landowners, was a highly effective and emotive way of disassociating God from the claims of the latter group. It reasserted his sovereign independence as the righteous judge who was not fooled by outward appearance.

> The eyes of the LORD are on the righteous
> and his ears are attentive to their cry;
> the face of the LORD is against those who do evil (Ps. 34:15f.).

7
Law and the legal system

For the newcomer to Old Testament law, the most daunting prospect is most likely the Pentateuch itself. Laws of every kind seem to be jumbled together, interspersed with narrative and descriptive sections. So in this chapter our aim is to introduce some clarity and order into the subject by giving a broad classification of the laws, in two dimensions. First we shall simply outline the major blocks of text where most of the laws are found. Then, secondly, we shall analyse the different kinds of law that are there. In conclusion we shall reflect on some of the relevant principles and implications of this material for ourselves.

THE MAIN LEGAL BLOCKS

There are, of course, isolated laws, precedents, and judgments scattered throughout the narrative sections, especially in Exodus and Numbers. But the bulk of the pentateuchal laws are contained in three major blocks or collections, in addition to the Decalogue itself, with which we begin.

1. THE DECALOGUE: EXODUS 20:2–17; DEUTERONOMY 5:6–21
'Decalogue' comes from the Greek rendering of the literal Hebrew expression, 'the ten words', found in Exodus 34:28, Deuteronomy 4:13; 10:4. In the Sinai narrative of Exodus 19 – 20 (repeated in Deuteronomy 5), the Decalogue was given to Israel by God. Though Moses was the mediator, as of the rest of the

laws attributed to him, his role in respect of the Ten Commandments was minimal. They were said to have been spoken and inscribed in stone by God himself. There was something 'self-contained' and final about them, captured in the deuteronomic observation, 'These are the commandments the LORD proclaimed . . . and he added nothing more' (Dt. 5:22). That and the awe-inspiring, earth-shaking phenomena that accompanied their promulgation at Sinai assured them of a special place in Israel's traditions. This simple but comprehensive summary of the essential stipulations of the covenant relationship provided a 'boundary fence' of the behaviour consistent with covenant membership, a 'policy statement' which determined the ethos and direction of the rest of the detailed legislation.

Because of its importance, the Decalogue has been the object of a vast quantity of scholarly scrutiny and argument, some of which is referred to in the bibliographical notes. The debate has swung in this century from questions of authorship and date of origin, to what kind of law the Decalogue is and how it functioned in Israelite life and worship. The arguments are still unabated by any consensus, except on the fact itself of the importance of the Decalogue in Israel. Two comments are worth quoting.

> Whatever one thinks about the authorship, the fact that the Decalogue early held a central position in Israelite life remains as the most important result of recent research. . . . [It] stood in association with the review of the Sinai events as the binding charter expressing the will of the divine Lord of the Covenant.[1]

> The evidence that it was assigned a unique place of importance by the Old Testament itself, and not just by subsequent Jewish and Christian interpreters, is manifold . . . the reflection of the commandments in the prophets (Hos. 4:1ff., Jer. 7:9ff.), and in the Psalms (50 and 81) testify to this influence upon Israel's faith.[2]

---

[1] J. J. Stamm, *The Ten Commandments*, p. 39.
[2] B. S. Childs, *Exodus* (SCM, 1974), p. 397.

2. THE BOOK OF THE COVENANT: EXODUS 20:22 – 23:33

This is the name given to the section of laws immediately following the Decalogue. It is referred to as such in Exodus 24:7, where it was read to the people in preparation for the sealing of the covenant.

After a prologue which underlines the uniqueness and holiness of God (20:22–26), the section of laws opens with the title, 'These are the *mishpatîm* . . .' (21:1) – *i.e.* 'cases'. The laws which follow are mainly civil laws (see below) concerning disputes over property, damage, assault, negligence, *etc.* There is also an important section on social responsibilities for the weaker members of society (22:21–27), regulations concerning judicial procedure (23:1–9), and a section of cultic law (see below) to do with offerings and festivals (23:14–19). The collection concludes with an epilogue looking forward to the invasion of Canaan and reinforcing the exclusiveness of the LORD's demand upon his people, thus returning to the theme of the prologue.

While, again, there has been a large amount of study and debate among scholars on the various sections of the Book of the Covenant, as to whether they were originally separate, and if so at what stage and by whom they were edited into the present shape, the universal agreement is that this is the oldest of the collections of law in the Old Testament.

3. THE LEVITICAL COLLECTION

Leviticus consists almost entirely of laws and regulations, with only brief narrative descriptions of the ordination of Aaron and the work of the priests (chs. 8 – 9), and of the death of Nadab and Abihu (ch. 10). The first seven chapters contain regulations for the various sacrificial offerings, while chapters 11 – 15 list clean and unclean foods and give detailed instructions on hygiene and cleanliness, both personal and domestic. The duties of priesthood combined something of doctor and public health inspector. At the centre of the book stands chapter 16 with instructions for the Day of Atonement.

Leviticus 17 – 26 has been regarded by scholars for about one hundred years now as a separate law collection, which has been given the title '*the Holiness Code*' (H for short), because of its repeated reference to and demand for holiness. But as we saw in chapter 1, holiness for Israel was far from merely ritual or pious. These chapters are full of very practical laws for the regulation of family life sexually (18 and 20) and of social life generally (especially 19), as well as additional rules for the priestly work and the various festivals (21 – 24). Chapter 25 contains important laws concerning the sabbatical and jubilee years, redemption procedures, and general economic compassion, while chapter 26 concludes the collection with characteristic promises of blessing for obedience and threats of judgment for the disobedience that was all too foreseeable.

4. THE DEUTERONOMIC COLLECTION

The setting which Deuteronomy paints for itself in its opening verses is that of Israel encamped in the plains of Moab, some forty years on from the great events of the exodus and Sinai, on the verge of entering Canaan at last. The whole book is thus a 'covenant renewal' document (*cf.* Dt. 29:1), in which the historical experiences of the people are recounted (1 – 3) in order to stir up gratitude and wholehearted obedience (4 – 11). As with the 'Holiness Code', there are concluding blessings and curses (27 – 28). In between comes the section of laws proper, *chapters 12 – 26.*

The word 'Deuteronomy' is a Greek construction meaning 'a second law'. Although it is based on no Hebrew original, it is a reasonably apt description of the legal section of the book. The sense intended is not that it is a *new* law, but that it reiterates and amplifies the earlier laws. Thus many of the laws of the Book of the Covenant recur in Deuteronomy, but often with slight changes, expansions, or added motivation. It has been described as 'preached law', and indeed that is what Deuteronomy 1:5 says Moses was doing: 'Moses began to *expound* this law'. There is repetition, exhortation, pleading, coaxing, motivating and warning – all typical of 'preaching', and all showing that, for Israel, the law was indeed more than a crust of legalism: it was the very bread of life. 'They are not just idle words for you – they are your life' (Dt. 32:47).

THE DIFFERENT KINDS OF LAW

In our Prologue it was suggested that to approach Old Testament law in the traditional hope of being able to lay bare a distinct category of 'moral law', as opposed to 'civil' and 'ceremonial' law, was not a very fruitful way in to discovering the ethical relevance of the law as a whole. Rather, we need to study and classify the laws against their own social background in ancient Israel, and then discuss what significant moral features or principles emerge from *each* category so identified. Thus our classification will not be designed to answer the question, 'Which laws are, and which are not, still relevant to us?' Rather, it will enable us to work out the moral relevance of the whole in an authentic context.[3]

1. CRIMINAL LAW

A 'crime' is any offence which any particular state regards as contrary to the best interests of the whole community. Accordingly, a 'criminal' is punished on behalf of the whole community in the name of the highest authority within the state. Criminal law is therefore distinct from civil law, which is concerned with private disputes between citizens, in which the state may judicially intervene but is not the offended party.

Now Israel was a state. But because they owed their existence to the historical redemptive activity of God, they accorded to him the supreme authority within the state. That is the meaning of 'theocracy'. They also believed that their relationship to God was their very *raison d'être*, so that their survival and security were bound up with maintaining that relationship. Therefore, any act which was a fundamental violation of that covenant relationship was a threat to the very security of the whole nation. An offence against God was an offence against the state which depended on him. Such offences were treated, therefore, as 'crimes' and dealt with in an appropriately serious way. Israel being a theocracy, the social and theological realms fused into one in the matter of delineating the substance of 'crime'.

In this context we see once again the central importance for Israel of the *Decalogue*, as an expression of certain fundamental kinds of behaviour which were required or prohibited on the authority of the God by whose grace and power they were now

---

[3] There has been considerable variety in the approaches of scholars to understanding Israelite law – in its origins, form and function. Some of the major figures in the field have been Mowinckel, Alt, Noth, Mendenhall, and Gerstenberger. Details are to be found in the bibliography. The classification offered in this chapter is based upon a similar scheme suggested by A. Phillips, *Ancient Israel's Criminal Law*. While the book has weaknesses, I find the basic functional division of the laws broadly convincing.

a free nation. The Decalogue, in itself, was not a 'criminal law code' in our sense, inasmuch as it incorporated no detailed legislation or specified penalties. But it set out the boundaries and obligations of the covenant, and thus defined the nature and extent of what, for Israel, would constitute serious crime. Other laws spelt out the legal entailments.

It is signficant that all the offences for which there was a statutory *death penalty* in Old Testament law can be related, directly or indirectly, to certain of the Ten Commandments. In the light of the nature of 'crime', as just described, these instances of capital punishment should not be thought of as 'primitive' or fired by vengeful religious fanaticism. They are simply an eloquent testimony to the seriousness that was attached to the covenant and the importance of protecting it from violation which would endanger the whole community. The national interest was bound up with preventing and punishing crime against the covenant in a sufficiently serious manner.

On the other hand, although all death penalty offences can be linked to the Decalogue, the reverse is not true: not every Commandment was sanctioned by the death penalty. The Tenth (prohibiting coveting) was by its very nature not open to *any* judicial penalty, least of all death. But that in itself is ethically important, since it shows that a person could be thought of as morally 'criminal' before God without having committed an external, judicially punishable, offence. Jesus applied the same principle to other Commandments (Mt. 5:21–24, 27f.). The Eighth (prohibiting stealing) concerns property, and no property offence was capital in Israelite law. However, because of the importance of a family's land and substance, theft was nevertheless a serious matter, and therefore included within the core of covenant law.

2. CIVIL LAW

Very many of the laws in the Pentateuch begin with 'If . . .' or 'When . . .', then go on to describe a situation, and conclude with provisions or penalties to cover the circumstances described. This is 'case' law or, as sometimes called, 'casuistic' law. Some of the best examples are in the Book of the Covenant, where there are cases of damage, negligence, assault, accidental injury, disputes over loaned or hired property and so on. This kind of civil law, covering disputes between citizens, is of course a common feature of most societies, and there are many points of comparison between Israel's law and other ancient Near Eastern legal collections, especially from Mesopotamia, *e.g.* the Code of Hammurabi.

However, it is sometimes the differences that are significant. One striking difference in Israel's civil law can be seen in the laws on slaves. Three Old Testament civil laws are quite unparalleled in any other ancient Near Eastern code. Exodus 21:20f. and 21:26f. take up the case of slaves injured or killed *by their own masters*, and Deuteronomy 23:15f. grants asylum to a runaway slave. Each of these is discussed in chapter 8.

There can be no doubt that this 'swimming against the stream' in Israel's slave laws is the result of the theological impact of her own historical experience. The action of God on her behalf when in slavery transforms her attitude to slavery into something quite distinctive from contemporary custom and seminal for the future. This shows up the inadequacy of the 'moral/civil' distinction, if it assumes that the 'moral law' rests on the permanent moral will of God, whereas the 'civil law' was entirely contingent to Israel and ethically irrelevant. For in this case, it is precisely by careful study of the *civil* law that we find powerful theological forces at work, applying the character and action of God to the civil realm. You will not find a section of 'moral law' denouncing slavery, not even in the Ten Commandments. But you do find a moral *principle* operative within the civil law, which, when put alongside other Old Testament passages on the subject (*e.g.* Lv. 25:42; Ne. 5:1–12; Jb. 31:15; Je. 34; Am. 2:6), questions and undermines the whole institution.

3. FAMILY LAW

In ancient Israel the household had a major judicial role. This was one aspect of that social centrality of the family and larger kinship groupings which we shall discuss in more detail in chapter 8. The head of a household had the primary responsibility for, and legal authority over, all his dependants. That would include his married sons and their families while they resided within the patrimonial estate. A good example of this is the way Gideon, though himself a married man with teenage sons (Jdg. 8:20), was afraid of his 'father's house' (Jdg. 6:27), and yet was effectively protected by his father Joash (6:30f.) from a possible lynching.

On many routine matters, and some larger ones, the head of the household could act on his own legal authority without recourse to civil law or the external authority of a court of elders. Family law took precedence in some things over civil law. Such matters included parental discipline, which extended beyond childhood. Such discipline stopped short, however, of the right of life and death over a member of one's family. If the circumstances grew as serious as that, then family law gave way to civil law and the matter was referred to the court of elders (see Dt. 21:18–21). Marriages were also arranged within family, not civil, jurisdiction, except where there had been a prior offence (intercourse with the unbetrothed daughter of another man, in which case the civil law specified clear obligations: Ex. 22:16f., modified in Dt. 22:28f.), or there was a dispute between husband and father of a bride concerning her pre-marital chastity (Dt. 22:13–21). Divorce, too, fell within family jurisdiction, the civil law concerning itself only with regulating the post-divorce circumstances (Dt. 24:1–4). We have seen that the civil law took an interest in the fair treatment of slaves, but the ceremony by which a slave might voluntarily accept permanent attachment to one household, instead of freedom after six years, was a domestic ceremony – another case of internal family law (Ex. 21:5f.;[4] Dt. 15:16f.).

As well as these matters, there were laws and institutions designed to protect the family and its land inheritance. These included levirate marriage (Dt. 25:5–10), inheritance laws (Dt. 21:15f.), redemption of land and persons and the jubilee (Lv. 25:23ff.). Then, too, we must remember that the family was the chief educational agency, within which the rest of the laws were taught and explained (Dt. 6:7–9, 20–25).

Now under the old 'moral/civil/ceremonial' scheme, all this family law would presumably have to be included under 'civil law'. But clearly it needs a separate category, for sociologically it was a different kind of law. Its importance arises from the legal dimension it gives to the social, economic and theological role of the family which we shall discuss in more detail in chapter 8. Its ethical significance therefore lies in the same factors that our previous study uncovered. Exploring these

---

[4] The translation 'before the judges' (NIV, v. 6) is in my view a misinterpretation. The expression, as in the margin, is literally, 'before God', and probably refers to a ceremony at the household shrine, as in the presence of God.

deposits of ancient Israel's family law adds a 'three-dimensional' richness to the familiar 'sanctity of the family' motif, which is otherwise usually pinned on to the Fifth Commandment alone.

4. CULTIC LAW

The 'ceremonial' category, under the old division, is that which is said to prefigure the work of Christ and therefore to have been fulfilled and rendered obsolete by him. For this reason, many people's concept of the ceremonial, or cultic, law of the Old Testament is controlled by the Letter to the Hebrews and limited to the blood-sacrifices, priestly ordinances, and the ritual of the Day of Atonement. All of these are assuredly vital parts of the cultic law, but by no means the whole of it. For an Israelite, cultic life embraced such matters as dietary and hygiene regulations with their division between clean and unclean, sabbaths and other festivals, as well as a range of practical, material requirements which had important social effects, such as offerings, tithes, the first-fruits and gleanings of harvest.

Even the major economic institution of the *sabbatical fallow year* on the land with, under deuteronomic law, an accompanying release of pledges held for debts had a cultic rationale. It was based on the concept of divine ownership of the land, and was described as 'a Sabbath to the LORD' (Lv. 25:4) and 'the LORD's time for cancelling debts' (Dt. 15:2). So the material obligations and sacrifices that were involved in keeping this sabbatical institution were thought of as obligations to *God* himself. Yet the intended practical effect of it was the *humanitarian* concern for the impoverished and the debtor. This is spelt out explicitly in each of the three occurrences of the law (*cf.* Ex. 23:11; Lv. 25:6f.; Dt. 15:2, 7–11). You honoured God by keeping a law which benefited your poorer brethren.

Here again, then, in this unlikely-looking corner of Old Testament *cultic* law, we come upon a basic *moral* principle which pervades biblical ethics – namely that the service of God and mutual human care are inseparably bound together. God will not be worshipped acceptably by those who neglect justice and compassion. This ancient Israelite sabbatical institution, which might otherwise be deemed quite outdated and culturally (and agriculturally) irrelevant, presents us with a concrete, economic paradigm of a fundamental principle of biblical ethics – that we go a long way towards fulfilling our duty to God when we display responsible, sensitive and sacrificial care for our fellow men. Echoes of this could be multiplied.[5]

5. CHARITABLE LAW

Here we have a category that we would not regard strictly as law at all, in the judicial sense. Indeed, the injunctions which one gathers together under this heading could not have been regarded as enforceable legislation in Israel either. Yet such is the compassionate drift of the moral principles we have discerned in other categories of actual law, and such is the degree of penetration of Israel's theological beliefs into the practicalities of legal life, that it comes as really no surprise to find hosts of these charitable and humanitarian instructions scattered throughout the legal codes.

The breadth of situations covered by this category of law is very impressive. It includes: protection for the weak, especially those who lacked the natural protection of family and land, namely widows, orphans, Levites, immigrants and resident aliens; justice for the poor; impartiality; generosity at harvest time and in general economic life; respect for persons and property, even of an enemy; special care for strangers; prompt payment of wages earned by hired labour; sensitivity over articles taken in pledge; consideration for people in early marriage, or bereavement; even care for animals, domestic and wild, and for fruit trees. Again, it would be well worth pausing with a Bible to read through the passages in the footnote, to feel the warm heart-beat of this material.[6]

The practical outcome of this material, as we have said, is humanitarian. But the origin and motive are theological, and this is what is ethically most significant about it. It is here that we see the clearest illustration of the point made in chapter 1, namely that a wholehearted covenant commitment to God requires that his people reflect his character, as revealed in his actions on their behalf. The primary, compelling, and repeated reason why, if you had been an Israelite, you were to observe this charitable law towards the weak, the enslaved or the impov-

[5] *Cf.* Dt. 24:10–15; Jb. 31:16ff.; Pss. 15; 41:1ff.; Pr. 19:17; Is. 1:10–17; 58:1–7; Je. 7:4–11; Zc. 7:4–10.

[6] *Cf.* Ex. 22:21–27; 23:4–9; Lv. 19:9f., 13–18, 23–25, 33–36; Dt. 14:28f.; 15:12–14; 20:5–7, 19f.; 21:10–14; 22:1–4; 23:24f.; 24:5f., 10–15, 17–22; 25:4; 27:18f., 25.

erished, was that it was modelled on the way God had actually behaved towards you, when you were in similar conditions. 'Remember that *you* were slaves in Egypt and the LORD your God redeemed *you* from there. *That is why* I command you to do this' (Dt. 24:18, my italics).

Now to obey God's commands is to love him. The two are equivalent ideas for Deuteronomy (*cf*. Dt. 10:12f.). Love for God and love for one's neighbour thus stand united here as well. Indeed we remember that Jesus was quoting from the Old Testament when he framed the two 'Greatest Commandments': 'Love the LORD your God with all your heart and with all your soul and with all your strength' (Dt. 6:5), and 'love your neighbour as yourself' (Lv. 19:18). And with the motivation of God's experienced grace as the dynamic of this category of Old Testament law, we can see that Jesus was but drawing out to its infinite extent the same principle when he commanded us to 'love each other *as I have loved you*' (Jn. 15:12, my italics).

Now that we have outlined the different kinds of law operating in ancient Israel, we can see how futile it is to think of isolating a separate category of 'moral law'. There is too much overlap between the categories. Some laws can be a combination of, say, cultic and criminal, or civil and charitable, *etc.*, and there are moral principles to be found in all the categories. Not even the Decalogue is 'simple moral law'. It contains requirements which Israelites would have regarded as cultic (First to Fourth), family (Fifth), and civil (Sixth and Ninth) in their legislative outworking, whilst they all remain 'criminal' law in the sense carefully defined above.

So the task of interpreting the laws for our own ethical instruction requires careful thought. We need to see how any particular law functioned in its own Israelite context and what moral principles underlie it. It is those principles (or 'middle axioms') which then feed our ethical thought and action in our own environment.

In some cases, of course, the moral principle involved lies very 'close to the surface' of the law itself and is readily deduced. Indeed a law may in effect be a direct expression of the moral principle. We spoke earlier of the special nature of the Decalogue within the Old Testament itself as the 'policy statement' which outlines the principles and direction of the rest of Israel's laws. In line with that, I would consider that stipulations already embody and express moral principles, and that these in turn are illustrated and exemplified in specific legislation appropriate to Israel's historical and cultural setting.

On the other hand, many an individual specific law may have only a limited significance in and of itself, precisely because it relates so closely to Israel's own socio-economic or cultural life. Nevertheless, it remains as a concrete paradigm of some principle, and God has seen fit to leave it within the total context of the canon of Scripture for some reason that is 'profitable'. At the very least it will keep us earthed, by showing that general principles must have particular outworking and affect the local, culture-bound specifics of human life. Indeed, the very fact that a law seems irrelevant to us just as it stands because it is so specific to its own cultural context is evidence of the seriousness that the Old Testament gives to the earthy particulars of everyday life before God. If our ethics are all vague generalities, then we have not listened to Old Testament law.[7]

REFLECTIONS ON OLD TESTAMENT LAW

THEOLOGICAL ORIENTATION

Although we may find it helpful to categorize the laws into various sociological and functional divisons, as we have done, there is a higher category which stands above them all: for an Israelite, all the law was *God's law*. It was the gift of God's grace and the demand of God's covenant. To break or neglect the law was not just a criminal, civil, cultic offence, nor even just a lack of charity. It was *sin*. God stood above and behind the law, so that keeping the law was by no means an end in itself, but rather the way to 'knowing God' in personal covenant relationship. In that sense, the law was indeed 'life'. It was in living as God commanded that they would be the people he wanted and so fulfil his purpose in the world (Ex. 19:5f.).

This is not the place to linger in the complex minefield of the status of Old Testament law within New Testament theology and ethics. However, it does seem to me that at least one clue

[7] On the specificness of Old Testament law, see further John Goldingay, *Approaches to Old Testament Interpretation* (IVP, 1981), especially ch. 2, 'The Old Testament as a way of life'.

to understanding that issue lies in this matter of the covenant relationship which stands behind and is prior to the law itself.

It was emphasized in chapter 1 that the law was given to frame the response to a redemption and a relationship *already accomplished* by God's grace. The whole law, especially the Decalogue, enshrines both the vertical and the horizontal dimensions that are integral to the covenant: God's redemptive act and man's responsive obedience, expressed in love for God and for one another. It is this covenant dimension which provides the bridge between the status of the law in the Old Testament and the use made of it, particularly of the Decalogue, in the New. It is not that the Decalogue is some universal moral law imposed inexorably and equally upon Israel and the church. It is rather the fact of the continuity of relationship between God and his people and the nature of that relationship which is the constant factor. There was an old covenant and there is a new covenant, but in both cases we are dealing with *covenant* and in both cases it is the prior action of the same God in redemptive grace demanding our response of love and obedience.

In Christ we are granted that intimate covenant relationship with God to which the Old Testament law pointed. Even the pre-Christ experience of it filled devout Israelites with joy. We need to remind ourselves often that the ancient Israelite looked on the law not as a burden but as a gift of grace, a delight, precisely because of the relationship with his God that it enabled and expressed (*cf.* Pss. 19 and 119). But also in Christ that part of the promise of the new covenant which related to the law is fulfilled in us:

> I will put my law in their minds
> and write it on their hearts (Je. 31:33).

So while the Christian is certainly no longer 'under the law' (Rom. 3:19; 6:14), *i.e.* bound by the law of the old covenant, he is nevertheless not 'without the law' (1 Cor. 9:21), as though it has nothing whatever to say to him. Rather, the power of the indwelling Spirit makes it possible 'that the righteous requirements of the law might be fully met in us, who . . . live . . . according to the Spirit' (Rom. 8:4). And the principal fruit of the Spirit is love, which is the fulfilling of the law, especially of the Commandments (Rom. 13:8–10). For to love God wholly and exclusively and to love your neighbour as yourself constitute the very essence of the Decalogue, and indeed of the whole law and the prophets. But both are ultimately possible only within the freedom of the new covenant relationship in Christ.

So the law has abiding theological and ethical validity, as Christ himself affirmed. This is not because of what it is in itself, but because of what it was the expression of, in the case of Israel, and for what it points towards, in our case – a redemptive, covenant relationship with God. There is, therefore, a continuity and discontinuity in biblical ethics as regards the *law*, which is parallel to the continuity and discontinuity in biblical theology as regards *redemption*.

The relationship in both cases is *typological*. We perceive the correspondence between the 'new thing' in Christ and the 'former things'. With Peter, we can say 'this is that . . .' (Acts 2:16, AV). Thus, we know that neither we nor our personal ancestors were delivered from slavery in Egypt, but we recognize *the redemptive purpose of the same God*, to whose victory in the cross and resurrection we trace our own redemption.

In the same way, we do not have oxen threshing our corn in our back gardens, so we are not bound by the letter of Deuteronomy 25:4. Nevertheless we can perceive the moral principle at work in it. We appreciate its Christian application made by Paul in a particular situation in 1 Corinthians 9:7–12. Paul's method and assumption should be ours as we read the law: 'Doesn't the Law say the same thing? For it is written in the Law of Moses . . . Surely he says this for us, doesn't he? Yes, this was written for us, because . . .' . . . because we recognize *the moral will of the same God* behind the specific, culture-related Israelite injunction and the principle applied to relationships within the Christian church.

There is also, however, a wider relevance in this theological orientation of the law. The God who, as their Redeemer, gave the law to Israel as his own people, was also known to be the Creator and Ruler of all mankind. The law is based on the assumption of Israel's accountability to the LORD as their covenant sovereign. But that in itself rests on the axiom of Old Testament creation faith that *all* people are morally accountable to God. In fact, canonically speaking, the creation narratives and their moral implications were *part* of 'the law', meaning the Pentateuch, to the Israelites.

There is an interesting sideways glance at the rest of mankind in Deuteronomy 4:6–8 which envisages a mixture of admiration and envy on their part when they see the quality of Israel's law.

> Observe them [the laws] carefully, for this will show your wisdom and understanding to the nations, who will hear about all these decrees and say, 'Surely this great nation is a wise and understanding people.' What other nation is so great as to have their gods near them the way the LORD our God is near us whenever we pray to him? And what other nation is so great as to have such righteous decrees and laws as this body of laws I am setting before you today?

Something similar is found in the eschatological vision of Isaiah 2:2–5, when all the nations flock to 'the mountain of the LORD'. The prophet envisages them living by the law of the 'God of Jacob'.

> The law will go out from Zion,
> the word of the LORD from Jerusalem.

One might also compare the global scope of the exercise of God's 'equity' in Psalms 96, 97 and 98.

So there is, within the Old Testament itself, an awareness that the law given in a unique way to Israel as a unique people had wider relevance for the rest of mankind, just as their call to be a 'holy nation' was so that they could be a 'priesthood', a 'light to the nations'. This frees us to explore the law with that wider purpose in mind and justifies what we described earlier as a *'paradigmatic'* approach. That is, we assume that if God gave Israel certain specific institutions and laws, they were based on principles which have universal validity. That does not mean that Christians will try to impose by law in a secular state provisions lifted directly from the laws of Moses. It does mean that they will work to bring their society nearer to conformity with the principles underlying the concrete laws of Old Testament society, because they perceive the same God to be both Redeemer and law-giver of Israel, and also Creator and Ruler of contemporary mankind.

This approach and assumption, then, is concerned with the implication, not just the application, of Old Testament law. It releases the ethical *potential* of the law, without short-circuiting the task of working at *actual* practical applications in varying cultural contexts. It does not guarantee or predetermine the results of such outworking. But it does justify, and indeed necessitate, the task itself.

ISRAEL'S SCALE OF VALUES

The relevance of Old Testament law to modern societies and the salutary impact its application could make on them are nowhere more evident than in its system of values. Take the order of the Commandments in the Decalogue itself. They begin with God and end with the inner thoughts of a man's heart. In a sense the Tenth and the First correspond to one another, inasmuch as covetousness by its nature puts other things in the position that should be occupied by God: 'covetousness which is idolatry' (Col. 3:5, RSV). After God and his day come parents, life, sex, property, and judicial integrity.

> Though every commandment expresses the will of God, and breach of any one of them is a sin calling down on the offender the wrath of God, their order is not haphazard: the most vital demands are placed first. This is confirmed by the penal law. Flagrant disregard of the first six commandments carried a mandatory death penalty. For the seventh death was probably optional, not compulsory. Only in exceptional cases would breach of the eighth and ninth commandments involve capital punishment. And it is most unlikely that the tenth commandment was ever the subject of judicial process. The order of the commandments thus gives some insight into Israel's hierarchy of values and this should be borne in mind in their exegesis.[8]

Two particular features of their scale of values are worth noting: the priority of life over property and the priority of persons over punishment.

Life and property
The sanctity of human life is one of the earliest explicit moral values in the Old Testament, based, as it is, on the creation of

[8] G. J. Wenham, 'Law and the legal system in the Old Testament' in *Law, Morality and the Bible*, p. 29.

man in God's image. God's words to Noah make the matter very clear:

> For your lifeblood I will surely demand an accounting. I will demand an accounting from every animal. And from each man, too, I will demand an accounting for the life of his fellow man.

> Whoever sheds the blood of man,
>   by man shall his blood be shed;
> for in the image of God
>   has God made man (Gn. 9:5f.).

The effect of this sanctity can be seen in some almost incidental features of certain laws. When an ox gores a human being to death, for example, the law requires that the ox itself be stoned. This is a unique Israelite detail in what is otherwise a very common law, found in most other ancient Near Eastern codes. It ties in with the concept of Genesis 9:5 that God holds even animals accountable for the lifeblood of man.

But the most outstanding effect is the fact that in Israelite law life and property are never measured against each other. That is, no property offence in normal legal procedure was punishable by death. (In abnormal cases like Achan's theft, the matter was a serious violation of a covenant demand – the 'ban' or devotion to destruction of pagan, 'polluted' things.) This feature of Israelite law stands in sharp contrast to many ancient law codes where certain thefts by certain people were punishable by death, and, indeed, to British law until comparatively recent times. On the other hand, theft of a *person* for gain (kidnapping) *was* a capital offence (Ex. 21:16; Dt. 24:7).

The other side of this principle is that if you had committed a capital offence with a mandatory death penalty, you could not get off by paying money instead. This was prohibited in Numbers 35:31–34. Again, this contrasts with ancient Near Eastern codes where many capital offences could be commuted to fines. There the system in effect favoured those wealthy enough to afford to 'pay' for their crimes. In the Old Testament the only exception to this rule was in the case of the fatally goring ox; the owner could ransom his life if the family of the ox's victim agreed, since the homicide was indirect (Ex. 21:30).

Even the life of a slave was protected in this way, notwithstanding the fact that in other respects he was his master's property (Ex. 21:20f.).

Human life, then, and material property were incommensurable. They were treated as qualitatively different, not to be equated with one another in judicial procedure. Like parallel lines, they did not meet or intersect.

Persons and punishment

This conviction of Old Testament ethics that persons matter more than things not only informs the hierarchy of serious offences and the distinguishing of capital and non-capital penalties, it also extends to the offender himself and the nature and extent of the punishment meted out. There is a humanitarian ethos in Israelite penal law which is acknowledged by all who have compared it with contemporary ancient Near Eastern collections of law.

The prototype example of God's concern for the rights of the criminal is the case of Cain. In other respects this is a curious case, for God himself waives the death penalty for Abel's murder. But he answers Cain's fear as to how others will treat him, the murderer, by making it quite explicit that other men will be held accountable to himself, God, for their treatment of Cain (Gn. 4:15).

This view that criminals remain human persons with rights protected by God is found in the provision in Deuteronomy 25:2f. If corporal punishment is administered, it has to have a clear limit – not exceeding forty lashes – explicitly so that the offender is not 'degraded'. He is still a brother. Apart from the death penalty by stoning, beating appears to have been the only other normal physical punishment in Israelite law.

No form of imprisonment is prescribed in the law, though it was a feature of later monarchic practice. When one thinks of some of the horrific features and long-term effects of our own 'civilized' prison system, it is arguable that the slavery prescribed by Old Testament law for some offences (*e.g.* unrepayable theft or debt) was, on humanitarian grounds, preferable to imprisonment. At least a slave was still free to enjoy his own marital and family life, remained within the community, sharing its seasons and festivals, and was engaged in normal, useful work alongside the rest of the community – things which imprisonment denies. Unlike other ancient Near Eastern codes which had some very nasty amputations for punishment, physical mutilation as a judicial penalty is absent from Old Testament law, except for one rather bizarre, extreme and somewhat unlikely circumstance (Dt. 25:11f.).

There is also no trace in Old Testament law of any gradation of penalties according to the social class and rank of the offended party. In Mesopotamian law an injury to a nobleman would commonly entail a far heavier penalty than an identical injury done to a commoner or slave. In Israel, by contrast, equality before the law for all social groups, including aliens and immigrants, is made explicit in Exodus 12:49, Leviticus 19:34 and Numbers 15:16. Furthermore, substitutionary punishment was excluded. For example, in the Code of Hammurabi, if a house collapsed and killed the owner's son, then the *son* of the housebuilder (not the man himself) was to be put to death. Deuteronomy 24:16 forbade this on principle, and in the law of the goring ox (again!) the penalty is clearly stated to be constant, even if the ox killed a son or daughter (Ex. 21:31).

A study of the penal provisions, particularly in Deuteronomy, shows up some clear and positive principles on which Israelite punishments operated. Taking Deuteronomy 19:18–20 and 25:1–3 as key examples, the following ingredients of punishment can be seen:

1. *Retribution.* The offender was to suffer his just legal deserts which should be appropriate to the offence. That is the significance and justification of the *lex talionis* ('an eye for an eye', *etc.*) principle. It was a very limiting law, preventing excessive or vengeful punishment.

2. *Purging.* Guilt had to be 'wiped away' from God's sight.

3. *Deterrence.* 'All Israel shall hear *and fear*', *i.e.* be afraid to do the same.

4. *Restoration.* The offender remained a brother and was not to be degraded.

5. *Compensation.* Restitution was made to the injured party – not to the state as a fine.[9]

There can be no doubt then, it seems to me, that the Old Testament provides us with a scale of values, concretely illus-

---

[9] For a full discussion of all this, *cf.* G. J. Wenham, *op. cit.*, and the literature cited there in footnotes, pp. 50–52.

trated in the judicial sphere, which has powerful ethical implications in comparable areas of our own socio-cultural environment. Once again, the matter of detailed outworking of these principles and values in the realm of, say, modern penology, has to be left to those whose expertise lies in that field. And again, it is the paradigmatic approach which will be found the most fruitful.

As an illustration, let us take an example which at first sight seems likely to be highly unhelpful – the law prescribing the stoning of the rebellious son in Deuteronomy 21:18–21. If we examine the text and context carefully, the following points may be observed:

1. The preceding verses are concerned with the right of the firstborn son, protecting him from the whim of a father who might show favouritism to another child. The law before us is a kind of balance, showing that sons had a reciprocal responsibility to their father and family. There is a balance in the rights of parents and children in respect of each other.

2. The law presupposes the necessity of family discipline, for the case is brought only after prolonged parental discipline has been disregarded.

3. The law is a limitation on the extent of family law. That is, the father did not have the right of life and death over his own children; such a serious matter had to be brought before the whole community, under civil law.

4. The law therefore recognizes a valid role for the civil law in domestic, family matters when they are serious enough to be a threat to the rest of the community.

5. Further protection for the son, in spite of his delinquency, is found in the requirement that *both* parents must together bring the charge; the son will not suffer for the malice of a vindictive father alone.

6. The offence was serious. It is not just a case of an unruly, high-spirited youngster. The law specifies several offences, including stubbornness, rebellion, persistent disobedience, and social delinquency, which both squandered the family's substance and was an infectious bad example. If the son in this law were the firstborn, as in the previous law, then his profligacy was endangering the whole family and its posterity. For if this was how he behaved as a minor, what would become of the family's substance when he inherited it? As Old Testa-

ment law reveals elsewhere, the welfare of every family was the concern of the whole community. That is why this case becomes a community problem and no longer just an internal domestic matter.

7. The penalty reflects the seriousness of the offence for Israel. It was a covenant crime, an offence against the Fifth Commandment, and therefore against God himself. It therefore threatened to bring judgment on the whole theocratic community and so had to be purged away. Now that can no longer be the rationale for any punishment in a secular state, so the demand for the death penalty no longer applies. Nevertheless, it remains as a reminder of the seriousness of the nature of the offence described, and suggests that there are grounds for supporting a degree of strictness and severity in the law's response to serious juvenile criminality. The punishment was explicitly said to be deterrent (v. 21c).

8. The whole community was to be involved, not only in the sense that the 'elders' represented the wider community, but also in that the punishment was to be carried out corporately. The issue was treated as a matter of serious social responsibility which all shared. That is certainly something which those involved with 'problem youth' would long to see in our own day.

'THE DUE PROCESS OF LAW'

To have admirable laws is one thing, but what really counts in practice for the ordinary man in everyday life is how justice and the law is actually administered. This is an abiding, ever relevant human concern in every age and society. Therefore it is of interest to reflect on the Old Testament's concern for the *process* of law as well as the promulgation of it.

Here, however, we come up against the problem of the big cultural gap between the Old Testament and modern social practice in this area. In ancient Israel, as we saw above under civil and family law, there was a combination of, and in some matters a progression between, familial and public means of administering or enforcing justice. For example, in cases of murder, the responsibility for punishing the criminal lay with the *gō'ēl* – the *kinsman* 'avenger of blood' – not with a 'public prosecutor'. The civic elders of a village or city fulfilled only an assisting role to the *gō'ēl* (Dt. 19:1–13), or acted as 'purgers' if the murderer could not be brought to justice (Dt. 21:1–9). The family thus had the primary duty in enforcing justice. This kinship responsibility extended to clan level as well, as the case described in 2 Samuel 14:5–11 shows. That case also shows, however, that appeal could be made beyond the jurisdiction of kinship to the civil authority, as high as the king himself.

This familial nature of the process of law had several significant results, which need to be taken into account in any application to contemporary processes of law. First, it encouraged a climate in which law was supposed to be known. A child's basic education was substantially education in the *tôrāh*. This included much that was not law in the judicial sense, but would nevertheless give the child a familiarity with the legal framework of the nation (Dt. 6:7ff.). Added to this was the teaching of the law which was supposed to be the role of the Levites (Dt. 33:10; Mal. 2:6f.). They were a kind of 'Citizens' Advice Bureau'! And on top of that there was the public reading of the law, at which everyone, including children, was expected to be present (Dt. 31:10–13). Since all this was supposed to take place and ensure that the law was known, one can understand Hosea's bitter complaint that the moral decline of the nation stemmed from lack of knowledge (Ho. 4:1–6), and the fact that he blamed the priests for the situation.

Secondly, the administration of justice was largely local. Most disputes, accusations, trials and cases took place in the local village assembly, and had a curiously democratic nature. It was a matter of local people arbitrating their own affairs through their own elders. Justice was not something remote, bureaucratic and imposed from above. Even the reforms of Jehoshaphat, by which judges were appointed by the king himself, applied only to the fortified cities and therefore probably left the local village courts largely unaffected (2 Ch. 19:5). Such a system of local and fairly 'unsupervised' courts could work well in the circumstances of broad social equality of families and wide distribution of land and wealth which the land division texts and other laws presuppose. Provided most families were economically viable and thus qualified to have their senior menfolk as elders, then there would be a broad base for social justice. But when families began to be deprived of land and driven into a kind of debt-serfdom, control of the courts and other forms of social power fell into the hands of the small class of wealthy land-owners. The administration of justice was thus very vulnerable to corruption and exploitation. The prophets saw clearly this link between the shift of balance in economic power and the accelerating corruption and denial of justice.

Thirdly, the initiative in justice was mainly private. As we have seen, it began as a family responsibility, and outside that, in any dispute, it was often a matter of self-help aided by the courts if necessary. There was no Director of Public Prosecutions, no police force, and no official intermediary profession of barristers and solicitors. This meant that a judge, or a group of elders sitting in judgment on a dispute, was much more directly involved with the plaintiff and defendant than in our society. This could be so even if the judge were the king (as in the case in 1 Sa. 14). And in a village society the judge might be a relative or workmate. Illustration of the way in which all sides in a case could be acquaintances, and other aspects of the Hebrew legal assembly, can be found in the revealing account in Ruth 4 and in Job's description of his former respected status in such assemblies in Job 29.

Against this background, the careful instructions on applying the law with rigorous fairness and the warnings against bribery and favouritism are all the more pertinent. So it is worth concluding this section with a look at *Exodus 23:1–8*, which is a concise summary of judicial ideals, and yet includes all three of the main parties in a legal case.

Verses 1–3 advise *witnesses* about their integrity, honesty and independence:

> Do not spread false reports. Do not help a wicked man by being a malicious witness. Do not follow the crowd in doing wrong. When you give testimony in a lawsuit, do not pervert justice by siding with the crowd, and do not show favouritism to a poor man in his lawsuit.

Verses 4–5 then address the *antagonists* in the case (the meaning in this context of the word 'enemy') and warn them not to neglect the normal requirements of brotherly obligation even though they are at odds judicially:

> If you come across your enemy's ox or donkey wandering off, be sure to take it back to him. If you see the donkey of

someone who hates you fallen down under its load, do not leave it there; be sure you help him with it.

Finally, verses 6–8 address those who must *judge* the issue, and command impartiality and incorruptibility:

Do not deny justice to your poor people in their lawsuits. Have nothing to do with a false charge and do not put an innocent or honest person to death, for I will not acquit the guilty. Do not accept a bribe, for a bribe blinds those who see and twists the words of the righteous.

When these paragraphs are set alongside similar injunctions in Leviticus 19:15, Deuteronomy 16:18–20 and Jehoshaphat's admirable brief to his appointed judges in 2 Chronicles 19:4–11, it can be seen how concerned the Old Testament is that the way the law is administered should match up to the standard of the content of the law itself. This corresponds well with a growing awareness in our day that people, especially the powerless, the poor, the illiterate, the immigrant, are as often hurt by the *process* of law, even good law, as they are victims of bad law or deliberate injustice. In this instance too, the Old Testament 'has been there before us', and should encourage and undergird Christians who are actively concerned for justice in the procedural side of our legal systems. This, after all, is only to apply the *Ninth Commandment*, 'You shall not bear false witness', in the sphere to which it originally applied, namely the protection of the integrity of legal procedures.

LIMITATIONS OF LAW

Our last reflection on the ethical relevance of the law is more negative. There is an awareness in the Old Testament itself that the law is limited in its capacity for sustaining righteousness and justice in society, if there is determination to avoid its demands. This brings a realistic caution to those who would put all the eggs of their concern for social righteousness in the basket of legislative reform – either by attacking laws which they regard as dangerously 'permissive', or by promoting laws which they deem morally 'protective'. This is not in the least to decry the work of Christians in this field. Its importance can be gauged by the depth of God's concern, witnessed in the Old

Testament, for the laws of a society. It is simply to deflate any expectation that society can be preserved or reformed by force of law alone.

In the Old Testament there are three aspects of this awareness. First of all, just laws may be unjustly used, or simply ignored. Amos 2:6 accused unscrupulous creditors of what was probably technically legal. People were taken into a form of debt-slavery as a 'working pledge' for unpaid debts; but this was being done for trifling debts and with callous disregard for the poor or their families. Likewise, the creditors of Nehemiah 5:1–13 were probably using the legal technique of the redemption of land from impoverished kinsmen to their own greedy benefit. Nehemiah appealed to their consciences, not to a court of law or any legal statute (except that of the charging of interest, which was making the burden even heavier and reducing people to debt-slavery all the quicker).

Secondly, where the law could be twisted or evaded, those with sufficient power and influence could promulgate unjust laws to their own advantage. Isaiah observed this extra bitter burden that was borne by the oppressed of his day.

> Woe to those who make unjust laws,
>   to those who issue oppressive decrees,
> to deprive the poor of their rights
>   and rob my oppressed people of justice,
> making widows their prey
>   and robbing the fatherless (Is. 10:1f.).

The Psalmist gives powerful expression to a similar complaint about oppression on the part of corrupt rulers in Psalm 94:20f.

Thirdly, mere changing of the law or invoking of old laws is an inadequate remedy, once injustice has taken deep root and become structurally ingrained and 'naturalized' in a society. In Jeremiah 34, for example, the wealthy and powerful proved themselves unable to fulfil a promise they had made to obey the ancient law on slave release, even after much prophetic exhortation and an abortive attempt to do so. Presumably, the whole exercise turned out to be too costly to be continued, and their economic heads silenced their fleetingly charitable (and obedient) hearts. This is the only occasion where a prophet appears to have campaigned for the enforcement of a specific statute law in circumstances of social and economic oppression. For the most part, the prophets see only two possibilities before the people, either God's direct judgment on a corrupt and incorrigible society, or else a *spiritual* change of heart, which only God can give (*cf.* Ezk. 18:31; 36:26ff.).

So again, we see the prior necessity of experiencing God's grace – redemptive or restorative – if genuine social justice is to be established, maintained or restored. The law by itself cannot achieve those ends. Justice flows from knowledge of God, not merely from knowledge of the law.

8
Society and culture

For all that Israel were called to be a holy nation, for all that they could be described in the words of Balaam's oracles as a 'people who live apart and do not consider themselves one of the nations' (Nu. 23:9), it is important to remember that they were not a 'clean slate'. They did not live in hermetically sealed isolation from the rest of humanity. On the contrary, they were an ancient people in a world of nations, indeed at the geographical crossroads of the already ancient civilizations of the Nile and of Mesopotamia, whose tides of influence ebbed and flowed across them throughout their history. So there are countless points of common culture, social norms and conventions, shared by Israel and her contemporaries. The question that is posed for our ethical enquiry is: How did Israel's unique religious faith relate to and interact with this social and cultural area of life?

Simple answers in so complex a field are perilous, but some broad classification of the spectrum of Israel's responses to contemporary culture may be attempted. One can discern a range that moves from outright rejection and prohibition of some customs, through toleration with careful regulation of others, to acceptance and affirmation with 'value added' theological interpretation. We shall look at each of these in its Old Testament context and then raise a few pointers to their relevance for Christian ethics.

REJECTION AND PROHIBITION

There were some practices of contemporary culture which were
abhorrent to God and were accordingly prohibited to Israel.
Most of these were connected directly or indirectly with
Canaanite religion, and the prohibition related not only to their
inherent wickedness but to their connection with the snare of
idolatry and 'other gods'. The adoption of any of the accoutre-
ments of the religion of Canaan was prohibited with uncompromising severity. The unceasing struggle of the prophets over
this issue, however, shows how difficult Israel seems to have
found it to resist the worship of the old gods of the land.

The social side-effects of Canaanite religion come under
similar condemnation. The practice of cultic prostitution was
outlawed, along with a variety of other kinds of sexual perversion. All kinds of occult practice were prohibited, including
spiritism, mediums, witchcraft, necromancy and divination.
The greatest horror was reserved for the practice of child
sacrifice, regarded by Deuteronomy as the worst manifestation
of this 'detestable' worship (12:31). The range of practices prohibited and the depth of feeling against them can be assessed by
reading through the references in the footnote.[1]

If Israel were to absorb these features of her surrounding
culture, rather than resist and destroy them, she would not
only cease to be distinctive, but would expose herself to the
same divine judgment as their present practitioners. They were
about to be 'vomited out', such was the divine revulsion at
these aspects of their 'culture'. The same standard of judgment
would be applied to Israel. Her holiness and these practices
could not be mixed.

TOLERATION WITH CONTROL

Some customs and practices common in the ancient world were
tolerated within Israel, without explicit divine command or
sanction, but with a developing theological critique which

[1] *Cf.* Ex. 22:18; 23:24; Lv. 18:3, 21–25; 19:26, 29, 31; 20:2–6, 22f., 27; Dt. 12:29–31; 18:9–13;
23:17–18.

regarded them as falling short of God's highest standards. The customs in question were then regulated by legal safeguards in such a way as to soften or eliminate their worst effects. In this category one could place polygamy, divorce and slavery.

POLYGAMY

Polygamy is certainly present in the Old Testament, but its extent should not be exaggerated. Examples are almost entirely confined to kings or those in positions of leadership or prestige of some kind. And even in these cases, with a few notable exceptions such as Solomon, it is mostly bigamy rather than polygamy that is evidenced.

Monogamy seems to have been the common practice of the populace. The patriarchs are sometimes held up as paragons of polygamy, a fact which causes amusement to some when they are cited as inspiration for monogamous fidelity in the marriage service of the Book of Common Prayer! But we must distinguish between polygamy (having more than one *wife*) and concubinage. The difference may seem immaterial to us, but it was an immense social distinction in the ancient world. A concubine was a slave woman, in a very different and inferior relation to her master compared with his wife. With that in mind, we realize that Abraham and Isaac were both mono*gamous*, while Jacob, who actually wanted only one wife, ended up with four women in his life (two wives and two concubines) by a combination of trickery and jealousy!

'But it was not this way from the beginning' (Mt. 19:8). These words spoken by Jesus about divorce could equally be applied to polygamy. For the creation narrative clearly implies a monogamous 'one-flesh' relationship between one man and one woman (Gn. 2:24). To this could be added passages in the wisdom literature which advocate, or at least would seem to presuppose, faithful monogamy (Pr. 5:15–20; 18:22; 31:10–31; Song) as well as the implications of the figure of marriage used for the *exclusive* relationship between God and Israel. Notwithstanding this theological awareness that polygamy was short of ideal, it was tolerated in Israel as a social custom. But there were laws, as we shall now see, which sought to limit its potentially exploitative effects on women.

As mentioned above, the status of a concubine was far inferior to that of a wife, yet the legal rights of concubines were explicitly laid down in Exodus 21:7–11. She could not be resold by her owner; she was to be treated as only one man's concubine, not a family plaything. If he took another concubine, he must not deprive the first of material provision and sexual rights. If these were the rights of concubines, the rights of wives in a polygamous situation cannot have been less. Deuteronomy 21:10–14 likewise protects the rights of a female captive of war who is taken to wife (whether as a first or additional wife is not said). She was to be treated with humanity and sensitivity and could not be treated as a slave. The inheritance law of Deuteronomy 21:15–17 tacitly acknowledges the prime criticism of bigamy, that a man cannot love two women equally, or rather that one may not be loved at all eventually. It then goes on to protect the unloved wife from the ignominy of having her son, if he was the firstborn, deprived of his inheritance. The story of Elkanah and his rival wives (1 Sa. 1) was hardly written for the primary purpose of criticizing bigamy, but it is a vivid illustration of the potential agonies it can produce.

DIVORCE

Polygamy, then, was tolerated without explicit approval, but with legal safeguards that were latent criticisms of it. *Divorce*, on the other hand, was also tolerated, but with eventual explicit disapproval. Divorce hardly features in Old Testament law at all, for the reason that, unlike our modern custom, neither marriage nor divorce were matters for civil law. They fell within the 'family law' jurisdiction of the head of a household (see chapter 7 for definition of these categories of law). A man did not have to go to court to get a divorce.

The laws which do involve divorce are concerned either with circumstances where divorce is ruled out, or with regulating relationships after divorce has happened. In both cases the protection of the woman seems to be the main point of the law. The first is Deuteronomy 22:28f., where a man is prohibited from divorcing a woman he has been obliged to marry as a result of pre-marital intercourse. The second is the regulation in Deuteronomy 24:1–4 which was the point of controversy between Jesus and the Pharisees. This law does not 'command' divorce; it presupposes it, requires a 'bill of divorce' (for the woman's protection, lest she or a future husband be accused of adultery), and forbids the first husband from taking her back if her next husband divorces her or dies. One might also mention again the case of the captive wife, who was to be divorced, not sold as a slave, if her captor-husband was dissatisfied. In this case, divorce appears as a lesser of two evils for the woman. At least it preserved some shreds of dignity and freedom, in contrast to slavery (Dt. 21:14).

So divorce, too, was tolerated, within legal limits. But it falls much further short of God's ideal than seems to have been the case with polygamy. On divorce there is the uncompromising attack of Malachi 2:13–16, culminating in the blunt denunciation: ' "I hate divorce," says the LORD God of Israel'. Nothing as sharp as this, or with such powerful theological argument, is directed at polygamy. Presumably this is because, whereas polygamy is a kind of 'expansion' of the ordinance of marriage beyond the monogamous limit intended by God, divorce is a severing destruction of it. It is a 'covering oneself with violence', as Malachi puts it. Polygamy multiplies relationships where God intended a single relationship; but divorce destroys, or presupposes the destruction of, relationships.

SLAVERY

The Old Testament, like the apostle Paul, receives a large measure of criticism for tolerating *slavery*. And, of course, so it does. Slavery was such an integral part of the social, economic and institutional life of the ancient world contemporary with Old Testament Israel that it is difficult to see how Israel could have existed without it or effectively abolished it. Nevertheless, two things can be said at once.

First, slavery in relatively small societies like Israel was qualitatively vastly different from slavery in the large imperial civilizations, both the contemporary ancient Near Eastern empires, and especially the later Greek and Roman empires. There the slave markets were glutted with captives of war and displaced peoples and slaves were put to degrading and dehumanizing labour. In the pastoral-agricultural society of Israel, slaves were largely residential, domestic workers, complementing, but not a substitute for, the labour of free members of the household. In other words, slave labour was not a means by which free Israelites were released from physical labour, as was the case in classical Greece, for example. Provided they were humanely treated (as the law required), such slavery could be said to be little different *experientially* from many kinds of paid employment in a cash economy. And the evidence shows, as we shall see below, that slaves in Israel had more legal rights and protection than in any contemporary society. Indeed, slaves enjoyed more explicit legal and economic security than the technically free, but landless, hired labourers and craftsmen.

Secondly, slavery in the Old Testament was not simply tolerated with a 'rubber stamp' of uncritical approval. There are aspects of Old Testament thought and practice in this area which virtually 'neutralized' slavery as an institution and were the seeds of its radical rejection in much later Christian thinking. Certainly these aspects, to which we now turn, made Israel unquestionably unique in the ancient world in its attitude to slavery. This is a fact unanimously acknowledged by ancient Near Eastern scholars. Three points are worth noting.

The first and most influential factor in Israel's theological and legal attitude to slavery was her own history. The Israelites never forgot that they started out, in terms of national origin, as a rabble of freed slaves. This in itself is unusual, if not unique, among epics of national origins. Most ethnic myths glorify their nation's ancestral past. Israel, by contrast, looked back to four centuries of slavery in a foreign land, which had become increasingly oppressive, inhumane and unbearable. The experience coloured their subsequent attitude to slavery enormously. On the one hand, Israelites were not supposed to subject one another to slave status or conditions of labour. Such action was incompatible with the equality of being redeemed brothers, slaves of the LORD alone (*cf*. Lv. 25:42f., 46, 53, 55). On the other hand, their treatment of aliens within their own society, whether those aliens were the technically free but landless 'tenant' workers, or actual bought slaves, was to be marked with compassion, born of the memory of Egypt where it had been denied to themselves. This principle is quite explicit in the earliest legal code of the Old Testament, the Covenant Code of Exodus 21 – 23: 'Do not oppress an alien; you yourselves know how it feels to be aliens, because you were aliens in Egypt' (Ex. 23:9; *cf*. 22:21; Dt. 15:15).

In the second place, however, these historically generated attitudes were translated into specific legislation which accorded to slaves in Israel a degree of status, rights and protection unheard of elsewhere. Slaves were included within the religious life of the community. They could be circumcised and partake of the Passover (Ex. 12:44). They were to be allowed to join in the feasting and rejoicing of the great festivals (Dt. 16:11–14; note v. 12). Probably most relevant of all, in view of their occupation, was the command that slaves, male and female, be included in the weekly sabbath rest (Ex. 20:10); indeed it is said to be for their prime benefit – along with working animals – in Exodus 23:12.

This socio-cultic inclusion of slaves was extended into the realm of the protection of civil law. Exodus 21:20f., 26f. are two laws from the Covenant Code – therefore very early laws[2] – which deal with a master's treatment of his own slaves. That in itself makes them unique in ancient Near Eastern law. In other codes there were abundant laws concerning assault or murder of *another* person's slaves, but not of your own. If a master administered a beating of such severity that it was immediately fatal, the slave was to be 'avenged'. That is the literal meaning of the verb used, and in any other context would mean that the guilty party would be liable to death himself at the hands of his victim's family. Though some commentators are reluctant to accept it, this law's natural sense is that the murderous master was to be executed by the legal community on behalf of the slave, who had no family to avenge him.

The second law protected a slave from actual bodily harm. If it were inflicted, the slave was to be set free. The mention of a 'tooth' shows that it was not just because the slave's work capacity was impaired. There is here a deeper concern for the personal humanity of the slave. It should be stressed that these were civil laws, not charitable exhortations. They must imply that in such circumstances a slave could appeal to the court of elders against his own master. This too would be a unique right. Yet it seems to be a possibility that Job had in mind when he claimed never to have denied justice to any of his slaves in any legal complaint they had had against him (Jb. 31:14).[3]

After six years of service a slave was to be given the opportunity of freedom in the seventh year. Since he would still not

---

[2] The early date of these laws is stressed in order to show that Israel's uniquely humane slave laws were not a late product of a developing ethical sensitivity, but were part of the legal expression of her theology from the earliest period.

[3] The significance of these laws and the light shed by Job 31:14 is discussed more fully in C. J. H. Wright, *God's People in God's Land* (Paternoster, forthcoming).

own any land,[4] it is unlikely that such 'freedom' would mean much more than a change of employer. Deuteronomy 15:13f. expands the original law with a generous gift that was a primitive form of unemployment benefit. Proof that slavery was not necessarily oppressive is found in the fact that the law presumes that a slave would often prefer the security of his present residence to freedom (Dt. 15:16f.).

But the most astonishingly unique slave law in the Old Testament is the law of asylum in Deuteronomy 23:15f. A runaway slave, far from being punished or sent back, was to be given freedom of residence in a village of his choice. The universal law of the rest of contemporary societies not only punished the runaway but laid severe penalties on anyone who harboured him. Israel's law not only allowed his freedom, it *commanded* his protection.

> Is it not extraordinary – not to say amusing – that the one society in the ancient Near East that had a law protecting runaway slaves was that society that traced its origin to a group of runaway slaves from Egypt? . . The point is that Israel has experienced God as the one who is sympathetic to runaway slaves. So this law is not just an ethical or legal principle in defence of human rights, but a reflex of Israel's own religious experience – a fundamental characteristic of Biblical ethics.[5]

So starkly different in this law, that some scholars think it can have applied only to foreign slaves seeking asylum in Israel. The law does not state that. But even if that were true, it would still be unique, and would also show that Israel was an attractive society for a slave to seek refuge in. If, on the other hand, it applied within Israel, it represents a radical undermining of the institution of slavery itself. Slavery as such is not protected or

---

[4] See above, chapter 4, footnote 2, on the point that the 'Hebrew' in the slave release laws of Ex. 21:2–6 and Dt. 15:12–18 is not just a synonym for 'Israelite', but refers to a landless, rootless and often stateless substratum of society, found throughout the ancient Near East. It accurately described the state of the Israelites while in Egypt (Ex. 2:11ff.), and of David and his outlaws while in the land of the Philistines (1 Sa. 29:3). So the 'Hebrew slave' who was to be freed after six years was landless, and quite different from the Israelite landowner who mortgaged land because of increasing debt and poverty, but who was to be restored to his land and freedom in the jubilee (fiftieth) year (Lv. 25:39–41).

[5] D. J. A. Clines: 'Social Responsibility in the Old Testament', a Shaftesbury Project Working Paper, p. 8.

rendered sacrosanct under Israelite law. At the very least it can be said that such a law probably presumes that runaway slaves will be the exception, not the rule. This lends further weight to the view that normally slavery in Israel was not oppressively harsh. It would certainly not have been, if the spirit of the slavery laws of Exodus and Deuteronomy were put into practice.

The third thing to be said about slavery in the Old Testament arises from the remark above about slavery not being sacrosanct. It is that slavery was never viewed as 'natural'. In other words, it was not regarded as a divinely ordered part of creation itself, as though slave and free were different degrees of humanity. The very first mention of slaves and slavery is in the context of a *curse*. In Genesis 9:25–27 the future slave status of Canaan is attributed to the curse of Noah. Slavery is seen as unnatural, fallen and accursed, in no way an essential and unchangeable part of the 'nature of things'. But the highest point of the Old Testament's ethical critique of slavery is found again on the lips of Job and affirms the created equality of master and slave. Speaking of his own slaves he says,

> Did not he who made me in the womb make them?
> Did not the same One form us both within our
> mothers? (31:15).[6]

This gem from the creation ethic comes closer than anything else in the Old Testament to the finality of Paul's assertion that slave and free are one in Christ (Gal. 3:28). And if, in the light of the latter text, the abolition of slavery was not accomplished in Christendom for centuries, let alone by the New Testament church, we can hardly stand in critical judgment on Old Testament Israel for tolerating it with such a high degree of humanity and compassion.

---

[6] A similar application of the created equality of all mankind is found elsewhere in the wisdom tradition, *cf.* Pr. 14:31; 17:5; 29:13.

ACCEPTANCE AND AFFIRMATION

The clearest example of a socio-cultural pattern which Israel shared with surrounding societies was that of the importance of kinship, and the range of rights and responsibilities it conferred on individuals. The family is, of course, a vital basic unit of all human society. In ancient Semitic culture it took the larger form of the 'extended family', a household incorporating several generations vertically and several nuclear families horizontally, plus slaves, and resident employees. Here in particular it was of prime importance in social structure and cohesion.

Two features of family life in this wider Semitic culture stand out. First, there was the strength of the bonds of kinship, and the obligation felt towards them. This was not only so in terms of 'lateral' kinship – the demands of brotherhood. It also had a 'vertical' dimension in two directions. On the one hand there was a powerful respect for one's ancestors. In some cultures this amounted to veneration, if not actual worship. At any rate, one's present activities were either a credit or a shame to them, and even stronger was the degree of submission to the authority of one's living parents and grandparents. On the other hand, it was of prime importance to preserve the family line into the future by the birth of children, especially sons. One 'survived', in a sense, through one's descendants, or one was 'cut off' by childlessness or the death or destruction of one's posterity.

Secondly, there was the sacredness of family land. The preservation of the ancestral inheritance was vital for two reasons particularly that corresponded to the two directions of the vertical line of kinship. On the one hand, it was the place where one's ancestors were buried, and where you too would eventually be 'gathered to them'. On the other, keeping land in the family was vital to the economic survival of the next and succeeding generations. Kinship and land, then, were tightly bound together in this cultural matrix.

THE FAMILY IN THE OLD TESTAMENT

Now this kind of socio-economic pattern of family life would to some degree have been true of Israel as an ancient Semitic people, whether or not they had come to regard themselves as the people of Yahweh. But, given that they did in fact so regard themselves, and given that the maintenance of the national relationship with Yahweh was of paramount importance, the role of the kinship-land basis of society had an even greater significance. Briefly put, the household-plus-land unit was central to the triangle of relationships between God, Israel and the land, outlined in Part One. It will be helpful at this point to revive our diagram and add to it.

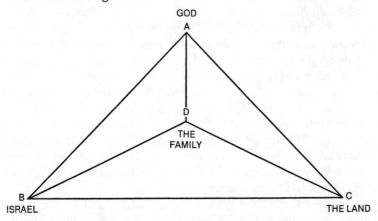

You will remember that the outer triangle represents the three major relationships of Israel's self-understanding. There was the primary covenant relationship between God and Israel (AB); God was the ultimate owner of the land (AC); and the land was given to Israel for an inheritance (CB). Now the family, which will stand as shorthand for what I have described as the extended family plus its land, was the basic, central unit in each of these dimensions. First, it was the basic unit of Israelite social and kinship structure (BD), with important military and judicial functions. Second, it was the basic economic unit of Israelite land tenure (CD). We saw some of the implications of this in terms of rights and responsibilities in chapter 3. Third, it was of pivotal importance in the experience of the covenant relationship (AD). It was by belonging within such a family that an individual could claim membership of the covenant people, whether by birth or (as in the case of slaves or resident aliens) by residence. It was by the teaching that was laid upon *parents* as a duty (*cf.* Dt. 6:6–9, 20–25; 11:18–21) that knowledge of the covenant and its obligations would be preserved from one generation to another. And it was within the family that some of the primary cultic acts took place, such as circumcision, Passover and the redemption of firstborn sons (Ex. 12; 13).

So all three realms, social, economic and theological, were closely bound together (as we have already seen), and all three had the family as their focal point. It can at once be appreciated, therefore, how anything which threatened to break up the 'lower triangle' (BCD), the socio-economic fabric of the nation, would *thereby* endanger the national covenant relationship with God. It would undermine its roots and soil, the network of free land-owning families. In view of all this, it is not at all surprising to find that there is a deep concern in the Old Testament to protect the family, both by affirming with theological support those customs which were already part of the kinship culture and by specific protective legislation.

This protection was both internal and external. *Internally*, the family was legally protected from the disruption of its domestic authority structure. Respect for parents and acceptance of their teaching and disciplining role were reinforced with heavy religious sanction. Likewise also, it was protected from disruption of its sexual integrity. Adultery and other irregular sexual liaisons were severely prohibited. *Externally*, the law sought to protect a family from the diminution or total loss of its material substance and thereby of its economic viability and social standing.

This brings into much sharper focus the importance of some of the social Commandments of the Decalogue. When we see them within this Israelite, covenantal and social, context, then we can relate the Fifth and Seventh Commandments (commanding honour for parents and prohibiting adultery respectively) to the internal protection of the family, and the Eighth and Tenth (prohibiting theft and coveting) to its external protection. None of these moral requirements is in itself unique to Israel. All of them are well documented in other contemporary societies and would have been found in Israel simply as a human society. In terms of an overall view of biblical ethics, we can say that such moral requirements are part of the way God has ordered human society as a whole. However, because Israel were conscious of a unique relationship with God, and because they grounded the experience and perpetuation of that relationship in their own family-centred socio-economic system, these Commandments took on a much more powerful theological rationale. Alongside the more obviously 'religious' first four Commandments, these social Commandments took their place as bulwarks of the covenant relationship in its social manifestation. This is evident even from the simple fact that they are included in the Decalogue, that summary of covenant law so closely associated with the sealing of the covenant between God and Israel at Sinai.

The importance of each of these Commandments can then further be seen in the small galaxies of supporting laws, exhortation and motivation which surround them. The Fifth Commandment, 'the first commandment with a promise' (Eph. 6:2), incorporates its own motivation in a promise significantly to do with life in the land. But it was sanctioned also by specific legislation concerning respect for parents[7] as well as by the theological motif of the filial relationship between Israel and God. Sonship demanded obedience.[8] The Seventh Commandment was translated into specific legislation also.[9] Interestingly, the polemic against adultery in the wisdom tradition is concentrated on its social and economic effects.[10] And again, the abhorrence and destructiveness of adultery is underlined by the theological employment of it as a figure for Israel's unfaithfulness to God.[11]

The Eighth Commandment subsumes a large number of laws to do with property offences of all kinds.[12] Elsewhere theft is condemned as incompatible with covenant allegiance (Ps. 50:16–18) and Zechariah pronounces a fearsome curse on the thief (5:3f.), just as Micah had seen covetousness as the 'crime' behind the economic oppression of his day (2:1f.). Alongside this one could place the protection of one's estate by the prohibition on removing boundary stones (Dt. 19:14; 27:17), the remedial institutions such as the redemption of the land of an impoverished kinsman and the jubilee (Lv. 25:23ff.) and the levirate marriage to preserve a childless man's inheritance (Dt. 25:5–10).

In all these ways, then, the family's socio-economic and cultural importance was affirmed and its instinctive protection was amplified and transformed into a major ethical imperative

---

[7] *E.g.* Ex. 21:15, 17; Dt. 21:18–21; 27:16. *Cf.* Pr. 1:8; 30:17.
[8] *Cf.* Dt. 14:1; Is. 1:2; Mal. 1:6.
[9] The following laws refer to a wide range of sexual offences, as well as adultery, which would threaten the sexual stability and integrity of the extended family: Lv. 18; 20:10–21; Nu. 5:11–31; Dt. 22:13–30.
[10] See Pr. 2:16–22; 5; 6:24–35; 7.
[11] *E.g.* Je. 3; Ezk. 16; Ho. 1 – 3.
[12] *E.g.* Ex. 22:1–15; Lv. 6:1–7.

grounded in Israel's own distinctive historical and redemptive theology. At this point covenant and culture coalesced.

CHRISTIANS AND CULTURE

We now have to ask whether the Old Testament's approach to the social and cultural aspects of its own day has anything to teach us as Christians about our response to the society and culture in which we live. The first thing to be said is that the variety of the Old Testament response rules out simplistic views on our part. We can neither wholly accept the culture of our society as good or at least tolerable, nor wholly reject it as irretrievably evil and abhorrent. A discriminating approach is clearly called for.

In the first place, the Old Testament leads us to expect that there will be some aspects of fallen human society which must be rejected as abhorrent to God. The only Christian response to them is renunciation and separation. It also gives us some clue on how to identify such features. Broadly one could say that the categories of what was socially prohibited to Israel included the following four in particular: the idolatrous, the perverted, that which was destructive of persons and callousness to the poor.

Do we not need the severity of the Old Testament's strictures against the subtle, as well as the blatant, idolatries of our age and culture? Christians are often as prone as Israel to relegate God unconsciously to salvation and Sundays, while we serve the golden calves and Baals of materialistic, secular culture in 'real life'.

Do we not need the cold clarity of the Old Testament's exposure of perversion, in an age where every moral value is questioned or turned inside out? It is significant how closely Paul links idolatry with perversion, *not only* in the realm of sexual practice, but also in a whole intellectual climate and in the realm of truth and falsehood (Rom. 1:18–32).

Do we not need the indignant revulsion of the Old Testament at the destruction of the weak and innocent, in such practices as ritual prostitution and child sacrifice? The pornography trade has elements of both in taking over from the economic exploitation of women and children in earlier eras – not that the latter is by any means eradicated.

Do we not need the Old Testament's uncompromising critique of all that oppresses and callously 'tramples on the heads of the poor' (Am. 2:7; Mi. 3:2f. is even more blood-curdling)? If the sin of Sodom was to be 'arrogant, overfed and unconcerned' and callously unhelpful to the poor and needy (Ezk. 16:49), then large sections of the Christian church are dwelling at ease, not in Zion, but in Sodom.

No doubt the reader can add his own contemporary and local content to what may be regarded as idolatrous, perverted, destructive or callous. Here at least is a framework. Israel was called to fight these things. There is a battle for the church as well.

In the second place, the experience of Old Testament Israel prepares us to allow for the fact that society is fallen. Even God does so! That is the point of Jesus' saying that while, from the beginning, God's creation purpose was lifelong marriage, nevertheless he 'allowed' divorce 'for your hardness of heart' (Mt. 19:8, RSV). If divorce could be tolerated within Israel as God's redeemed people, though not without criticism and the teaching of the higher standard, it seems to me we must agree to its being tolerated within secular society. Not that it should pass without criticism and, more than that, positive working to uphold the highest, absolute standards and to enable people to approximate to them.

This principle must then apply to wider areas of social and political life. Christians are constantly in the position of having to live and work in, and cope with, situations and structures which they know fall short of God's standards. Some things have to be tolerated while at the same time we work, like salt or yeast, for change.

Polygamy, for example, may no longer be a live ethical issue in the West, but in other parts of the world it still faces Christians and demands an answer. From the perspective of a full biblical ethic we have to insist, of course, that polygamy is morally contrary to God's intention for marriage. The divorce sayings of Jesus, by regarding as an adulterer a man who divorces a wife and marries another, by implication rule out the taking of other wives as a valid option for Christians. So certainly a Christian may not *become* a polygamist. But what of the situation where a man in a polygamous culture already has several wives, and then becomes a Christian? Are we to say that his only course is to divorce all his wives but one? The Old Testament would surely regard that as replacing a lesser evil with a far greater one – from the wives' point of view. An Israelite might have gone on to give some pragmatic justification for tolerating polygamy. In a society without normal gainful employment for women, without welfare benefits for the single, divorced or widowed, and where childlessness was deepest shame, he might have argued that it was unquestionably better for every woman to be some man's wife, even polygamously, than to face the alternative – usually either prostitution or the parlous plight of widowhood. Some degree of toleration, combined with a radical and theological critique and a proclamation of the higher ideal, seems to be suggested by the light of the Old Testament.

One might also note Paul's handling of a comparable moral problem as regards marriage and divorce. He commanded that a Christian should not marry an unbeliever. But if one partner in a marriage *became* a Christian, he or she was not to divorce the unbeliever – unless the latter wished to divorce, in which case he granted the believing partner freedom. His principle seems to have been that personal commitments undertaken before conversion should be honoured from the new Christian's side. To remain married to an unbeliever was preferable to initiating divorce. It is arguable that Paul would have adopted a similar approach and toleration to the converted polygamist (*cf.* 1 Cor. 7:12–24).

Similarly, though we may have technically abolished slavery, there remain structures of economic and industrial life which fall far short of God's standards for human dignity. Christians have to tolerate these to the extent of being able to work within them and address them. At the same time, however, they must seek to challenge and reform them in the light of the Old Testament's own clear principles of justice, fair trade and compassion for the weakest.

Once again, the incarnation of God in Jesus greatly assists and inspires us in this task. In becoming man – one particular man – God accepted all the limitations of the far from perfect society of first-century Palestine. Without compromising his own holiness he was able to tolerate the institutions and structures of his day, while at the same time challenging and undermining them with the revolutionary message of God's dynamic rule among men. The church, as the continuing agent and vehicle of God's kingdom, is entrusted with the same dual task. Yeast has to 'tolerate' the dough. But it will not leave it unchanged.[13]

In the third place, the Old Testament shows that there are aspects of human social and cultural life that can be taken over by God's people and affirmed positively. The church through the ages has done this in a myriad ways. It has, for example, harnessed the arts, music, painting and drama to its own ends. It has taken over pagan festivals and given them a disinfected, Christian content. Sometimes it has done so at the cost of compromising its own distinctive nature; when it took over the trappings of empire, political domination and hierarchical power structures, in principle it was doing something similar to Israel when it accepted monarchy.

But what of the example we took from Israel's social structure, the family? Surely here is something Christians can affirm as God-given and make every effort to support. Indeed so, but we need to be careful how and where we are applying our biblical insights, and whether our insights really take the *whole* biblical model into account. The warning lights of the Prologue flash again! Beware the short cut and the short circuit!

In my view, the Old Testament teaching on the family can be ethically applied in two directions: with reference to the family in ordinary secular society, on the one hand, and with reference to the church, especially the local church, as the family or household of God, on the other. In the former case our interpretation needs to be *paradigmatic*; in the latter, *typological*.

THE FAMILY IN SOCIETY

Having perceived its centrality in biblical thought, it is easy to champion the family with great zeal as at once the bedrock, bricks and cement of a healthy society. This tends to go along with an attitude which loads the family with great expectations and responsibilities, and is quick to blame families, especially parents, for many of the ills and troubles of society at large. The danger here lies in not seeing the whole model of which

---

[13] *Cf.* J. Gladwin, *In the Circumstances*, Grove Booklet on Ethics, no. 29.

the family was a functioning part. That is not applying the whole paradigm, but selling it short. For, as we have seen, the family in the Old Testament stood at the centre of a conceptual framework which gave it a pre-eminent place and which gave it social and economic support. It was only as part of that larger structure that it was able to perform its vital role in the moral and religious life of the people. So if we want to assert the importance of the family in society along truly biblical lines, we must also ask serious and critical questions about the nature of society itself.

Now, of course, we must take into account the vast sociological difference between Israelite society and modern 'Western' society. Israel was a comparatively simple society, based on a relatively stable kinship network where family ties, both horizontally in the 'present' living generation, and vertically in genealogical descent, were all-important. The 'normal' family was an extended household. This cluster of related, two-generation families between them spanned up to four generations under a single head, with their servants and other dependants. It was economically largely self-supporting and bound in to the collective security of the clan and tribe.

Modern society, as it has developed especially since the industrial revolution, has generated a wide plurality of other social bonds quite unrelated to kinship, such as profession, class, sport, regional loyalties, ethnic and religious identities in a plural society, and others. Families are smaller and splintered by social mobility. Many of the social functions once attended to by the ties of kinship are now in the hands of the state or 'para-family' agencies and organizations. This is another area where serious sociological study needs to be allied to biblical insights and principles. Such work as is being done, both Christian and secular, far from concluding that kinship and family are irrelevant and dispensable in modern society, seems to me rather to point to the urgent necessity of rethinking and refortifying the role of the family in society.[14]

Granted, we cannot load the shrunken nuclear family with the same burdens as the broad-shouldered extended household of old. Nevertheless, the nuclear family is still a fundamental factor in society, just as it was, after all, the basic unit within

[14] See especially, S. B. Clark, *Man and Woman in Christ*; also a much briefer essay, J. Gladwin, *Happy Families!*, and the secular literature referred to there.

the extended household. The extended household was like a molecule formed by the adhesion of several kinship nuclei. It was not an amorphous, free-for-all commune. On the contrary, the internal boundaries of legitimate and illegitimate sexual relationships within the close-knit kinship framework were carefully defined in a way that protected the integrity of the constituent nuclear families (see Lv. 18; 20).

Granted also that no modern society is a redeemed, covenant nation, standing in the same triangular pattern of relationships as did Israel, we can nevertheless allow that pattern to function paradigmatically in this, as in matters considered earlier. Applying it in that way to wider human society, we can still aim towards a pattern of family-in-society which in some sense reflects the Old Testament ideal. This would mean that we work towards the following goals for society:

1. Families could feel that they have a central social significance and value in the community rather than being statistical pawns of the state machine (the social angle).

2. Families could enjoy a degree of economic independent viability based on an equitable sharing of the nation's wealth (the economic angle).

3. Every family could have the opportunity of hearing the message of divine redemption in all its fullness of meaning and the freedom to respond to it and live it out through succeeding generations (the theological angle).

Idealistic? Perhaps. At least it is an idealism based on the overall biblical model. It may also be more realistic than looking for a morally revitalized society by calling for greater family cohesion, without at the same time tackling the economic pressures and evils that undermine the very thing called for. In other words, although the 'support-the-family' line is admirable as far as it goes, it does not do adequate justice to the whole biblical model unless at the same time we are striving to create social conditions in which family cohesion is economically possible, socially worthwhile and spiritually nourished.

Even less adequate is the 'blame-the-family' line. Certainly the Bible as a whole places great responsibility on the shoulders of parents. That is unquestionable, and needs to be reasserted in every generation. As well as the laws and the exhortations of wisdom to that effect, there were the sad examples of the sons of Eli (1 Sa. 2:12 – 3:18) and of Samuel (1 Sa. 8:1–3), though

Eli was blamed and Samuel was not, and the law recognizes the problem of stubborn incorrigibility (Dt. 21:18–21).

But when Israel began to fall apart morally, spiritually, economically and politically, in the later centuries of the monarchy, you do not find the prophets blaming the families for the social ills of the nation. Rather they condemned those whose greed, oppression and injustice were destroying families. The destructive and divisive effect of poverty and debt and the sheer powerlessness of ordinary families in the face of ruthless economic forces was later poignantly expressed in the plea of distraught fathers to Nehhemiah:

> We have had to borrow money to pay the king's tax on our fields and vineyards . . . we have to subject our sons and daughters to slavery . . . *but we are powerless*, because our fields and our vineyards belong to others (Ne. 5:4f.).

This is a cry with some very modern echoes.

THE FAMILY OF GOD

'We are his household (*oikos*)', says the Letter to the Hebrews, addressing Christian readers (3:2–6). The writer is referring to Numbers 12:7, where the term refers to the people of Israel as the household of God with Moses as chief steward. This is one of the many places in the New Testament where language and pictures originally applied to ancient Israel are used of the Christian church, justified by the typological relationship that exists between them, focused on Jesus the Messiah. The expression 'house of Israel' was common in the Old Testament, as was the idea of Israel as the 'house of the LORD' (in contrast to their plight when they had been in Egypt, the 'house of bondage'). The 'house of God', of course, also commonly referred to the temple in Jerusalem, but occasionally it was used figuratively of the whole people and land of Israel combined, as the household, the family, the inheritance, of God.[15] The point of the metaphor was that they were not just a nation or a collection of individuals, but a community with a sense of family oneness, a household belonging to God.

The background and content of the metaphor derive from the

[15] *E.g.* Je. 12:7; Ho. 8:1; 9:15; Mi. 4:2.

nature of the actual Israelite family, which we have already looked at in some detail. Two of its features may be emphasized in this context. First, it was a centre of worship, teaching and a vital agent in maintaining the continuity of the traditions and faith of the nation from generation to generation. Secondly, it was the place of inclusion, belonging and protection for the individual. It was where the individual found the substance and experience of his status as a member of the covenant people of God. That was the major reason for the special care commanded for widows, orphans and strangers – those who lacked the natural inclusion and protection of a household.

In the New Testament, the Christian church, as we have noted, saw itself as the true inheritor of the title 'House of Israel', as the family of God, both in the sense of the whole church (corresponding to the nation of Israel),[16] and in the sense of the smaller local church communities (corresponding in several ways to the Israelite extended family household). It is the second that is of greater interest to us here. The use of family and household imagery for the local Christian churches was, of course, greatly facilitated by the historical fact that many of them originated as converted households and actually met in homes.

> What could be conveyed by the idea of the family of God had, in fact, already come into being in the primitive Christian community through the house churches. The household as a community . . . formed the smallest unit and basis of the congregation. The house churches mentioned in the NT (Acts 11:14; 16:15, 31, 34; 18:8; 1 Cor. 1:16; Phlm. 2; 2 Tim. 1:16; 4:19) no doubt came into being through the use of homes as meeting places.[17]

Accordingly, the two features of the old Israelite family mentioned above are both seen to be operative in the New Testament local church family. It was the place of worship and teaching. Homes were used for the preaching of the gospel (Acts 5:42; 20:20). The Lord's Supper was celebrated there (Acts 2:46), and baptism was administered (1 Cor. 1:16; Acts 16:15).

---

16 *Cf.* Lk. 1:33; Eph. 2:19; Heb. 3:3–6; 8:8–10.
17 J. Goetzmann, 'House' in C. Brown (ed.), *New International Dictionary of New Testament Theology*, 2 (Paternoster, 1976), p. 250.

And the letters of Paul to his churches envisage them as living, learning and worshipping together in a 'household' spirit. Indeed, Paul operates the correspondence between church and actual family life in reverse, when he insists that those who exercise authority within the pastoral and teaching life of the church family must have proved themselves capable of managing their own household (1 Tim. 3:4f., *cf.* 3:15).

But it was also the place of belonging and inclusion. From an ethical point of view, this is perhaps the feature to be emphasized here. Christians are born into and so belong within the family of God. Therefore, in company with the other members among whom he has placed us, we share the responsibilities and the privileges of family membership. Among the responsibilities comes an obligation to share the family's 'substance', in the social and economic demands of genuine *koinōnia* fellowship, which we discussed in chapter 4. This also extended to a more general sense of mutual obligation within the family, as summed up by Paul: 'Therefore, as we have opportunity, let us do good to all people, especially to those who belong to the family of believers' (Gal. 6:10). The pervasive New Testament ethical emphasis on 'love for the brethren' is another expression of the 'family first' motif.

The primary privilege is, of course, that of full inclusion within the family of God, thus sharing all the blessings of the promised inheritance. The Christian believer, Jew or Gentile, is no longer, like the guest or resident alien, a 'para-family' person (*paroikos*), but has been given the status of a blood-relative (Eph. 2:19). But another important function of the church family was seen to be the provision of a kind of spiritual compensation in cases where the natural human family ties of a member had been disrupted as a result of his response to the gospel. This disruption of natural family relationships was also something foreseen in the Old Testament and commented on by Jesus himself.

The way in which the Gospels take up Micah's prophecy of the end-time (Mic. 7:6 = Matt. 10:35f.; Lk. 12:53) indicates that the primitive community had to reckon with the disruption of the family for the sake of the Gospel. Those who take this upon themselves are promised 'now in this time' new 'houses and brothers and sisters and mothers and children' (Mk.

10:29f.; Matt. 19:29; Lk. 18:29f.). The place of the disrupted family is taken by the family of God, the Christian community.[18]

One has to ask whether many local church families are sufficiently aware of this dimension of their reason for existence. Are they providing that social care and inclusion for those who, perhaps through very costly deliberate choice, come to them in circumstances that correspond to the widow, the orphan and the stranger of the Old Testament?

So, once again we find that social and cultural aspects of ancient Israel's life feed through typologically into our understanding of the New Testament people of God, and then issue forth into new and perpetually relevant ethical principles. In this context it is therefore very interesting to notice that one of the paramount blessings commonly discovered by churches which experience a renewal of their spiritual life is a revival of a truly biblical fellowship. There is a rediscovery of the true social nature and function of the church as the household of God and of the privileges and responsibilities it entails. It is satisfying to realize that this has a depth and richness that owes much to the Old Testament soil in which the New Testament church had its roots and from which it drew its ethical nourishment – even if many of those in today's church who are enjoying this rediscovery are, as yet, unaware of these origins.[19]

---

[18] *Ibid.*

[19] *Cf.* R. Davidson's comment, referring to the impact of the covenant community ethic of the Old Testament, 'We need not be surprised that, with the failure to take the Church with full seriousness as a basic datum for the Christian ethic, we find ourselves in a situation where, on the one hand, we hear repeated appeals concerning the need to rediscover the meaning of Christian fellowship, and on the other, the Church has by and large lost the sense of corporate discipline . . .' ('Some Aspects of the Old Testament Contribution to the Pattern of Christian Ethics', *Scottish Journal of Theology*, 12, 1959, p. 386).

9
The way of the individual

THE INDIVIDUAL IN COMMUNiTY

We arrive now, in the concluding chapter, at the point where some might have expected us to begin, namely Old Testament personal ethics: the moral demand God makes upon the individual in his whole course of life and in his daily living. This order has been quite deliberate. It is our contention, as noted in chapter 2, that the individual aspects of Old Testament theology and ethics cannot be appreciated apart from an understanding of the community that God called into being in his election and redemption of Israel. That is why we have devoted the foregoing chapters to the social aspects of Israel as a nation before narrowing the focus to the individual. In fact, the distinction between social and personal ethics is not always helpful or appropriate in the Old Testament, for individual ethics are 'community-shaped'.

We have to undergo a certain reorientation in our habitual pattern of ethical thought in this matter if we are to see things from an Old Testament perspective. We tend to begin at the personal level and work outwards. Our emphasis is to persuade people to live a certain kind of life according to this and that moral standard. If enough individuals live up to such-and-such a morality, then, almost as a by-product, society itself will be improved or at least maintained as a healthy, happy, safe environment for individuals to pursue their personal goodness. *This* is the kind of person you must be; *that* kind of society is a bonus in the background.

The Old Testament tends to place the emphasis the other

way round: here is the kind of society that God wants. His desire is for a holy people for his own possession, a redeemed community, a model society through whom he can display a prototype of the new humanity of his ultimate redemptive purpose.

Now if that is the kind of society God wants, what kind of person must you be once you belong to it? How can anyone 'live a life worthy of the calling you have received' (*cf.* Eph. 4:1)? Individual ethics are thus derivative from the theology of the redeemed people of God. Put another way, individual ethics in the Old Testament, just as much as social ethics, are *covenantal*. The covenant was established between God and Israel as a nation, but its moral implications affected every individual within it.

This feature of Old Testament ethics is wholly in accord with the ethical emphasis of the New Testament. Much of the ethical instruction there is given in the context of the nature of the community God has called into being in Christ, *i.e.*, in the context of the church, living, learning and worshipping together and serving Christ in the world. Thus, for example, the great ethical chapters of Ephesians 4 – 6 begin with the call to 'live a life worthy of the calling you have received'. From the preceding chapters this means the calling to be a member of God's new society, the miracle of social and spiritual reconciliation he has created through Christ. The *personal* moral standards of the later chapters are asserted on the basis of membership of the redeemed *community* expounded in the earlier ones.

So, one possible way to assemble a substantial quantity of the moral requirements of God upon the individual would be to work through the foregoing chapters on Israelite society and produce appendices containing the logical moral implications for the individual. For example, if God desired a society characterized by economic equality and compassion, then it required individuals to forgo selfishness and resist the temptation to cash in unjustly on the misfortunes of a neighbour. If he wanted a society founded on justice and ordered by laws known and upheld, then it was up to individual judges to act impartially and incorruptibly. And so one could go on through the whole spectrum of social characteristics, drawing out their individual entailments.

Since readers can make their own deductions, they would

find it tedious to wade through lengthy lists of results which are fairly obvious. The only point we want to establish here is this matter of perspective: it is the nature of the *community* God seeks (and will, in the eschatological vision, ultimately create) which governs the kind of *person* he approves. Social and personal are inseparable in Old Testament ethics.

PERSONAL RESPONSIBILITY

However, having made that point, we must be careful to stress that this does not mean that such a community-orientated ethic in any way replaces, let alone diminishes, the responsibility of the individual. The obligation of an individual oarsman to pull his weight is no less, just because the object of the exercise is for the whole crew to fulfil the expectations of their coach and win races. Likewise, for all its emphasis on the corporate aspect of God's moral demand, the Old Testament never loses sight of, never waives, the obligation on the individual to live uprightly before God. The personal accountability implicit in the first question in the Bible, addressed to Adam, 'Where are you?' (Gn. 3:9), extends to every human individual he represented. So, too, does the accountability for our fellow human beings implicit in God's question to Cain, 'Where is your brother?' (Gn. 4:9). Such Godward accountability for ourselves and for one another is of the essence of being human.

The story of the redeemed nation begins with the faith and obedience of an individual, Abraham. The patriarchal narratives are models of the power, providence and patience of God in the lives of individuals, especially of Jacob/Israel, which would in due course be so manifest and necessary in the history of the nation. At Sinai the covenant made with the individual Abraham for the sake of his descendants is renewed and expanded with the redeemed generation of those descendants, and then applied to every individual. The essence of the covenant relationship is corporate: 'I shall be your God; you shall be my people.' Here 'you' and 'your' are plural. But the primary demand of the covenant is addressed to the individual, with a singular 'you': 'You shall have no other gods before me.' The same is true of the rest of the Ten Commandments, and indeed of a substantial number of the detailed laws of the Pentateuch. The earliest law code, the 'Book of the Covenant' (Ex. 21 – 23), operates legislatively on the unmistakable ground of individual responsibility and liability before the law. Indeed, as we saw in chapter 7, vicarious or collective forms of punishment, which excused or diminished the individual's liability, were legally excluded in the realm of normal, human judicial procedure (Ex. 21:31; Dt. 24:16).

Moving from the law to the prophets, it is, of course, obvious that the primary calling of the prophets was to address the nation, or individuals who represented the nation, such as kings and other leaders of national influence. However, in the midst of this social and corporate task, they did not hesitate to confront individuals with the moral challenge of the word of God addressed to specific individual acts. Deborah rebuked Barak for his lethargy (Jdg. 4:8f.). Samuel challenged Saul regarding his disobedience (1 Sa. 15:22f.). Nathan confronted David with his adultery and murder (2 Sa. 12:1–10). Elijah denounced Ahab for injustice and murder (1 Ki. 21:17ff.). Isaiah, failing to inspire trust in God in King Ahaz, rebuked him for his faithless disobedience (Is. 7:1–13). Jeremiah opposed the false prophets, collectively (Je. 23:9–40) and individually (Je. 28).

Ezekiel has often been credited with the introduction of his insight on individual responsibility as though it were something new in the ethical thought-world of Israel (Ezk. 18). But this view has been abandoned by those who have looked more closely both at the true relationship between corporate and individual in Israelite thought, and at what Ezekiel was actually arguing. On the one hand, the fact that Israel had a strong concept of corporate solidarity did not mean, as some scholars in the past have maintained, that they had little sense of individual responsibility. The individuality of the early legal texts, centuries before Ezekiel, proves that.

On the other hand, Ezekiel was involved in an 'evangelistic' exercise (see the ending of ch. 18), for the purpose of which he needed to clear away false notions which were being used as a pretext to avoid responsibility. The exiles were blaming their fate on previous generations. Ezekiel makes them face up to their own guilt and responsibility. He does so by refuting a popular proverb (18:2) and then expounding a doctrine of personal ethics quite consistent with Deuteronomy 24:16. His sermon certainly gives a new depth and challenge to personal responsibility; he sets out clearly the life or death issues involved in moral choices and habits. But it is a development of well-established Old Testament faith, not a radical innovation.

MODELS OF MORALS

We move on now from the general considerations of the last two sections to something more specific. For the Old Testament provides us with a number of models of the kind of personal ethical life that is pleasing to God (and of the opposite). It is not the multitude of actual individuals who populate the pages of Old Testament history that we have in mind, though these constitute a rich quarry for personal moral lessons, as every Sunday school teacher knows. Rather, our concern now is with the character portraits which occur in various forms, giving an identikit picture of the typical qualities of the righteous person. We shall look at three such models.

1. THE WISE MAN
The Wisdom literature of the Old Testament, for all its international connections and assimilations, stands firmly within the mainstream of Israel's Yahwistic faith. As its theme verse insists, 'The fear of the LORD is the beginning [or first principle] of wisdom' (Pr. 9:10).[1] The Wisdom literature has a deep social concern, like the law and the prophets, but the bulk of its sayings are directed at the individual, to inform, forewarn, correct, and guide in that path of life which is both pleasing to God and in the individual's own best interests.

Although the prevailing interest of Proverbs appears to be man and his daily living, there is an interesting and indirect God-centredness underlying it. So much of the human character, behaviour and values which are commended do in fact reflect the known character of God, as revealed elsewhere in the Old Testament. In this respect the personal ethics of Proverbs bear out the point made in chapter 2 about Old Testament ethics, including a strong element of imitation of the ways

[1] For a study of this meaning of the text, see Henri Blocher, 'The fear of the LORD as the "principle" of wisdom' in the *Tyndale Bulletin*, 28, 1977, pp. 3–28.

of God himself. A few examples will sketch in the outlines of this particular model.

'*God created man in his own image. Male and female he created them.*' Human sexuality is a dimension of the image of God in man, and is therefore infinitely precious. The wise man therefore avoids any abuse of it, especially the destructive consequences of seduction and adultery (Pr. 2:16–22; 5; 6:20–35; 7). Instead, he finds continually fresh delight and joys in faithful marriage (5:15–19; 31:10–31; *cf.* Song).

God is father. The parent–child relationship is used as a figure for God's relationship to his people. So we find that a lot of the teaching in Proverbs is cast in a 'father-to-son' form, which has a divine–human ambiguity about it. But there is nothing ambiguous about the authority that is expected of human fathers and mothers, or the discipline and punishment which is affirmed as a function, not a denial, of familial love (Pr. 13:24; 15:5; 19:18; 22:15). Conversely, humility and obedience are required of the 'wise son' (13:1, 18); the sage feels the joys and pains of parenthood as keenly as God feels for his wayward people (10:1; 17:21; 19:26; 23:24f.).

God is righteous, both as king and judge. So Proverbs has plenty to say to the individual who finds himself in either of those offices. Political and judicial justice matter as much to the sage as to the law-giver and prophet (Pr. 16:10, 12–15; 17:15; 18:5; 20:8, 26; 22:22; 28:3, 16; 29:14; 31:1–9).

God is love. His unmerited kindness and infinite faithfulness were keynotes in the praises of Israel. Such qualities are to be reflected in human friendships. One of the most attractive features of the wise man of Proverbs is the quality of his friendship, the subtlety and maturity of his social skills. He knows the value of tact (15:1), confidentiality (11:13), patience (14:29), honesty (15:31f.; 27:6), forgiveness (17:9), loyalty (17:17; 18:24), considerate behaviour (25:17; 27:14), and practical help (27:10). And he knows the dangers of bought friendship (19:4), of gossip (20:19), anger (22:24f.), flattery (27:21) and misplaced sympathy (25:20).

God is compassionate and generous. The history of Israel, including the delivery from slavery and gift of the land, proved that. Practical concern for the poor was therefore laid on the shoulders of every Israelite. Many of the sayings of the sage concerning wealth and poverty and economic justice have a thoroughly modern relevance (Pr. 11:24f.; 14:31; 17:5; 19:17; 21:13; 22:9, 16).

God is a worker, whose infinite skill in creation (*cf.* Pr. 8) he has transmitted in a finite degree to man, his own image. Man, too, is a worker by nature and design (*cf.* ch. 4). Accordingly, the virtues and rewards of work are set before the individual in Proverbs, contrasted with the 'sluggard'. This latter figure is portrayed vividly in tragi-comic colours. But he is more than a laughing-stock. His deliberate, habitual and absurdly rationalized laziness is a denial of his humanity and an insult to his Maker (Pr. 12:11; 14:23; 18:9; 22:13; 24:30–34; 26:13–16; 28:19).

God speaks. This is one of the chief and most distinctive features of the *living* God of Israel, and one of his highest gifts to humanity is the boundless power of verbal communication. Words matter deeply to the sage, for he sees them as no less powerful vehicles of good or evil than deeds. So he has a lot of advice for the 'wise man' about his use or abuse of words (Pr. 12:19, 22; 13:3; 14:5; 15:2, 23; 18:6–8, 20f.).

Above all, *God is sovereign.* He has given to each person freedom and responsibility in his moral deliberation and choice, but in the end it will be God's will that counts (Pr. 16:1f., 9; 19:21; 21:1f., 30f.). The essence of wisdom, therefore, is to accept this ultimately incomprehensible truth and to seek God's guidance in the humility of commitment and obedience (3:5ff.; 16:3). This, in a great variety of shapes, is the meaning of the pervasive message, 'seek wisdom'. Conversely, 'the fool' in Proverbs is not merely intellectually defective (he may be very clever indeed). Rather he is the person whose life is lived deliberately, boastingly, even scoffingly, without reference to God. Wisdom and folly in the Old Testament are not primarily intellectual concepts, but moral and spiritual.

2. THE MORAL APOLOGIA

The Wisdom literature includes Job. That powerful reflection on the relationship between personal morality and undeserved suffering furnishes us with another example of the identikit model of personal ethics – the moral apologia, or self-defence. Job, of course, defends his own moral uprightness throughout the book. His whole case is that his suffering has not been brought about by his own wickedness. But the climax of his case comes in chapter 31, a chapter of superb poetic and ethical power, in which Job invokes a long series of self-curses in support of his claim to have led an upright life.

Because of the curse-formula of the speech, the ethical points are necessarily framed in the negative. Job is rehearsing the kind of deeds he has not been guilty of, the kind of person he has not been. But the negatives can easily be processed into positive prints, snapshots of the kind of person Job actually was, or was claiming to be. In summary, the list includes the following:

- to have refrained from lust (1)
- and from actual adultery (9–12)
- to have been honest in trade (5f.)
- to have acted justly with his slaves (13–15)
- to have been generous and compassionate to all classes of the poor (16–23)
- to have eschewed idolatry, whether in the form of materialism or of astrology (24–28)
- to have controlled his thoughts and tongue (29f.)
- to have shown hospitality (31f.)
- not to have avoided open confession of sin (33f.)[2]
- to have followed the economic laws of Israel regarding both land and labourers (38–40).

Two things are worthy of comment. One is the breadth of moral behaviour that is included. It extends from the thoughts of the heart, through words, private actions, sexual and family affairs, to economic, judicial, social and public conduct. The other is the role played by God in the moral reasoning. He is all-seeing (4), and evaluates every act (6, 14). He is the Creator of all men and therefore the protector of their equal rights (15). He holds the sanction of judgment upon wrongdoing (23), especially on idolatry which is disloyalty to him (28). In short, he is the inescapable God, and the whole of life is lived before him, under his moral inspection. As another sage had said,

> Death and Destruction lie open before the LORD –
> how much more the hearts of men! (Pr. 15:11).

---

[2] This factor shows that Job was not claiming absolute moral perfection.

A second example of this moral self-defence is found on the lips of Samuel in his farewell speech when he hands over political power to Saul (1 Sa. 12:2–5). It is much shorter and refers only to the sphere of social morality, as was appropriate to the occasion. Samuel was handing in the accounts for his public leadership, and desired public testimony of his incorrupt tenure of office. Nevertheless, his list of questions and the people's response, exonerating him from any charge of theft or extortion (personal profit from public office), and from bribery (personal profit from judicial power), indicate the qualities of public integrity that were expected even then. Indeed, it was the failure of Samuel's sons to maintain his standards that triggered the successful bid for kingship (1 Sa. 8:1–5).

A third list of virtues and vices that might be included here is the repeated list in Ezekiel 18. It is not so much a particular individual's moral apologia, as God outlining the typical features of righteousness and unrighteousness as they manifest themselves in succeeding generations. Again the list is specific, and overlaps with Job and Samuel at several points. The sins there said to be avoided by the righteous person are:

- idolatry
- adultery and other sexual offences
- oppression of the poor, such as by failing to return pledges taken for debt
- robbery
- failure to feed the hungry and clothe the naked
- lending for exorbitant profit through usury
- failure to judge fairly in law-suits
- violence and murder.

We note again how the Old Testament intermingles what we tend to keep in separate compartments as 'private' and 'public' morality. Also noteworthy is the point that failure to do positive good is a sin. The complacent attitude that every minister battles with, 'Of course I'm a Christian; I never do anyone any harm', would have been curtly dismissed by Ezekiel! It was not enough, in defining the righteous, to say, 'He does not commit robbery' (18:7), without adding,

> but gives his food to the hungry
> and provides clothing for the naked (18:16).

Here is a clear foreshadowing of the moral teaching of Jesus himself.

3. THE ACCEPTABLE WORSHIPPER

There are other lists of virtues and vices in the prophets which occur in the contexts of one of the prophets' most prominent concerns: the link between morality and worship. It was a link they too often saw broken. Some of their most stinging vehemence is directed at those who presume to perform the rituals of worship while living in blatant wickedness. There was no shortage of religion and ritual in Amos's day, but the rampant social injustice made a blasphemous mockery of it. Amos said so and was ejected (Am. 4:4f.; 5:21–27; 8:5f.). Isaiah echoed the same note (Is. 1:10–17). Both have short lists of positive social ethics (Is. 1:17; Am. 5:14f.).

The shortest and yet most comprehensive positive list comes in Micah 6, and again, in the context of what constitutes acceptable worship. Having heard God's indictment of his people in 6:1–5, Micah wonders what will be appropriate as a sacrifice fit for repentance, 'With what shall I come before the LORD?' After questioning the adequacy of any offering, even of his own firstborn, he utters the memorable declaration, inescapably individual in its challenge and relevance,

> He has showed you, O man, what is good.
> And what does the LORD require of you?
> To act justly and to love mercy
> and to walk humbly with your God (Mi. 6:8).

Jeremiah was sent to the very gate of the temple, there to confront the approaching worshippers with the moral demands of the God of the covenant whom they claimed to worship and whose protection they presumed upon (Je. 7:1–11). He outlines the kind of practical behaviour that would be evidence of true repentance and contrasts it with what they are actually doing. The details of his indictment include:

- oppression of the alien, the orphan and the widow
- shedding innocent blood
- idolatry
- presumptuous false security and complacency
- theft
- adultery
- perjury.

In this context one might add Isaiah 58, which contrasts a merely ritual fasting with the ethics of true repentance. The latter include justice and provision for the poor especially and observance of the Sabbath.

It is not hard to detect echoes of the Decalogue in these passages (similarly in Hosea 4:1f.). Indeed, some scholars think that the Ten Commandments were used in public liturgy as part of the 'entrance requirements', in which case Jeremiah was reawakening people to the demands of what may have become a toothless ritual. Certainly, whether or not the Decalogue was used in this way, we do have two other clear examples of 'entrance requirement' liturgy, in Psalms 15 and 24.

> LORD, who may dwell in your sanctuary?
> Who may live on your holy hill?
> He whose walk is blameless
>   and who does what is righteous (Ps. 15:1f.).

The Psalm goes on to outline the acceptable worshipper: a person of true speech and motive; avoiding hurtful action, words and thoughts; discriminating in his associations; loyal to his word; uncorrupted by the lure of money, either through usury or judicial bribery. More succinct is Psalm 24, which brackets outward act and inward motive in the phrase 'He who has clean hands and a pure heart' (Ps. 24:4) and adds the primary qualification for acceptable worship: rejection of idolatry.

These are only the clearest examples of a theme which runs throughout the Psalms, and indeed many parts of the Old Testament: acceptable worship is inseparably linked with acceptable living. The liturgy of Israel is saturated with moral contrasts. The tone is set in the very opening Psalm. For all the depth of the Psalter's corporate awareness, the dividing line of righteousness and wickedness, blessedness and judgment meets the steps of every individual: 'Blessed is the *man* who . . .'. It is in worship that the demands of the covenant with the whole nation confront afresh the individual, even in the secret places of the heart and regarding sins hidden from public view or detection. This was the function of the list of curses in Deuteronomy 27:14–26, which left no loophole for the excuse, 'It's all right so long as nobody finds out'. Again, the contents of that list are significant, tying in with the other lists we have noted, both in general intention and in some specific details. It includes curses upon:

- idolatry
- dishonour to parents
- removal of boundary stones (economic fraud)
- leading the blind astray (social callousness)
- withholding justice from alien, orphan or widow
- sexual offences, including adultery, bestiality and incest
- secret murder
- accepting bribery for 'judicial murder'
- general failure to keep the law.

It is also in worship that moral perspectives are sharpened and readjusted to see things from God's point of view rather than through the confusion and frustration of outward appearances. This is the experience profoundly described in Psalm 73. The poet is scarcely able to hold on grimly to his personal moral integrity and his belief in God's moral justice in the face of the prosperity of the wicked and suffering of the righteous (vv. 1–16). But when he went to worship in the sanctuary (v. 17), his insight and moral assurance were restored by a fresh vision of God's ultimate purposes.

FAILURE AND FORGIVENESS

To see things from God's perspective is, of course, much more uncomfortable when one's gaze is directed at oneself. For then that awareness of personal sin, failure and inadequacy becomes acute. This brings us in our concluding section to one of the most profound and important ethical features of the Old Testament, and one of its central contributions to the faith and ethics of biblical religion, Jewish and Christian.

We have had occasion to reckon with the effects of the fall in all the areas of social ethics hitherto considered. There is no less radical and comprehensive a recognition of the effect of sin upon every aspect of personal human life as well. The verdict of Genesis could scarcely be more total: 'every inclination of the thoughts of his heart was only evil all the time' (Gn. 6:5); 'every inclination of his heart is evil from childhood' (Gn. 8:21). Thus the sage enquires rhetorically:

> Who can say, 'I have kept my heart pure;
> I am clean and without sin'? (Pr. 20:9)

He expects no answer.

So Old Testament ethics stand on a foundation of realism. Without lessening the great moral absolutes of God's demand, they take full account of man's moral predicament, ranging from sheer frailty to outright obstinate rebellion. Jeremiah, who perhaps had closer prolonged contact with wickedness than many another, saw the penetration of evil to the depths of man's constitution:

> The heart is deceitful above all things
> and beyond cure.
> Who can understand it? (17:9)

He also saw that sin could not be erased by one's own effort:

> Can the Ethiopian change his skin
> or the leopard its spots?
> Neither can you do good
> who are accustomed to doing evil (13:23).
>
> Although you wash yourself with soda
> and use an abundance of soap,
> the stain of your guilt is still before me (2:22).

But this was not a realism of despair. Awareness of sin and failure is not the paralysis of ethics in the Old Testament.

Knowing your sin does not stop you walking in the way of the LORD; it simply tells you where you have to start from, before you can set foot on it. That starting point was God's objective provision of atonement and the subjective experience of forgiveness. In the Old as well as the New Testament, gospel precedes ethics. So we can see that the detailed provisions of the elaborate Levitical sacrificial system had its ethical significance. Not only did it enable the Israelite to receive cleansing for past misdeeds, through the atoning (literally, 'covering') blood of sacrifice. It also thereby reassured him of his continuing inclusion within the covenant people of God, the only position in which the Word and will of God could be known and obeyed in the future.

But Israel also knew that God's redeeming power and purpose as well as mankind's need for forgiveness and ethical empowering both transcended the rituals of sacrifice. Even the bleak verdicts of Genesis, quoted above, are set in the context of God's miraculous deliverance of Noah, the prototype of redemption. Jeremiah, for all his pessimism, looked forward to the new covenant when,

> I will forgive their wickedness
> and will remember their sins no more (31:34).

Ezekiel, too, could see the transforming power of God, replacing hearts of stone, calloused in evil, with hearts of flesh, reborn and filled with his Spirit (36:25–27; 37:1–14).

Again we find it is the Psalmists who reveal most deeply the meaning of repentance, forgiveness and the ethical freedom and joy that issues from them. Both Psalms 25 and 32 pray for forgiveness of sins, the latter after deep conviction and confession; and both link the experience of forgiveness to the expectation of both guidance and ability in the ethical sphere. It is the *forgiven* sinner whom God enables to live as pleases him:

> . . . he instructs sinners in his ways.
> He guides the humble in what is right (Ps. 25:8f.)
> . . . you forgave the guilt of my sin.
> I will instruct you and teach you in the way you should go
> (Ps. 32:5, 8).

Perhaps no-one knew this better than David, a man who descended to the lowest of evil, yet could be called 'a man after God's own heart'. As king, he was called to give moral guidance, by example and instruction, to his people. But how could a flawed character lead others? Only by the supernatural grace of a forgiving, cleansing, renewing God.

> Create in me a pure heart, O God,
>   and renew a steadfast spirit within me.
> *Then* I will teach transgressors your ways,
>   and sinners will turn back to you (Ps. 51:10, 13).

But let us give the final word to Isaiah. For it was to people whom he had accused of being filled with the blood of wickedness and oppression, whose worship was a wearisome, sickening abomination to God, that he addressed the breath-taking invitation of God's saving 'reasonableness':

> 'Come now, let us reason together,'
>   says the LORD.
> 'Though your sins are like scarlet,
>   they shall be as white as snow;
> though they are red as crimsom,
>   they shall be like wool.'

But this saving word of gospel is at once followed by the inescapable ethical challenge:

> 'If you are willing and obedient,
>   you will eat the best from the land;
> but if you resist and rebel,
>   you will be devoured by the sword.'
>   For the mouth of the LORD has spoken
>   (Is. 1:18–20).

It is in the same book that we find the great vision that ultimately the focus of atonement will not be a place or an object, but a person, the Servant of the LORD. We see him, in the climactic 'servant song', Isaiah 52:13 – 53:12, suffering vicariously, victoriously and effectively, for sins not his own but ours. For in his redemptive purpose,

> the LORD has laid on him the iniquity of us all.
> It was the LORD's will to . . .
> make his life a guilt offering (53:6, 10).

Here is the Calvary of the Old Testament. Here, too, is the essential basis of the unity of gospel and ethics, of faith and life, in both Testaments – the sovereign grace and mercy of God. For the cross of the Messiah is the gateway, not only to life, but to living.

Bibliography

The following bibliography has been classified to follow the subject-matter of the chapters of the book, though obviously there is bound to be considerable overlap in certain areas. The main aim of these lists is to give some guidance to the student who wishes to take his researches further into the general field of Old Testament ethics, or into one of the more specialized areas.

The non-specialist reader should find that the works bearing an asterisk will deepen his understanding without being over-technical. Most of them also ought to be accessible, either in print or through libraries.

ABBREVIATIONS

ASTI	*Annual of the Swedish Theological Institute*
BA	*Biblical Archaeologist*
Bib.	*Biblica*
BJRL	*Bulletin of the John Rylands Library*
BR	*Biblical Research*
BTr	*Bible Translator*
BZAW	*Beihefte zur Zeitschrift für die alttestamentliche Wissenschaft*
CBQ	*Catholic Biblical Quarterly*
CTJ	*Calvin Theological Journal*
EQ	*Evangelical Quarterly*
ERT	*Evangelical Review of Theology*
ExT	*Expository Times*
HUCA	*Hebrew Union College Annual*
Interp.	*Interpretation*
JBL	*Journal of Biblical Literature*
JBR	*Journal of Bible and Religion*
JCSE	*Journal of Christian Social Ethics*
JETS	*Journal of the Evangelical Theological Society*
JJS	*Journal of Jewish Studies*
JNES	*Journal of Near Eastern Studies*
JQR	*Jewish Quarterly Review*
JR	*Journal of Religion*
JSOT	*Journal for the Study of the Old Testament*
JTS	*Journal of Theological Studies*

Bibliography

OudSt	Oudtestamentische Studiën
PEF/Q	Palestine Exploration Fund/Quarterly
PTR	Princeton Theological Review
RdSO	Rivista degli Studi Orientali
RIDA	Revue Internationale des Droits de l'Antiquité
RTR	Reformed Theological Review
SJT	Scottish Journal of Theology
SVT	Supplements to Vetus Testamentum
TB	Tyndale Bulletin
TGUOS	Transactions of the Glasgow University Oriental Society
VT	Vetus Testamentum

GENERAL WORKS WITH A BEARING ON OLD TESTAMENT ETHICS

Bahnsen, G. L., *Theonomy in Christian Ethics* (Craig Press, Nutley, NJ, 1979).

Barton, J., 'Natural Law and Poetic Justice in the Old Testament', *JTS* 30, 1979, pp. 1–14.

'Understanding Old Testament Ethics', *JSOT* 9, 1978, pp. 44–64.

Bream, H. N., *et al.* (ed.), *A Light unto my Path: Old Testament Studies in Honour of J. B. Myers* (Temple UP, Philadelphia, 1974).

Crenshaw, J. L. and Willis, J. T. (ed.), *Essays in Old Testament Ethics* (Ktav, New York, 1974).

*Davidson, R., *The Old Testament* (Hodder and Stoughton, 1964).

Eichrodt, W., 'The Law and the Gospel: The Meaning of the Ten Commandments in Israel and for us', *Interp.* 11, 1957, pp. 23–40.

Theology of the Old Testament II (SCM, 1967).

Ellison, H. L., 'The Significance of the Old Testament Today', *Churchman* 74, 1969, pp. 231–238.

Elmslie, W. A. L., 'Ethics', in *Record and Revelation*, ed. H. Wheeler Robinson (OUP, 1938), pp. 275–302.

*Forster, G., *Christian Ethics in the Old Testament*, Grove Booklet on Ethics, 35 (Grove Books, 1980).

Gehman, H. S., 'Natural Law and the Old Testament', in *Biblical Studies in Memory of H. C. Alleman*, ed. J. M. Myers *et al.* (Augustin, New York, 1960), pp. 109–122.

*Goldingay, J., *Approaches to Old Testament Interpretation* (IVP, 1981).

*Goldsworthy, G., *Gospel and Kingdom: Christian Interpretation of the Old Testament* (Paternoster, 1981).

Greene, W. B., 'The Ethics of the Old Testament', *PTR* 27, 1929, pp. 153–193, 313–366.

Hammershaimb, E., 'On the Ethics of the Old Testament Prophets', *SVT* 7, 1959, pp. 75–101.

Johnston, L., 'Old Testament morality', *CBQ* 20, 1958, pp. 19–25.

Kevan, E. F., *Keep His Commandments: The Place of Law in the Christian Life* (Tyndale Press, 1964).

*Kidner, F. D., *Hard Sayings* (IVP, 1972).

*Martens, E. A., *Plot and Purpose in the Old Testament* (IVP, 1981).

*Muilenburg, J., *The Way of Israel: Biblical Faith and Ethics* (Harper Torchbooks, 1961).

Nielsen, E., *The Ten Commandments in New Pespective: A Traditio-historical Approach* (SCM, 1968).

Porteous, N. W., *Living the Mystery: Collected Essays* (Blackwell, 1967).

'The Relevance of the Old Testament as the Rule of Life', in *Studia Biblica et Semitica*, Vriezen Festschrift, ed. W. C. van Unnik and A. S. van der Woude (Veenman, 1966), pp. 278–289.

Shepherd, J. J., 'Man's Morals and Israel's Religion, *ExT* 92, 1981, pp. 171–174.

Stamm, J. J., and Andrew, M. E., *The Ten Commandments in Recent Research* (SCM, 1967).

Westermann, C. (ed.), *Essays on Old Testament Interpretation* (SCM, 1963).

*Wright, C. J. H., *Using the Bible in Social Ethics*, Grove Booklet on Ethics, 51 (Grove Books, 1983).

Wright, D. F., 'The fulfilment of the Law', *Christian Graduate* 29, 1976, pp. 99–105.

CHAPTER 1: THE THEOLOGICAL ANGLE

Albrektson, B., *History and the Gods* (Gleerup, Lund, 1967).

Barr, J., 'Revelation through History in the Old Testament and in Modern Theology', *Interp.* 17, 1963, pp. 193–205.

Engelhard, D. H., 'The Lord's Motivated Concern for the Underprivileged', *CTJ* 15, 1980, pp. 5–26.

Fletcher, V., 'The Shape of Old Testament Ethics', *SJT* 24, 1959, pp. 47–73.

Freedman, D. N., 'Divine Commitment and Human Obligation: The Covenant Theme', *Interp.* 18, 1964, pp. 419–431.

Gemser, B., 'The Importance of the Motive Clause in Old Testament Law', *SVT* 1, 1953, pp. 50–66.

Hasel, G. F., 'The Problem of History in Old Testament Theology', Andrews University Seminary Studies 8, 1970, pp. 23–50.

*Kline, M. G., *The Structure of Biblical Authority* (Eerdmans, 1972).

McCarthy, D. J., 'Notes on the Love of God in Deuteronomy and the Father-Son Relationship between Yahweh and Israel', *CBQ* 27, 1965, pp. 144–147.

CHAPTER 2: THE SOCIAL ANGLE

Allen, L. C., 'Micah's Social Concern', *Vox Evangelica* 8, 1973, pp. 22–32.

Baron, S. W., *A Social and Religious History of the Jews* (New York, 2nd revised edition, vol. I, Columbia UP, New York, 1952).

Davidson, R., 'Some Aspects of the Old Testament Contribution to the Pattern of Christian Ethics', *SJT* 12, 1959, pp. 373–387.

Gottwald, N. K., *The Tribes of Yahweh: A Sociology of the Religion of Liberated Israel 1250–1050 BCE* (SCM, 1979).

Kelly, B. H., 'Word of Promise: The Incarnation in the Old Testament', *Interp.* 10, 1956, pp. 3–15.

May, H. G., 'A Sociological Approach to Hebrew Religion', *JBR* 12, 1944, pp. 98–106.

von Rad, G., *God at Work in Israel* (Abingdon, Nashville, 1980).

von Waldow, H. E., 'Social Responsibility and Social Structure in Early Israel', *CBQ* 32, 1970, pp. 182–204.

Weber, M., *Ancient Judaism* (Glencoe, Illinois, 1952); and a review of same by N. N. Glatzer, *JR* 34, 1954, pp. 133–135.

Weinfeld, W., 'The Origin of Humanism in Deuteronomy', *JBL* 80, 1961, pp. 241–249.

Bibliography

Wolf, C. U., 'Some Remarks on the Tribes and Clans in Israel', *JQR* 36, 1946, pp. 287–295.

'Terminology of Israel's Tribal Organization', *JBL* 65, 1946, pp. 45–49.

'Traces of Primitive Democracy in Ancient Israel', *JNES* 6, 1947, pp. 98–108.

Wright, C. J. H., 'The Ethical Relevance of Israel as a Society', *JCSE* (forthcoming).

CHAPTER 3: THE ECONOMIC ANGLE

Bergheim, S., 'Land Tenure in Palestine', *PEF*, 1894, pp. 191–199.

*Brueggeman, W., *The Land* (Fortress, 1977).

Davies, W. D., *The Gospel and the Land* (University of California Press, 1974).

Henry, K. H., 'Land Tenure in the Old Testament', *PEQ*, 1954, pp. 5–15.

Miller, P. D., jr., 'The Gift of God; the Deuteronomic Theology of the Land', *Interp.* 23, 1969, pp. 451–465.

von Rad, G., 'The Promised Land and Yahweh's Land in the Hexateuch', in *idem*, *The Problem of the Hexateuch* (Oliver and Boyd, 1966), pp. 79–93.

Robinson, T. H., 'Some Economic and Social Factors in the History of Israel', *ExT* 45, 1933–34, pp. 264–269, 294–300.

von Waldow, H. E., 'Israel and her Land: Some Theological Considerations', *A Light unto my Path*, ed. H. N. Bream, R. D. Heim, C. A. Moore (Temple UP, Philadelphia, 1974), pp. 493–508.

CHAPTER 4: ECONOMICS AND THE LAND

Anderson, B. W., 'The Earth is the Lord's: An Essay on the Biblical Doctrine of Creation', *Interp.* 9, 1955, pp. 3–20.

Barr, J., 'Themes from the Old Testament for the Elucidation of the New Creation', *Encounter* 31, 1970, pp. 25–30.

'Man and Nature – The Ecological Controversy and the Old Testament', *BJRL* 55, 1972–3, pp. 9–32.

Gamoran, H., 'The Biblical Law against Loans on Interest', *JNES* 30, 1971, pp. 127–134.

Ginsberg, E., 'Studies in the Economics of the Bible', *JQR* ns 22, 1932, pp. 343–408.

*Hengel, M., *Property and Riches in the Early Church* (SCM, 1974).

Lang, B., 'The Social Organization of Peasant Poverty in Biblical Israel', *JSOT* 24, 1982, pp. 47–63.

McFadyen, J. E., 'Poverty in the Old Testament', *ExT* 37, 1925, pp. 184–189.

McKenzie, J. L., 'God and Nature in the Old Testament', *CBQ* 14, 1952, pp. 18–39, 124–145.

*Moss, R., *The Earth in our Hands* (IVP, 1982).

Neufeld, E., 'The Prohibitions against Loans at Interest in Ancient Hebrew Laws', *HUCA* 26, 1955.

'Socio-economic Background of *Yobel* and S^emittah', *RdSO* 33, 1958, pp. 53–124.

North, R., *Sociology of the Biblical Jubilee*, Analecta Biblica IV (Pontifical Biblical Institute, Rome, 1954).

'The Biblical Jubilee and Social Reform', *Scripture* 4, 1951, pp. 323–335.

Porteous, N. W., 'The Care of the Poor in the Old Testament', in *idem*, *Living the Mystery* (Blackwell, 1967), pp. 143–155.

Rogerson, J. W., 'The Old Testament View of Nature: Some Preliminary Questions', *OudSt* 20, 1980, pp. 67–84.

Sloane, R. B. jr., *The Favorable Year of the Lord: A Study of Jubilary Theology in the Gospel of Luke* (Bethel Press, 1977).

Stein, S., 'The Laws on Interest in the Old Testament', *JTS* ns 4, 1953, pp. 161–170.

Sulzberger, M., 'The Status of Labor in Ancient Israel', *JQR* ns 13, 1922–23, pp. 245–302, 397–459.

*Wright, C. J. H., *What does the Lord Require?* (Shaftesbury Project Publications, Nottingham, 1978).

God's People in God's Land (Paternoster, forthcoming).

*Zimmerli, W., *The Old Testament and the World* (SPCK, 1976).

CHAPTER 5: POLITICS AND THE WORLD OF NATIONS

*Bruce, F. F., *Israel and the Nations* (Paternoster, 1963).

*Clements, R. E., *God's Chosen People: A Theological Interpretation of the Book of Deuteronomy* (SCM, 1968).

Dumbrell, W. J., 'Spirit and Kingdom of God in the Old Testament', *RTR* 33, 1974, pp. 1–10.

*Ellul, J., *The Meaning of the City* (Eerdmans, 1970).

* *The Politics of God and the Politics of Man* (Eerdmans, 1972).

Fensham, F. C., 'Legal Aspects of the Dream of Solomon', *Fourth World Congress of Jewish Studies*, Papers Vol. I (Jerusalem, 1967), pp. 67–70.

*Gladwin, J., *God's People in God's World* (IVP, 1979).

Gordis, R., 'Democratic Origins in Ancient Israel – The Biblical *edah*', in *Alexander Marx Jubilee Volume*, ed. S. Lieberman (Jewish Theological Seminary, New York, 1950), pp. 369–388.

Heaton, E. W., *Solomon's New Men: The Emergence of Ancient Israel as a Nation State* (Thames and Hudson, 1974).

Johnston, O. R., 'God and the Nations', *ERT* 1, 1977, pp. 83–93.

Lewis, A. H., 'Jehovah's International Love', *JETS* 15, 1972, pp. 87–92.

Lind, M. C., 'The Concept of Political Power in Ancient Israel', *ASTI* 7, 1968–9, pp. 4–24.

Malamat, A., 'Organs of Statecraft in the Israelite Monarchy', *BA* 28, 1965, pp. 34–65.

May, H. G., 'Aspects of the Imagery of World Dominion and World State in the Old Testament', in Crenshaw and Willis (ed.), *Essays in Old Testament Ethics* (Ktav, New York, 1974), pp. 57–76.

Mendenhall, G. E., 'The Relation of the Individual to Political Society in Ancient Israel', in *Biblical Studies in Memory of H. C. Alleman*, ed. J. M. Myers, O. Reimherr, H. N. Bream (Augustin, New York, 1960), pp. 89–108.

Mettinger, T. N. D., *Solomonic State Officials: A Study of the Civil Government Officials of the Israelite Monarchy*, Coniectanea Biblica, OT Series 5 (Lund, 1971).

Neufeld, E., 'The Emergence of a Royal-Urban Society in Ancient Israel', *HUCA* 31, 1960, pp. 31–53.

Noth, M., 'God, King and Nation in the Old Testament', in *idem*, *The Laws in the Pentateuch and other studies* (Oliver and Boyd, 1966), pp. 145–178.

Simon, U., 'The Poor Man's Ewe Lamb . . . Judicial Parable', *Bib.*, 1967, pp. 207–242.

Wolf, C. U., 'Traces of Primitive Democracy in Ancient Israel', *JNES* 6, 1947, pp. 98–108.

Yeivin, S., 'Social, Religious and Cultural Trends in Jerusalem under the Davidic Dynasty', *VT* 3, 1953, pp. 149–166.

CHAPTER 6: RIGHTEOUSNESS AND JUSTICE

Bloom, A., 'Human Rights in Israel's Thought', *Interp.* 8, 1954, pp. 422–432.
Goldingay, J. E., 'The Man of War and the Suffering Servant; The Old Testament and the Theology of Liberation', *TB* 27, 1976, pp. 79–113.
Kapelrud, A. S., 'New Ideas in Amos', *SVT* 15 (1966), pp. 193–206.
Lofthouse, W. F., 'The Righteousness of Jahveh', *ExT* 50, 1939, pp. 341–345.
*Marshall, I. H., *The Biblical Concept of Justice*, Shaftesbury Project Working paper, 8 Oxford Street, Nottingham.
Nahmani, H. S., *Human Rights in the Old Testament* (Tel Aviv, 1964).
Schofield, J. N., 'Righteousness in the Old Testament', *BTr* 16, 1965, pp. 112–116.
*Snaith, N., *The Distinctive Ideas of the Old Testament* (Epworth Press, 1944).
Stek, J. H., 'Salvation, Justice and Liberation in the Old Testament', *CTJ* 13, 1978, pp. 133–165.
*Wright, C. J. H., *Human Rights: A Study in Biblical Themes*, Grove Booklet on Ethics, 31 (Grove Books, 1979).
* *Peace and Justice in the Bible*, Shaftesbury Project Working Paper, 8 Oxford Street, Nottingham.

CHAPTER 7: LAW AND THE LEGAL SYSTEM

Alt, A., 'The Origins of Israelite Law', in *idem*, *Essays in Old Testament History and Religion* (Blackwell, 1966), pp. 81–132.
Andersen, F. I., 'The Social-Judicial Background of the Naboth Incident', *JBL* 85, 1966, pp. 46–57.
Beattie, D. R. G., 'The Book of Ruth as Evidence for Israelite Legal Practice', *VT* 24, 1974, pp. 251–267.
Bellefontaine, E., 'Deuteronomy 21:18–21 – Reviewing the Case of the Rebellious Son', *JSOT* 13, 1979, pp. 13–31.
*Boecker, H. J., *Law and the Administration of Justice in the Old Testament and Ancient Near East* (SPCK, 1981).
*Bullimore, J., *Christianity and Due Process of Law*, Grove Booklet on Ethics, 32 (Nottingham, 1979).
Diamond, A. S., 'An Eye for an Eye', *Iraq* 19, 1957, pp. 151–155.
Falk, Z. W., *Hebrew Law in Biblical Times: An Introduction* (Wahrmann, Jerusalem, 1964).
Gerstenberger, E., 'Covenant and Commandment', *JBL* 84 (1965), pp. 38–51.
Greenberg, M., 'Some Postulates of Biblical Criminal Law', in *Yehezkel Kaufmann Jubilee Volume*, ed. M. Haran (Magnes, Jerusalem, 1960), pp. 5–28.
Jackson, B. S., *Essays on Jewish and Comparative Legal History*, Studies in Judaism in Late Antiquity 10 (Brill, Leiden, 1975).
Leggett, D. A., *The Levirate and Goel Institutions in the Old Testament with Special Attention to the Book of Ruth* (Mack, New Jersey, 1974).
McKay, J. W., 'Exodus 23:1–3, 6–8 – a Decalogue for the Administration of Justice in the City Gate', *VT* 21, 1971, pp. 311–325.
McKeating, H., 'Sanctions against Adultery in Ancient Israelite Society with

some Reflections on Methodology in the Study of Old Testament Ethics', *JSOT* 11, 1979, pp. 57–72.

McKenzie, D. A., 'Judicial Procedure at the Town Gate', *VT* 14, 1964, pp. 100–104.

Mendenhall, G. E., 'Ancient Oriental and Biblical Law', *BA* 17, 1954, pp. 26–46.

Napier, B. D., 'Community under Law: On Hebrew Law and its Theological Presuppositions', *Interp.* 7, 1953, pp. 404–417.

Nicholson, E. W., 'The Decalogue as the Direct Address of God', *VT* 27, 1977, pp. 422–433.

Paul, S. M., 'Studies in the Book of the Covenant in the Light of Cuneiform and Biblical Law', *SVT* 18, 1970.

Phillips, A., *Ancient Israel's Criminal Law: A New Approach to the Decalogue* (Blackwell, 1970).

'Another Example of Family Law', *VT* 30, 1980, pp. 240–243.

'Another Look at Adultery', *JSOT* 20, pp. 3–25.

'Another Look at Murder', *JJS* 28, 1977, pp. 105–126.

'Should the Primate of All England Eat York Ham? Christians and the Old Testament', *Theology* 85, 1982, pp. 339–346.

*Wenham, G. J., 'Law and the legal system in the Old Testament', in *Law, Morality and the Bible*, ed. B. N. Kaye and G. J. Wenham (IVP, 1978).

Wiseman, D. J., 'Law and Order in Old Testament Times', *Vox Evangelica* 8, 1973,pp. 5–21.

CHAPTER 8: SOCIETY AND CULTURE

Andersen, F. I., 'Israelite Kinship Terminology and Social Structure', *BTr* 20, 1969, pp. 29–39.

Brichto, H. C., 'Kin, Cult, Land and Afterlife – a Biblical Complex', *HUCA* 44, 1973, pp. 1–54.

Burrows, M., *The Basis of Israelite Marriage*, American Oriental Series 15 (American Oriental Society, New Haven, 1938).

Chamberlain, J. H., *Man in Society: The Old Testament Doctrine* (Epworth, 1966).

Clark, S. B., *Man and Woman in Christ* (T. & T. Clark, 1981).

Ellison, H. L., 'The Hebrew Slave: A Study in Early Hebrew Society', *EQ* 45, 1973, pp. 30–35.

Fensham, F. C., 'Widow, Orphan and Poor in Ancient Near Eastern Legal and Wisdom Literature', *JNES* 21, 1962, pp. 129–139.

Gladwin, J., *Happy Families!*, Grove Booklet on Ethics, 39 (Grove Books, 1981).

Kennett, R. H., *Ancient Hebrew Social Life and Culture as Indicated in Law, Narrative and Metaphor*, Schweich Lecture, 1931 (OUP, 1933).

*Köhler, L., *Hebrew Man* (SCM, 1956).

*Mace, D. R., *Hebrew Marriage: A Sociological Study* (Epworth, 1953).

Mendelsohn, I., *Slavery in the Ancient Near East* (OUP, New York, 1949).

Mendenhall, G. E., *The Tenth Generation* (Johns Hopkins UP, 1973).

Milgrom, J., 'The Biblical Diet Laws as an Ethical System: Food and Faith', *Interp.* 17, 1963, pp. 288–301.

McKenzie, J. L., 'The Elders in the Old Testament', *Bib.* 40, 1959, pp. 522–540.

Pedersen, J., *Israel: Its Life and Culture*, I-IV (OUP, 1926 and 1940).

van der Ploeg, J., 'Slavery in the Old Testament', *SVT* 22, 1972, pp. 72–87.

Porter, J. R., *The Extended Family in the Old Testament*, Occasional Papers in Social and Economic Adminstration 6 (London, 1967).

Rodd, C. S., 'The Family in the Old Testament', *BTr* 18, 1967, pp. 19–26.

Bibliography

Rogerson, J. W., *Anthropology and the Old Testament* (Blackwell, 1978).

*de Vaux, R., *Ancient Israel: Its Life and Institutions* (Darton, Longman and Todd, 1961).

*Wolff, H. W., *Anthropology of the Old Testament* (SCM, 1974).

Wright, C. J. H., 'The Israelite Household and the Decalogue: The Social Background and Significance of some Commandments', *TB* 30, 1979.

Yaron, R., 'On Divorce in Old Testament Times', *RIDA*, 3rd series 4, 1957, pp. 117–128.

CHAPTER 9: THE WAY OF THE INDIVIDUAL

Brockington, L. H., 'The Hebrew Conception of Personality in Relation to the Knowledge of God', *JTS* 47, 1946, pp. 1–11.

Daube, D., 'Communal Responsibility', in *idem, Studies in Biblical Law* (CUP, 1947), pp. 154–189.

Fohrer, G., 'Action of God and Decision of Man in the Old Testament' in *Biblical Essays*, ed. A. H. Van Zyl (University of Stellenbosch, 1966), pp. 31–39.
'The Personal Structure of Biblical Faith', in *Fourth World Congress of Jewish Studies*, Papers Vol. I (Jerusalem, 1967), pp. 161–166.
'The Righteous Man in Job 31', in *Essays in Old Testament Ethics*, ed. J. L. Crenshaw and J. T. Willis (Ktav, New York, 1974).

Johnson, A. R., *The One and the Many in the Israelite Conception of God* (University of Wales Press, 2nd edition, 1961).

Kennedy, J., 'Riches, Poverty and Adversity in the Book of Proverbs', *TGUOS* 12, 1944–46, pp. 18–22.

Klein, W. L., 'The Model of a Hebrew Man', *BR* 4, 1959, pp. 1–7.

May, H. G., 'Individual Responsibility and Retribution', *HUCA* 32, 1961, pp. 107–120.

Mendenhall, G. E., 'The Relation of the Individual to Political Society in Ancient Israel', *Biblical Studies in Memory of H. C. Alleman*, ed. J. M. Myers, O. Reimherr, H. N. Bream (Augustin, New York, 1960), pp. 89–108.

McKenzie, J. L., 'Divine Sonship and Individual Religion', *CBQ* 7, 1945, pp. 32–47.

Porter, J. R., 'The Legal Aspects of the Concept of "Corporate Personality" in the Old Testament', *VT* 15, 1965, pp. 361–380.

von Rad, G., 'The Early History of the Form Category of I Corinthians 13:4–7', in *idem, The Problem of the Hexateuch* (Oliver and Boyd, 1966), pp. 301–317 (on Job 31).

Robinson, H. Wheeler, 'The Hebrew Conception of Corporate Personality', *BZAW* 66, 1936, pp. 49–62.

Rogerson, J. W., 'The Hebrew Conception of Corporate Personality: A Re-examination', *JTS* ns 21, 1970, pp. 1–16.

Tang, S. Y., 'The Ethical Content of Job 31: A Comparative Study', unpublished dissertation, Edinburgh University, 1967.

Index of biblical references

Genesis
1   68, 104
2   91, 105, 176
3   71, 90, 105, 199
4   105, 137, 165, 199
6   105, 209
8   209
9   164, 182
10   107
11   34, 106f.
12   33f., 107
14   106
15   48
18   28, 106, 125, 136f.
19   106, 126
23   46
41   109, 128
50   25
Exodus
1–24   21f.
2   21f., 74, 181n.
3   22, 75, 90
4   53, 95, 142
5   110
6   22, 75
9   75, 110, 142
10   110
12   109, 166, 180, 185
13   85, 185
15   53, 57, 111
19   22, 40f., 110, 125, 148, 159
20   22, 78, 148ff., 180
21–23   134, 179, 200
21   26, 77f., 154f., 164ff., 177, 180, 181n., 186n., 200
22   80, 84, 147, 155, 157n., 175n., 179, 186n.
23   26, 36, 48, 79, 85f., 156, 157n., 170f., 175n., 179f.
24   150
32   23, 28, 53
33   23, 47
34   23, 85, 148
40   47
Leviticus
6   186n.
8–15   150
17–26   150f.
18   47, 175n., 186n., 192
19   26f., 78, 80, 86, 134f., 157n., 158, 166, 171, 175n.
20   47, 142, 175n., 186n., 192
21–22   40
24   109
25   29, 56ff., 61, 78,

82ff., 86, 154ff., 179, 181n., 186
26   29, 47, 49, 78, 91
Numbers
5   186n.
12   193f.
13–14   47
15   166
23   174
26   54
32   47
34   48, 54
35   164
Deuteronomy
1–5   23
1–11   47, 151
4   35f., 53, 148, 162
5   78, 148f.
6   36, 155, 158, 169, 184
7   36, 51, 109
8   29f., 51, 53f., 72, 85, 90
9   51, 109
10   27f., 75, 147f., 158
11   54, 91, 184
12   53, 175
12–26   47, 151
14   85f., 157n., 186n.
15   26, 29, 53f., 61, 77, 79, 84, 86, 101, 155f., 157n., 179ff.
16   78, 171, 180
17   38, 84, 116ff., 144
18   77, 175n.
19   53, 83, 166, 168, 186
20   157n.
21   155, 157n., 167ff., 177f., 186n., 193
22   79, 155, 157n., 177, 186n.
23   84, 86, 154, 157n., 175n., 181
24   78, 80, 84, 86, 155, 157n., 158, 164, 166, 177, 200
25   79, 86, 134f., 155, 157n., 161, 165f., 186
26   52f., 86
27   84, 157n., 186, 208
27–28   151
28   48f., 91
29   36, 48, 151
31   169
32   53, 57, 104, 133, 151
33   40, 169
34   48
Joshua
1   48
13–19   54

Judges
4   144, 200
5   138, 144
6   154
8   118, 154
Ruth
2   86
4   87, 170
1 Samuel
1   177
2–3   192
7   48, 144
8   38ff., 48, 58, 61, 117f., 192, 205
12   205
14   170
15   200
24   25
29   181n.
31   48
2 Samuel
7   119
8   48
9   28
10   48
12   120, 200
14   120, 169
1 Kings
3   120
5   78
9   78
11   78, 121
12   78, 121
13   121f.
14   121
17   129
18   36, 73, 129
20   119
21   55, 200
2 Kings
8   120
9–10   129
14   121
2 Chronicles
19   169, 171
Nehemiah
5   84, 154, 172, 193
Job
10   137
24   84
29   170
31   137, 154, 157n., 180, 182, 203f.
Psalms
2   119
8   68
9   137
15   157n., 207
19   160
23   119, 134
24   68, 207

Psalms (cont.)
25 28, 210
32 210
34 147
35 138
36 135
41 157n.
45 144
47 110
50 149, 186
51 211
58 144
67 110
71 138
72 28, 119f., 144
73 137, 208
81 149
85 135
89 75, 136
94 172
95 85
96–98 162
96 137
97 92
98 110
99 41, 110
115 68, 75
119 160
136 52
137 49
145 137
146 28, 137, 147
147 137

Proverbs
1 186n.
2 186n., 202
3 28, 82, 203
5 176, 186n., 202
6–7 186n., 202
8 203
9 28, 201
10 28, 82, 202
11 202f.
12 203
13 73, 202f.
14 137, 147, 182n., 202f.
15 202ff.
16 145, 202f.
17 137, 182n., 202f.
18 176, 202f.
19 157n., 202f.
20 202, 209
21 203
22 147, 202f.
23 84, 202
24 203
25 202
26 203
27 202f.
28 202f.
29 145, 182n., 202
30 82, 186n.
31 145, 176, 202

Ecclesiastes
2 72
4 72
5 72f., 145
6 73
9 72

Isaiah
1 30, 36f., 107, 146, 157n., 186n., 206, 211
2 91f., 162
5 30, 56, 135, 145f.
7 200
9 147
10 146, 172
11 81, 91
13–14 85
15–16 124
19 125, 131
23 85, 124, 131
24 108
27 102
35 91, 102
40 108
41 138, 140
42 41f., 140
43 50
44 41
45 138, 140
46 138
48 42
49 41ff.
50 41
51 42
52–53 41, 211f.
56 95
58 37, 78f., 146n., 157n., 207
60 131
61 102, 133

Jeremiah
2 30, 209
3 186n.
4 110
7 30, 62, 79, 146n., 149, 157n., 206
12 137, 193n.
13 209
17 79, 209
22 78, 119, 146n.
23 50, 119, 139, 200
28 200
29 126f.
31–33 85
31 91, 160, 210
32 50, 82f., 122
34 154, 172
38 129

Ezekiel
16 30, 61f., 107, 109, 146n., 186n., 188
18 146n., 173, 200, 205f.
20 30
22 146n.
26–28 124
28–29 125
31 125
34 119
36 173, 210
37 210
47 77, 95

Daniel
2 128
3 128, 130
6 128

Hosea
1 129
1–3 186n.
2 60, 81, 91
4 40f., 115, 146, 149, 169, 207
5 84
8–9 193n.
10 135
12 146n.
13 30

Amos
1–2 123
2 30, 56, 146n., 154, 172, 188
3 141
4 107, 146, 206
5 49, 56, 146, 206
6 146n.
7 49, 122
8 79, 146n., 206
9 36, 81, 109, 140

Micah
2 55f., 82, 146n., 186
3 37, 146n., 188
4 77, 81, 92, 193n.
6 30, 135, 146n., 206
7 146n., 195

Habakkuk
1 137

Zephaniah
3 130

Haggai
2 131

Zechariah
5 186
7 146n., 157n.,
14 131

Malachi
1 186n.
2 41, 169, 178
3 146n.

Matthew
5 27, 153
6 74
8 43n.
10 195
11 101
12 43n.
18 31, 99
19 176, 188f., 195
25 92

Mark
10 43n., 195

Luke
1 194n.
4 43n., 101
9 111
12 195
18 195

John
1 105
4 94
13 31
15 23, 31, 158

Acts
2 98, 161, 194
4 98, 101
5 194
11 194

16	94, 194	*Ephesians*		*Philemon*	
17	104	1	132, 148		194
18	194	2	96f., 194n., 195	*Hebrews*	
20	194	3	96	1	105
Romans		4	99, 198	3	193, 194n.
1	187	5	27, 44	8	194n.
3	93, 160	6	74, 186	12	91
6	160	*Philippians*		13	98
6–7	31	1	98	*James*	
8	31, 160	2	44, 99	2	99
9–11	93	3	93	5	80
12	23, 98	4	98	*1 Peter*	
13	92, 160	*Colossians*		1	98
15	98, 127	1	105, 132	2	31, 44, 127
1 Corinthians		2	111	*2 Peter*	
1	194	3	82, 99, 163	3	91f.
7	189	*2 Thessalonians*		*1 John*	
9	160f.	3	69	2	99
15	92, 102	*1 Timothy*		3	31, 92, 99
2 Corinthians		2	127	4	23, 99
8–9	98f.	3	195	*Revelation*	
Galatians		6	98	11	131
2	98	*2 Timothy*		18	85
3	97, 182	1	194	21	91f., 131
5	93	3	16, 64	22	92
6	93, 98, 195	4	194		

Subject index

Abraham, 33, 34, 35, 46, 63, 74f., 92, 94, 97, 107, 125f., 199
adultery, 177, 185f., 188, 200, 202, 204f.
agriculture, 61, 101
alien, 28, 51, 57, 77, 86, 95f., 176, 179
animals, 50, 59, 61, 143, 164, 180

Babel, 33f., 105f., 130
Babylon, 49f., 85, 105f., 126, 129

Canaan, Canaanite, 36f., 47f., 57f., 150, 175, 182
canon, 64
charitable law, 157ff.
church, 92, 100, 127, 190, 198
circumcision, 180, 185
civil law, 153ff.
compassion, 124, 126, 151, 198

concubine, 176f.
covenant, 22, 34, 36, 40, 46ff., 51, 53, 55, 62f., 74f., 87, 94f., 111, 115, 135, 149–152, 157, 159f., 179f., 182, 184ff., 192, 194, 198
creation, Creator, 67f., 76, 87, 89, 90f., 104, 130, 137, 141, 162, 182, 203
crime, criminal law, 55, 152f., 158, 167
cult, cultic, 158, 185
culture, cultural, 159, 167
curse, 71, 83, 90

death penalty, 153, 164f.
debt, debtor, 55, 58, 61, 79, 86, 172
Decalogue, 22f., 143, 148f., 152f., 158, 160, 162, 185f., 207 (*see also* Ten Commandments)
demonic, 73, 108
divorce, 155, 177f., 188f.

earth, 67–71, 90f.
Eden, 90f., 125
economics, 37f., 54ff., 59ff., 76, 82, 85, 99, 101, 124, 185, 204
elders, 38, 168
election, 51, 63, 75f., 109
employment, 59, 69, 79, 179, 189
equality, egalitarian, 56, 112, 198
eschatology, 76f., 80f., 88, 90f., 95, 100, 102, 131, 199
exile, 49, 60, 200
exodus, 34, 57, 98, 111, 142

fall, 71, 73, 103, 105, 209
fallow year, 58, 60, 78f., 86
family, 37f., 50, 55, 58, 95, 112f., 167f., 180, 183–186, 190–196
fellowship, 97, 99f., 195f.
forgiveness, 210f.
freedom, 25, 56, 112f., 178, 203

Subject index

generosity, 98, 202, 204
Gentiles, 61, 93, 96f., 103
grace, 23, 109, 159f., 173
gratitude, 21–24, 151

harvest, 52f., 59f., 96, 157
history, 24, 33, 46, 51, 53, 60
holiness, 26f., 40f., 43, 47, 123, 134, 150f.
household, 37, 57f., 96, 177f., 190–196

idolatry, 121f. 143, 162, 175, 187f., 204
image of God, 31, 68, 104, 164, 202
imitation of God, 27f.
immigrants, 57, 167, 171 (see also aliens)
inalienability, 82f.
incarnation, 41, 43f., 110, 189
individual, 54, 183, 197ff.
inheritance, 53–59, 95, 184
injustice, 56, 106, 142, 146, 200, 206
interest, 84
international, 103, 105, 110, 123f.

Jesus Christ, 92–100, 105, 111, 182, 189, 193
Jews, 93, 94, 96, 149
jubilee, 60, 79, 87, 101f.
judgment, 122, 124, 126, 134, 142, 144, 148
justice, 38, 119, 133ff., 156, 169–171, 202

king, kingship, 37ff., 48, 54, 58, 61, 78, 84, 110, 141, 144f., 169, 200, 202, 211
Kingdom of God, 26, 37, 45, 99f., 102, 131
kinship, kinsman, 37, 58f., 86, 95f., 99, 169, 183ff., 191f., 205

land, 37f., 46–59, 63, 71, 75–78, 82f., 86, 88–100, 155, 157, 183–186, 200ff.
law, 22f., 47, 58f., 63, 85, 89, 91, 112, 133, 143, 148ff., 181f., 185, 200

Levirate marriage, 59, 86, 155
life, 149, 151, 163f., 187
love, 51f., 109, 135, 160, 202

marriage, 105, 155, 176, 186, 188f.
Messiah, Messianic, 61, 93f., 96f., 99, 118, 139, 193
monarchy, 38f., 61, 116f., 190, 193 (see also king, kingship)
motive, motivation, 29, 137

nations, 33f., 37, 39, 51f., 54, 61, 88, 90, 103f., 122f., 139, 169, 200
nature, 52, 80, 91, 191
neighbours, 58

obey, obedience, 48, 54, 98, 151, 186, 202f.
oppression, 48, 52, 56, 106, 121, 142–147, 173, 207, 211
orphans, 77, 86, 157, 195f.

Palestine, 92, 94, 189
parable, parabolic, 120
paradigm, paradigmatic, 40–45, 61f., 64, 88f., 92, 100f., 162, 167f., 190ff.
parents, 155, 167, 184ff., 192, 202, 208
peace, 48, 96, 126, 135
pledges, 79, 84, 86, 156, 172
politics, 38, 101, 103ff., 139, 141
polygamy, 176ff., 188f.
poor, poverty, 54, 61, 82, 86, 98f., 101, 144–147, 170f., 187f., 193, 202, 205
priest, priestly, priesthood, 40f., 49, 110, 125f., 150, 162, 169
property, 54, 59, 68f., 71, 150, 157, 163.
prosperity, 54, 72, 81, 126
providence, 139–141, 199
punishment, 55, 163, 165f., 168, 200, 202

race, 109
redemption, 22f., 25, 33–35, 46, 50, 52, 59, 60f., 63, 74–76, 86–94, 98, 103, 107,
114, 130, 137, 139, 140f., 155, 158, 160f., 187, 192, 197f., 210f.
repentance, 120, 210
responsibility, 25, 54, 58f., 63, 69, 119, 142, 150, 190, 200f., 203
revolution, 129
righteousness, 51, 86, 91, 133ff., 171, 201, 205, 208
rights, 54, 56, 58, 63, 99, 142, 204

sabbath, sabbatical year, 58, 60, 78f., 101, 143, 156, 207
sacrifice, 87, 156, 210
Servant of God, 41–43, 211f.
sex, 177, 187, 191f., 202, 204
sharing, 68, 70, 85, 87
sin, 33, 61, 105f., 121, 188, 208ff.
Sinai, 22, 40, 46, 53, 60, 63, 148f., 151, 186, 199
slavery, 78, 86, 143, 154, 161, 165, 172, 178–182, 189, 202
society, social life, 34f., 37, 40f., 44, 50, 57, 61, 99, 101, 103f., 146, 150f., 179, 188, 191f., 196, 197f.
Sodom, 28, 61f., 106, 125, 137, 188
Spirit, 97, 104, 126, 160
stewardship, 57, 68, 70, 85

Ten Commandments, 35, 113, 142, 149, 160, 185f., 199 (see also Decalogue)
theocracy, 112, 118f., 152
tithes, 52, 54, 58, 85f.
Trinity, 104f.
typological, 43, 88, 92, 96f., 99, 101, 161, 190, 193, 196
Tyre, 85, 124, 131

wages, 78
wealth, 38, 51, 55, 82, 192, 202
widows, 77, 86f., 147, 157, 194
Wisdom literature, 28, 144, 201, 203
work, 69, 71f., 77–81, 143, 165, 203
worship, 52, 60, 94, 138, 142, 147, 149, 175, 194f., 206ff.